The Best of McSweeney's
Volume 1

The Best of McSweeney's
Volume 1

EDITED BY DAVE EGGERS

HAMISH HAMILTON
an imprint of
PENGUIN BOOKS

HAMISH HAMILTON

Published by the Penguin Group

Penguin Books Ltd, 80 Strand, London WC2R ORL, England

Penguin Group (USA) Inc., 375 Hudson Street, New York, New York 10014, USA

Penguin Books Australia Ltd, 250 Camberwell Road, Camberwell, Victoria 3124, Australia

Penguin Books Canada Ltd, 10 Alcorn Avenue, Toronto, Ontario, Canada M4V 3B2

Penguin Books India (P) Ltd, 11 Community Centre, Panchsheel Park, New Delhi – 110 017, India

Penguin Group (NZ), cnr Airborne and Rosedale Roads, Albany, Auckland 1310, New Zealand

Penguin Books (South Africa) (Pty) Ltd, 24 Sturdee Avenue, Rosebank 2196, South Africa

Penguin Books Ltd, Registered Offices: 80 Strand, London WC2R ORL, England

www.penguin.com

This collection first published 2004

1

Collection copyright © McSweeney's Publishing, 2004
Introduction copyright © Dave Eggers, 2004
pp. 411–15 constitute an extension of this copyright page

Set in 12/14.75 pt Monotype Garamond 3
Typeset by Rowland Phototypesetting Ltd, Bury St Edmunds, Suffolk
Printed in Great Britain by Clays Ltd, St Ives plc

A CIP catalogue record for this book is available from the British Library

ISBN 0–241–14234–2
tradepaperback 0–241–14235–0

Contents

Introduction by Dave Eggers   vii

Yet Another Example of the Porousness of Certain Borders (viii)
DAVID FOSTER WALLACE   3

Four Institutional Monologues
GEORGE SAUNDERS   13

The Observers
PAUL LAFARGE   35

Walking on the Rings of Saturn
PAUL COLLINS   61

The Girl with Bangs
ZADIE SMITH   79

The Hypnotist's Trailer
ANN CUMMINS   89

Tedford and the Megalodon
JIM SHEPARD   101

Three Meditations on Death
WILLIAM T. VOLLMANN   123

Up the Mountain Coming Down Slowly
DAVE EGGERS   151

Contents

The Days Here
KELLY FEENEY   211

Haole Go Home!: Small Gestures from the Hawaiian Secessionist Movement
ZEV BOROW   227

Solicitation
REBECCA CURTIS   245

Fat Ladies Floated in the Sky Like Balloons
AMANDA DAVIS   251

In the Kingdom of the Unabomber
GARY GREENBERG   257

Mollusks
ARTHUR BRADFORD   341

The Republic of Marfa
SEAN WILSEY   349

Fire: The Next Sharp Stick?
JOHN HODGMAN   387

The Double Zero
RICK MOODY   395

About the Contributors   411

Introduction

The United States has more literary journals than any other nation – I haven't checked South Africa or Egypt or a few other countries, but I think you'll trust me on this – and I have no idea why this is the case. There are probably over a hundred high-quality literary journals, high quality meaning that they're bound as legitimate paperback books and are produced with the highest standards of editing, design, and production. Just about every state in the union has its own journal – from the *Mississippi Review* to the *Alaska Quarterly Review*, and I have yet to see one that doesn't make its constituents proud. Then there are of course the independent standard-bearers, the journals that have for decades broken new ground and discovered new writers: the *Paris Review*, *Callaloo*, *Epoch*, *StoryQuarterly*, *Conjunctions*, *Grand Street*. Add to that a spate of new entries, all of them excellent: *Open City*, *3rd Bed*, *Pineldyboz*, *Fence*. Beyond these are easily twenty-five great college- or university-sponsored journals – from the *Kenyon Review* to *Ploughshares* – and you see what I'm saying. And these are just the journals of the highest quality! There are easily a thousand more created with more limited means and more modest results. The US has long been short-story crazy, and the fact that so many journals can make their way is astounding.

So why would this country need yet another? There's really no good reason. I guess the only excuse I can offer is that, first of all, I just thought it would be an interesting project, a new form to explore, something to keep me and some friends from a life of petty vandalism and vindictive art criticism via small newspapers. Second, there was indeed a small sliver of elbow room in the field: that is, even with all that was being published, there were literary forms that were strangely underrepresented. In particular, there were only a handful of journals where experimental fiction and nonfiction were welcomed, and there were virtually no forums where literary humor could find a home.

So we started there. Actually, *McSweeney's* began while I was stalling on other things I was supposed to be doing, and while neglecting any duties I could be presumed to have while working at a glossy magazine in New York. I was employed at a men's magazine, ostensibly conceiving of and writing features, but I wasn't doing much of that; instead, I was trying to finish my first book. At the same time, I was procrastinating, every day and every night, from working on that first book, and, because I wanted to create the impression – to myself, I guess – that I was accomplishing something, I began thinking about a new quarterly.

I'd moved to New York from San Francisco a year earlier, and my introduction to the glossy world of glossy magazines was in many ways a shock. Writers I knew were having great work rejected everywhere, or having assigned articles killed for any conceivable reason – too long, too difficult, too timely, not timely enough, or too much emphasis on a giant glowing slug.

I began wondering if it were possible to start a new journal, assembled from these articles not fit for other magazines – a quarterly of orphaned stories. Simultaneously, I began fiddling with fonts and cover compositions. I'd been collecting and studying 19th-century pamphlets and front-matter layouts from old books, and on a trip to Cuba collected dozens of examples, classics from Spain and medical texts from France and Germany, and began modeling the look of a new magazine on these archaic books.

The first thing I wanted to do was to simplify the look of a magazine. I'd known too many great articles and stories that were edited brutally to make room for design elements – photographs, illustrations, pull-quotes, even cartoons. I wanted this new magazine to be limitless in the space and freedom allotted to writers. As a contrast to the aggressive design systems of many magazines, this new journal would use almost no images, and would be limited to one, classic font – in this case, Garamond 3. Garamond 3 had always been my favorite font, because it looked good in so many permutations – italics, small caps, all caps, tracked out, justified or not.

Around this time, I saw a show of photography by someone named Peter Garfield at a small Chelsea gallery. In the photographs, single-story homes seemed to be flying through the air, falling from the sky as if God was tossing heaven's defective domiciles. The pictures were incredible. I bought a catalog, which featured an interview between the artist and an Italian art historian, and many pictures documenting just how the home-falling photos were taken. There was a detailed explanation of how the homes were lifted, via military helicopter, and then dropped onto vacant fields; in the photos, Garfield and his team seemed purposeful and serious, and wore hard hats.

The only suspect part of the catalog was a small line on the inside cover, where these words were printed: MANUFAC-TURED IN ICELAND.

When I finally met the artist, he explained to me, laughing at my gullibility, that I'd fallen for an elaborate hoax. There were no helicopters, and no actual homes being dropped from the sky. The homes, he showed me, were models, about four inches high, that he tossed and photographed in his backyard. Actually, he said, the only true words in that whole catalog were the ones I most suspected – that the book had been printed in Iceland.

So this printer, Oddi Printing in Reykjavik, became the printer of this new magazine even before I'd really begun working on it in earnest. The name came next. When I was a kid, our family periodically received letters from someone who called himself Timothy McSweeney, and who claimed to be a member of our family (my mother's maiden name was Adelaide McSweeney). In his letters, which were nonsensical and customarily unsettling, he usually included train and plane schedules, and vague itineraries – he was always promising to visit – for a reunion! – sometime soon.

And so the name of a journal of stories that had been estranged from the family of acceptable literature – if they'd ever been related at all – became *Timothy McSweeney's Quarterly Concern*.

And while the first issue did contain a number of stories that had been rejected elsewhere, we quickly abandoned that limited scope, and, from the second issue on, the majority of what we published had been written with us in mind. Once we had figured out the basics of the journal's interior, we – we were now a staff of two or three – started fiddling with the exterior form as well. Each issue sought to outdo the one before, to reinvent itself. Issue One was simple enough, and Two doubled the cover's complexity, with Three tripling the second's, while also featuring a short story, by David Foster Wallace, printed on its spine. For each issue, I would fly from Brooklyn to Reykjavik, each time asking the printers there what was possible. Could we do a four-color foldout? Could we create an issue with fourteen separate booklets, all held together inside a cardboard box?

In each case, they said yes, and the elaborateness of each successive issue became something of a challenge – more often than not, we had to outdo ourselves every time. So Issue Four, the box of booklets, was followed by Issue Five, a full hardcover book with four different covers and three color foldouts. Issue Six featured a CD soundtrack by They Might Be Giants, included free inside each book, with song written to accompany each story. Issue Seven comprised another bunch of booklets, this time held together with cardboard and a giant rubber band.

The point of all this production fussiness? The only point is to see what can be done. Each issue must present new challenges for us; each issue must be begun as if it were our first or our last. And each issue must make itself ownable. That is, we always thought – and continue to think – that books should be beautiful, and that, if they're beautiful, people will be more likely to want to keep them, to display them, to touch them and come back to them again and again. We're in love with the tactility of books, and we try to reward those readers who love to hold them, save them, lay them on the floor and look at them.

So far this introduction has described just the exteriors of these journals, which we always emphasize is secondary to what goes on within the work of the writers we've been fortunate enough to publish. But the two aspects can't easily be separated. Part of the reason that we've been able to attract so many great writers is that the context within which their work appears is an aesthetically pleasing one, one that grants their work – even if it's humorous – some dignity.

That said, we feel really lucky that from the very start we had the pleasure of typesetting and printing work by many of our favorite people, writers who had been our heroes long before the journal was even a notion, people like George Saunders, Lydia Davis, Rick Moody, Jonathan Lethem, William T. Vollmann, and David Foster Wallace. And along with them, we've been happy to publish early work by writers who were just getting recognized, or got their recognition as a result of their appearance in our pages, writers like Paul Collins, Rebecca Curtis, Ann Cummins, Arthur Bradford, and even Zadie Smith, who was well known by the time we found her, but not yet as a writer of short stories.

At some point I should clearly, boldly define the unifying *McSweeney's* aesthetic, or even declare a rigid set of requirements for what we do and don't approve of in fiction. And while we may have showed certain tendencies over the years, in general our opinion is that there's nothing more effective at taking the life out of art than a unifying aesthetic or some kind of manifesto that even its writers are bored with within months. And though the first issues were more cohesive in form – or, at least, cohesive in their discomfort with traditional form – the later issues have concentrated on longer stories, well told, even if structurally traditional. Issue Eleven includes stories both experimental and traditional, and contains an excerpt from a novel about a talking monkey who aspires to be Jesus – all this while sharing space with a DVD including readings by everyone from Joyce Carol Oates to T.C. Boyle.

Included in this volume is a broad range of the stories we've published, with an emphasis on those stories that have survived the past few years, and which might survive translation. We hope you'll enjoy them.

Dave Eggers, 2004

THE BEST OF McSWEENEY'S
Volume 1

Yet Another Example of the Porousness of Certain Borders (viii)

DAVID FOSTER WALLACE

Then just as I was being released in late 1996 Mother won a small product liability settlement and used the money to promptly go get cosmetic surgery on the crow's feet around her eyes. However, the cosmetic surgeon botched it and did something to the musculature of her face which caused her to look scared all the time. You doubtless know the way someone's face looks in the split second just before they begin to scream. That was now Mother. It turns out that it only takes a minuscule slip of the knife one way or the other in this procedure and now you look like someone in the shower scene of Hitchcock. So, she went and had more cosmetic surgery to try to correct it. But the 2nd surgeon also botched it and the appearance of fright became even worse. Especially around the mouth. She asked for my candid appraisal and I felt as if our relationship demanded nothing less. Her crow's feet indeed were things of the past but now her face was a chronic mask of insane terror. Now she looked more like Elsa Lanchester when Elsa Lanchester 1st lays eyes on her prospective 'mate' in the 1935 classic *Bride of Frankenstein*. Now after the 2nd botched procedure even sunglasses were no longer of much help because still there was the issue of the gaping mouth and mandibular distention and the visible neck tendons and so forth. So, now she was involved in yet another lawsuit and when she regularly took the bus to the lawyer she'd chosen's office I escorted her. We rode at the bus's front in one of the two longer seats which face sideways instead of straight ahead. We had learned the 'hard way' not to sit further back in the rows of more regular seats which face ahead because of the way certain bus passengers would visibly react when they boarded and performed the seemingly reflexive action as they began to move down the aisle to a seat of briefly scanning the sea of faces facing them from the narrow rows of seats and would suddenly see Mother's distended soundlessly screaming face appearing to gaze back at them in abject horror. There were three or four embarrassing incidents and interactions before I applied myself to the issue and evolved a better seated location. Nothing in sources sufficiently explains why people perform the scan of the faces when they 1st board though on my anecdotal view it appears to be a defensive reflex species wide. Nor am I a good specimen to sit beside if she wanted to be inconspicuous because of the way my face usually towers above all others in the crowd. Physically I am a large specimen and have distinctive coloration, to look at me you would never know that I have such a studious bend. There also are the goggles worn and specially constructed gloves for fieldwork, it is far from impossible to find specimens on a public bus even though surveys as yet have yielded no fruit. No it is not as if I actively 'enjoy' riding with her while she exerts her willpower trying not to allow the self-consciousness about the chronic expression to make it even more terror stricken, or 'look forward' to sitting in a would-be-ostentatious reception area reading Rotary newsletters three times per week. It is not as if I do not have plenty of other things and studies to occupy my time. But what is one to do, the terms of my probation involve Mother's sworn statement to assume liability as my 'custodian.' But anyone privy to the reality of life together since the 2nd surgery would agree that the reality was the other way around because, due to despondency and fear of people's reaction she is all-but incapable of leaving the house and can answer the lawyer's wheedling summonses to his office only with my presence and protection throughout the long ride. Also I have never liked direct sunlight and burn with great ease. This time the lawyer smells a windfall if and when he can get Mother in a courtroom and let a jury see for itself the consequence of the cosmetic surgeons' negligence. I also carry a briefcase at all times since my own case. One today could call a briefcase a 'sematic accessory' to warn off predators. Since the original negligence I've primarily become immunized to Mother's chronic expression of horror but even so am myself made uncomfortable by some's reaction to us visually. A bus's circular steering wheel is not only larger but is set at an angle more horizontal than any taxi, private car or police cruiser's wheel I have seen and the driver turns the wheel with a broad all-body motion which is resemblant to someone's arm suddenly sweeping all the material off a broad surface in a sudden fit of emotion. And the long and perpendicular seats in the front comprise a good vantage from which to watch the driver wrestle with the bus. Nor did I have anything against the boy in any way. Nor is there anything in any state, county or local ordinance restricting what varieties you can work with or stipulating in any way that cultivating more than a certain number of them constitutes reckless endangerment or a hazard to the community at large. If the appointment is in the morning the driver also keeps a newspaper folded in a hutch by the automatic coin or token box which he tries to scan while idling at stoplights although it is not as though he will get much of his daily reading done that way. He was only nine which was repeatedly stressed as if his youth and innocence in any way strengthened any charge of negligence on my own part. A common Asian species has not only the sematic ventral insignia but a red line straight down the back, '. . . as if from a bursting seam,' leading to its indigenous name, 'Red Line on Back.' Standardized Testing has confirmed that I have both a studious bend and outstanding retention in study which she would not even deny. The theory I have evolved is, the morning driver scans his newspaper and wearily refolds and replaces it in the hutch in order to unconsciously communicate the boredom and contempt he feels in his paid job and a clinical- or court-appointed psychologist might diagnose the driver's newspaper as an unconscious 'Cry for help.' Our customary seat is the long perpendicular seat on the same side as the bus's door minimizing the likelihood that someone boarding will have a sudden frontal view of her chronic mask of insane terror. This too being a lesson we learned the 'hard' way. The only comedic interlude was, that when the 1st surgery's bandages came off and they brought her the mirror at first one could not verify whether the frightened mien in fact was a simple natural defensive reaction to what she was seeing in the mirror or if it itself was what she saw. Mother herself, who is a decent-hearted if vain, bitter and timid older woman who is not a colossus of the roads of the Intellect to put it blatantly, could not even determine at first if the look of abject terror there was her reaction or the stimulus and, if a reaction then a reaction to what exactly and so forth. The cosmetic surgeon himself was leaning forwards against the white wall with his face to the wall, a behavioral reaction which signaled, 'Yes' there was 'an objective' problem with the results of the cosmetic surgery. The bus is because we have no car, a situation this new attorney says he can now remedy in spades. The whole thing was carefully contained and screened off and even the State conceded that if he had not been up fiddling around on the roof of someone else's garage there is no way he could have come in contact with them in any form. This factored into the terms of probation. Sometimes, however, it's ½ amusing on the public conveyance to see the way passengers upon catching any glimpse of her frightened expression then will reflexively turn to look out whatever window to them Mother appears to be reacting to. Her fear of the phylum arthropodae is long standing which is why she never went into the garage and could contend 'ignorantia facti excusat,' a point of law. Ironically also hence her constant spraying of R—d© despite my impatient pointing-out that these species are long resistant to resmethrin and d-trans Allethrin. (The active ingredients in R—d©.) Granted 'widow' bites are a bad way to go because of the neurotoxin involved hence prompting a physician all the way in 1933 to comment, 'I do not recall having seen more abject pain manifested in any other medical or surgical condition,' whereas, the painless loxoceles or 'Recluse' toxin only causes necrosis and sloughing of the bitten area. Recluses however exhibiting a natural aggression which widows never share unless actively disturbed. Which he did. The bus's interior is flesh-colored plastic with endless advertisements for legal and medical services running horizontally above the bus's windows. The ventilation varies according to such criteria as fulness. The phobia becomes so extreme she will carry a can in her handbag until I always find it before leaving and firmly

7

say, 'No!' In one or two regrettable moments of insensitivity about it also I have quipped to her about taking the bus all the way through Santa Monica into the city itself and auditioning her as an 'extra' in one of the many movies in which crowds of extras are paid to look up in supposed terror of a Special Effect which is only later inserted into the movie through computerized design. Which I sincerely do regret, after all I'm all the support she has. To my mind though it is quite a stretch to say that an area of instability in a twenty-year-old garage roof equals failing to exercise due diligence or care. Whereas, Hitchcock and the other classics used cruder early Special Effects but to terrifying results. To say nothing of him trespassing and having no business up there anyway. In the deposition. To say nothing of claiming that not foreseeing a trespasser falling through a dry rotted portion of the garage roof and wholesale wrecking a complex and expensive tempered-glass container complex and crushing or otherwise disturbing a great many specimens and naturally due to the mishap allowing some decontainment and penetration of the surrounding neighborhood amounts to my failing due exercise of caution. This then is my argument for preferring the 'classics' of older film terror. Declining to ever place or slide the briefcase under the seat I keep it in my lap throughout the frequent rides. My position throughout the lengthy proceedings was a natural deep regret for the kid and his family but that the horror of what happened as a result of his fall did not justify hysterical or trumped-up charges of any kind. Quality counsel would have been able to translate this reasoning into effective legal language in legal briefs and arguments 'in camera.' But of course the reality is counsel proves to be abundant if you are the aggressor but not if you are merely the prey, they're parasites, cable television is infested with their commercials urging the viewer to wait patiently for the opportunity to attack, '. . . handled on a percentage basis, no fee of any kind if you are the aggressor!' One could see them come right out of the Woodwork after Mother's original product liability mishap. No one even knows for certain how the neurotoxin works to produce such abjectly horrible pain in larger mammals, science is baffled as to evolutionarily what advantage there is for a venom well in excess of required for this unique but common specimen to subdue its prey. Science is often confounded both by the luminous 'widow' and the more banal-looking Recluse. Plus the ones who say they will really get down in the dirt of the trench and really fight for you are Sleaze balls such as this supposed Oxnard negligence 'specialist' Mother has lined up. In another context the hysteria would have almost been humorous, any area as unkempt as our garage's neighborhood will be naturally infested with them in all the clutter and run-down homes. Clutter is their natural 'element,' specimens of varied size are to be found in basement corners, beneath shelves of utility rooms, 'linen' closets, in the infinite crevices of castaway litter and unkempt weeds. In the right-angles of most houses' shaded sides. Hence the clear goggles and polyurethane gloves are indispensable even in the shower whose right angles can be infested in just so many hours. Or outside the speeding bus in the palm trees people stand naively beneath in the shade to await the bus, 'Rent a ladder and check the undersides of those fronds sometime!' one is tempted to shout from the window. Once conditioned to know what to look for they are often almost everywhere, 'hiding' in plain sight. This very area and also further inland both contain the more exotic species of 'red' widow whose ventral hour-glass is brown or black as well as one of the Hemisphere's two 'brown' species in the further-inland desert regions. The 'red' widow's red lacks the spellbinding luster of the familiar 'black' variety, it is more a dull or matte red, and they are rare and both specimens escaped in his mishap and have not been reacquired. Here as so often in the arthropod realm, the female dominates as well. To be honest Mother's pain and suffering appeared somewhat inflated in the original product liability claim and she in reality coughs far less than during her deposition. Far be it from me however to deny her. But scientifically a large mammal would have to inhale a great deal of resmethrin or d-trans Allethrin for permanent damage to result which did impact the modesty of Mother's settlement. The facts are less than a centimeter either way is the only difference between smooth youthful eyes and the chronic expression of Janet Leigh in the shower in the 1960 classic of that name. The briefcase is aerated at select tiny points in each corner and 2.5 dozen polystyrene chocks distributed throughout the interior can protect the contents from jostling or trauma. Her new case's complexity is exactly how to distribute the liability claim between the original cosmetic surgeon whose negligence gave her the frightened eyes and forehead and the 2nd whose 'repair''s callous butchery left her with a chronic mask of abject terror and suffering that now can only cause confrontation in the case of someone in the opposing long perpendicular 'sideways' seat directly behind the bus's driver because the sole exposure to liability of Mother's seat here is that any such individual in the opposing seat hence will have the vantage of gazing frontally at us throughout the bus ride. And 'he' will on some occasions, if predisposed by environmental conditioning or temperament, appear to think

the 'cause' of the expression is me – with my size and distinctive mark, etc. – in that I have kidnapped this terrified-looking
middle-aged woman or behaved in a somehow threatening
manner towards her, saying, 'Ma'am is there some problem?'
or, 'Why don't you just leave the lady alone?' as she sinks into
her scarf in self-conscious fear over 'his' reaction but my own
evolved defensive response is to calmly smile and raise my
gloves in puzzled amusement as if to say, 'Why who knows
why anyone wears the public expression they do my good
fellow let us not leap to conclusions based on incomplete data!'
Her original liability was that a worker at the assembly plant
actually glued a can's nozzle on backwards. A clear-cut case
of failing to exercise due care. The 5th condition of the settlement was never to even mention again the name of the common
household spray in any connection to the liability-suit which
I am resolved to honor on her behalf, the 'law is the law.'
There was never one moment of consideration of using the
settlement to repair the garage roof or to rehabilitate the
damaged interior I have to say. I have been on several 1st
dates but there was insufficient chemistry, Mother is blackly
cynical in matters of the heart. Recently as the bus left Casitas
Springs as I looked down to check I saw accidentally protruding from one of the ventilation holes at the case's corner
the very slender tip of a black jointed leg, it was moving about
slightly and had the same luminous coloration as the rest of the
specimens, moving tentatively in an exploratory way. Unseen
against the more banal black of the briefcase's side. Unseen
by Mother whose expression I must ironically say would not
change in the least. Even if I opened up the entire case right
here on my lap and tipped it out into the central aisle allowing
rapid spreading-out and penetration of the contained environs.

This worse-case scenario would only occur if one confronts some duo of young 'punks' or would-be toughs in the long opposing seat facing us whose reaction to Mother's chronic expression might be an aggressive challenging returned stare or a hostile, 'What the "fuck" are you looking at.' It is ironically for just such a case that I am her public escort, with my imposing size and goggles one can tell beneath the face's insane rictus she believes I can protect her which is good.

Four Institutional Monologues

GEORGE SAUNDERS

I

(Exhortation)

MEMORANDUM
DATE: Apr 6
TO: Staff
FROM: Todd Bernie
RE: March Performance Stats

I would not like to characterize this as a plea, but it may start
to sound like one (!) The fact is, we have a job to do, we have
tacitly agreed to do it (did you cash your last paycheck, I know
I did, ha ha ha). We have also – to go a step further here –
agreed to do the job well. Now we all know that one way to
do a job poorly is to be negative about it. Say we need to
clean a shelf. Let's use that example. If we spend the hour
before the shelf-cleaning talking down the process of cleaning
the shelf, complaining about it, dreading it, investigating the
moral niceties of cleaning the shelf, whatever, then what happens is, we make the process of cleaning the shelf more difficult
than it really is. We all know very well that that 'shelf' is
going to be cleaned, given the current climate, either by you
or by the guy who replaces you and gets your paycheck,

so the questions boil down to: Do I want to clean it happy or do I want to clean it sad? Which would be more effective? For me? Which would accomplish my purpose more efficiently? What is my purpose? To get paid. How do I accomplish that purpose most efficiently? I clean that shelf well and I clean it quickly. And what mental state helps me clean that shelf well and quickly? Is the answer: Negative? A negative mental state? You know very well that it is not. So the point of this memo is: Positive. The positive mental state will help you clean that shelf well and quickly, and thus accomplish your purpose of getting paid.

What am I saying? Am I saying whistle while you work? Maybe I am. Let us consider lifting a heavy dead carcass such as a whale. (Forgive the shelf/whale thing, we have just come back from our place on Reston Island, where there were 1) a lot of dirty shelves, and 2) yes, believe it or not, an actual dead rotting whale, which Timmy and Vance and I got involved with in terms of the clean-up.) So say you are charged with, you and some of your colleagues, lifting a heavy dead whale carcass onto a flatbed. Now we all know that is hard. And what would be harder is, doing that with a negative attitude. What we found, Timmy and Vance and I, is that even with only a neutral attitude, you are talking a very hard task. We tried to lift that whale, while we were just feeling neutral, Timmy and Vance and I, with a dozen or so other folks, and it was a no-go, that whale wouldn't budge, until suddenly one fellow, a former Marine, said what we needed was some mind over matter and gathered us in a little circle, and we had a sort of a chant. We got 'psyched up.' We knew, to extend my above analogy, that we had a job to do, and we got sort of excited about that, and decided to do it with a positive attitude, and I have to tell you, there was something to that, it was fun, fun when that whale rose into the air, helped by us and some big straps that Marine had in his van, and I have to say that lifting that dead rotting whale on to that flatbed with that group of total strangers was the high point of our trip.

So what am I saying? I am saying (and saying it fervently, because it is important): let's try, if we can, to minimize the grumbling and self-doubt regarding the tasks we must sometimes do around here that maybe aren't on the surface all that pleasant. I'm saying let's try not to dissect every single thing we do in terms of ultimate good/bad/indifferent in terms of morals. The time for that is long past. I hope that each of us had that conversation with ourselves nearly a year ago, when this whole thing started. We have embarked on a path, and having embarked on that path, for the best of reasons (as we decided a year ago), wouldn't it be kind of suicidal to let our progress down that path be impeded by neurotic second-guessing? Have any of you ever swung a sledgehammer? I know that some of you have. I know some of you did when we took out Rick's patio. Isn't it fun when you don't hold back, but just pound down and down, letting gravity help you? Fellows, what I'm saying is, let gravity help you here, in our workplace situation: pound down, give in to the natural feelings that I have seen from time to time produce so much great energy in so many of you, in terms of executing your given tasks with vigor and without second-guessing and neurotic thoughts. Remember that record-breaking week Andy had back in October, when he doubled his usual number of units? Regardless of all else, forgetting for the moment all the namby-pamby thoughts of right/wrong etc. etc., wasn't that something to see? In and of itself? I think that, if we each look deep down inside of ourselves, weren't we each a little envious? God he was really pounding down and you could see the energetic joy on his face each time he rushed by us to get additional clean-up towels. And we were all just standing there like, wow, Andy, what's gotten into you? And no one can argue with his numbers. They are there in the Break Room for all to see, towering above the rest of our numbers, and though Andy has failed to duplicate those numbers in the months since October, 1) no one blames him for that, those were miraculous numbers, and 2) I believe that even if Andy never again duplicates those numbers, he must still, some-where in his heart, secretly treasure up the memory of that magnificent energy flowing out of him in that memorable October. I do not honestly think Andy could've had such an October if he had been coddling himself or entertaining any doubtful neurotic thoughts or second-guessing tendencies, do you? I don't. Andy looked totally focused, totally outside himself, you could see it on his face, maybe because of the new baby? (If so, Janice should have a new baby every week, ha ha.)

Anyway, October is how Andy entered a sort of, at least in my mind, de facto Hall of Fame, and is pretty much henceforth excluded from any real close monitoring of his numbers, at least by me. No matter how disconsolate and sort of withdrawn he gets (and I think we've all noticed that he's gotten pretty disconsolate and withdrawn since October), you will not find me closely monitoring his numbers, although as for others I cannot speak, others may be monitoring that troubling fall-off in Andy's numbers, although really I hope they're not, that would not be so fair, and believe me, if I get wind of it, I will definitely let Andy know, and if Andy's too depressed to hear me, I'll call Janice at home.

And in terms of why is Andy so disconsolate? My guess is that he's being neurotic, and second-guessing his actions of October – and wow, isn't that a shame, isn't that a no-win, for Andy to have completed that record-breaking October and now to sit around boo-hooing about it? Is anything being changed by that boo-hooing? Are the actions Andy did, in terms of the tasks I gave him to do in Room 6, being undone by his boo-hooing, are his numbers on the Break Room Wall miraculously scrolling downwards, are people suddenly walking out of Room 6 feeling perfectly okay again? Well we all know they are not. No one is walking out of Room 6 feeling perfectly okay. Even you guys, you who do what must be done in Room 6, don't walk out feeling so super-great, I know that, I've certainly done some things in Room 6 that didn't leave me feeling so wonderful, believe me, no one is trying to deny that Room 6 can be a bummer, it is very hard work that we do. But the people above us, who give us our assignments, seem to think that the work we do in Room 6, in addition to being hard, is also important, which I suspect is why they have begun watching our numbers so closely. And trust me, if you want Room 6 to be an even worse bummer than it already is, then mope about it before, after, and during, then it will really stink, plus, with all that moping, your numbers will go down even further, which guess what: They cannot do. I have been told in no uncertain terms, at the Sectional Meeting, that our numbers are not to go down any further. I said (and this took guts, believe me, given the atmosphere at Sectional): Look, my guys are tired, this is hard work we do, both physically and psychologically. And at that point, at

Sectional, believe me, the silence was deafening. And I mean deafening. And the looks I got were not good. And I was reminded, in no uncertain terms, by Hugh Blanchert himself, that our numbers are not to go down. And I was asked to remind you – to remind us, all of us, myself included – that if we are unable to clean our assigned 'shelf,' not only will someone else be brought in to clean that 'shelf,' but we ourselves may find ourselves on that 'shelf,' being that 'shelf,' with someone else exerting themselves with good positive energy all over us. And at that time I think you can imagine how regretful you would feel, the regret would show in your faces, as we sometimes witness, in Room 6, that regret on the faces of the 'shelves' as they are 'cleaned,' so I am asking you, from the hip, to try your best and not end up a 'shelf,' which we, your former colleagues, will have no choice but to clean clean clean using all our positive energy, without looking back, in Room 6.

This all was made clear to me at Sectional and now I am trying to make it clear to you.

Well I have gone on and on, but please come by my office, anybody who's having doubts, doubts about what we do, and I will show you pictures of that incredible whale my sons and I lifted with our good positive energy. And of course this information, that is, the information that you are having doubts, and have come to see me in my office, will go no further than my office, although I am sure I do not even have to say that, to any of you, who have known me these many years.

All will be well and all will be well, etc. etc.,

Todd Bernie
Divisional Director

II

(Design Proposal)

It is preferable, our preliminary research has indicated, for some institutional space to be provided, such as corridor, hallway, etc., through which the group may habitually move. Our literature search indicated that a tiled area is preferable, in terms of preventing possible eventual damage to the walls and floors by the group moving through the space. The review of published literature also indicated that it is preferable that this area to move through (henceforth referred to, per Ellis et al., as the 'Fenlen Space') be non-linear in areal layout, that is, should include frequent turning options (i.e., side hallways or corners), to give the illusion of what Ellis terms 'optional pathway choices.' Per Gasgrave, Heller et al., this non-linear areal layout, and the resulting apparent optional pathway choices, create a 'Forward-Anticipating' mindset. Per Ellis et al., the Forward-Anticipating mindset (characterized by an Andrew–Brison Attribute Suite which includes 'hope,' 'resolve,' 'determination,' and 'sense of mission') results in less damage to the Fenlen Space, as well as better general health for the Temporary Community, which in turn results in significantly lower clinic/medicinal costs.

Also in Ellis et al., the phrase 'Forward-Anticipating Temporary Community' (FATC) is defined to designate a Temporary Community which, while moving through a given Fenlen Space, maintains NTEI ('Negative Thought External Indicator') values below 3 per person/per hour. A 'Non-Forward-Anticipating Temporary Community' (NFATC) is defined as one for which NTEI values are consistently above 3 per person/per hour. NTEIs are calculated using the Reilly Method, from raw data compiled by trained staff observing from inside what are termed 'Amstel Booths,' one-way-mirror locales situated at regular intervals along the Fenlen Space.

For the purposes of this cost proposal, four Amstel Booths have been costed, along with the necessary ventilation/electrical additions.

As part of our assessment, we performed a statistical analysis of the NTEIs for four distinct Fenlen Spaces, using a standard Student's T-test, supplemented with the recently developed Anders–Kiley outlier correction model. Interestingly, the most important component of the Fenlen Space appeared to be what is referred to in the current literature as the Daley Realignment Device (DRD).

The DRD allows for quick changes in the areal layout of the Fenlen Space during time periods during which the Temporary Community is moving through another, remote, portion of the Fenlen Space. The purpose of the DRD is to prolong what Elgin et al. term the 'Belief Period' in the Fenlen Space; that is, the period during which the Temporary Community, moving through the recently realigned DRD, fails to recognize that the portion of the Fenlen Space being traversed by them has already in fact been traversed by them. Rather, the altered areal layout leads to the conclusion that the portion of the Fenlen Space being traversed is an entirely unfamiliar and previously untraversed place, thus increasing the Temporary Community's expectation that, in time, they will arrive at what Allison and Dewitt have termed the 'Preferable Destination.' At some facilities, a brief oral presentation is made to the Temporary Community shortly before the Community enters the Fenlen Space, during which it is strongly implied or even directly stated that the Community will be traversing the Fenlen Space in order to reach the Preferable Destination, which is described in some detail, especially vis-à-vis improvements in terms of cold/heat considerations, food considerations, crowding/overcrowding considerations, and/or perceived menace considerations. An 'apology' may be made for any regrettable past incidents. It may also be implied that the individuals responsible for these incidents have been dismissed etc. etc. Such presentations have been found to be extremely beneficial, significantly minimizing NTEIs and prolonging the Belief Period, and several researchers have mentioned the enthusiasm with which the Temporary Community typically enters the Fenlen Space following such a presentation.

Should Building Ed Terry wish to supplement its DRD with such a pre-traversing oral presentation, Judson & Associates would be pleased to provide the necessary technical writing expertise, a service we have already provided successfully for nine facilities in the Northeast.

In any event, some sort of DRD is strongly recommended. In a study of a Fenlen Space located in Canton, New Jersey, a device which was not equipped with a DRD, it was reported that, toward the end of Day 1, the Temporary Community went, within a few hours, from a strong FATC (with very low NTEIs, ranging from 0–2 per person/per hour) to a very strong NFATC (with NTEIs as high as 9 per person/per hour). Perhaps the most striking finding of the Canton study was that, once the Temporary Community had devolved from an FATC to a NFATC (i.e., once the Belief Period had expired), NTEI values increased dramatically and catastrophically, until, according to one Amstel Booth observer, the NTEIs were occurring at a frequency that was 'essentially impossible to tabulate,' resulting in the event being classified as 'Chaotic' (on the Elliot Scale), after which the Fenlen Space had to be forcibly cleared of the Temporary Community. In other words, once the Temporary Community perceived the Fenlen Space as a repetitious traversing of the same physical space, morale eroded quickly and, per clinical data, could not be restored. Needless to say, the forcible clearing of a Fenlen Space involves substantial risk and expense, as does the related interruption to the smooth flow of facility operations.

In contrast, since a DRD was added to the Canton facility, no further Chaos Situations have occurred, with one exception, which was later seen to be related to a small fire that occurred within one of the Amstel Booths.

Currently available DRDs range from manually rearranged units (typically featuring wallboard panels with quick-release bolts, which are placed into a floor-embedded grid) to electronic, track-based units which offer a large, practically unlimited range of configurations and are typically integrated using the ChangeSpace™ computer software package. The design we have submitted for Building Ed Terry includes cost estimates for the economical Homeway DRD6 (wallboard-grid model) as well as the higher-end Casio 3288 DRD (track-based, computer-operated unit). For the Homeway unit, we have included approximate costs for the physical labor involved in the manual rearrangement of the DRD. For the purposes of this proposal, we have assumed seven rearrangements a day, with four persons required for each rearrangement. This corresponds with a circumnavigation period of approximately three hours – that is, seven rearrangements a day, precluding the possibility that the Temporary Community would inadvertently encounter areal rearrangements in progress, which has been shown (in Percy et al.) to markedly decrease the Belief Period, for obvious reasons.

Judson Associates firmly believes that the enclosed proposal more than meets the needs described in your Request for Proposal of January 9. Should you desire further clarification, please do not hesitate to contact either Jim Warner or myself. We look forward to hearing from you, and to working with you on this exciting and challenging project, and on other projects yet to come.

Sincerely,

Mark Judson
President and CEO
Judson Associates

III

(A Friendly Reminder)

We in Knuckles herebuy request that those of you in Sorting refran from calling the Fat Scrap Box the Pizza Hut Box and refran from calling the Bone Scrap Box the Marshmallow Box and refran from calling the Misc. Scrap Box the Dog Food Box because we think that is insulting to our work and workplace in terms of why do you have to make fun of what we all of us do for a living as if it is shameful. Even though it is true that some of our offal might get used for pizza topping and mashmallows and dog food we do not like it when you are saying those names in a sarcasmic voice. Because new hires can be infected by these attitudes which are so negative and soon they will not be working their best but only laughing at your smartass dumb jokes, so in the future use the correct names (Fat Scrap and Bone Scrap and Misc. Scrap) for these boxes if you feel like you have to talk at all while working although also we in Knuckles suggest you just shut up and just work. For example when one of us in Knuckles throws a Knuckle but it misses the belt you do not have to call it a 'skidder' or act like you are a announcer on a basketball show by saying whoa he missed the hole. And also you dont have to say Ouch whenever one of our throwed Knuckles goes too far and hits the wall, it is not like the Knuckle could feel that and say Ow, because it is dead dumbass, it cannot feel its leg part hitting the wall, so we know you are being sarcasmic. And we dont think this is funny because when we miss the belt or hit the wall what do we have to do is we have to put down our knives and go get it which takes time. And already we are tired without that extra walking. Because what we do takes real muscle and you can easily see us if you look huffing and breething hard all day in the cold inside air, whereas you, although its true you are all hunched over, we never see you breething hard and you dont even work with knives and so never accidentally cut your friend. Which is why we think you have so much energy for yelling your 'funny' taunts that you say at us and have so much energy for making up dumb names of your Belts. So to summarize we do not appreciate all the sarcasmic things that are daily said by you in Sorting in your snotty voices, as it is not something to be ashamed about, people need meat and people like meat, it is good honest work you should be glad you got it, so straighten up and fly right, in other words fucken shut up while working and just do your work silencely and try to appreciate the blessing god give you, like your job of work, it could be worse and is worse for many peeple who have no work

IV

(93990)

A ten-day acute toxicity study was conducted using twenty male cynomologous monkeys ranging in weight from 25 to 40 kg. These animals were divided into four groups of five monkeys each. Each of the four groups received a daily intravenous dose of Borazadine, delivered at a concentration of either 100, 250, 500, or 10,000 mg/kg/day.

Within the high-dose group (10,000 mg/kg/day) effects were immediate and catastrophic, resulting in death within 20 mins of dosing for all but one of the five animals. Animals 93445 and 93557, pre-death, exhibited vomiting and disorientation. These two animals almost immediately entered a catatonic state and were sacrificed moribund. Animals 93001 and 93458 exhibited vomiting, anxiety, disorientation, and digging at their abdomens. These animals also quickly entered a catatonic state and were sacrificed moribund.

Only one animal within this high-dose group, animal 93990, a diminutive 26 kg male, appeared unaffected.

All of the animals that had succumbed were removed from the enclosure and necropsied. Cause of death was seen, in all cases, to be renal failure.

No effects were seen on Day 1 in any of the three lower-dose groups (i.e., 100, 250, or 500 mg/kg/day).

On Day 2, after the second round of dosing, animals in the 500 mg/kg/day group began to exhibit vomiting, and, in some cases, aggressive behavior. This aggressive behavior most often consisted of a directed shrieking, with or without feigned biting. Some animals in the two lowest-dose groups (100 and 250 mg/kg/day) were observed to vomit, and one in the 250 mg/kg/day group (animal 93002) appeared to exhibit self-scratching behaviors similar to those seen earlier in the high-dose group (i.e., probing and scratching at abdomen, with limited writhing).

By the end of Day 3, three of five animals in the 500 mg/kg/day group had entered a catatonic state and the other two animals in this dose group were exhibiting extreme writhing punctuated with attempted biting and pinching of their fellows, often with shrieking. Some hair loss, ranging from slight to extreme, was observed, as was some 'playing' with the resulting hair bundles. This 'playing' behavior ranged from mild to quite energetic. This 'playing' behavior was adjudged to be typical of the type of 'play' such an animal might initiate with a smaller animal such as a rodent, i.e., out of a curiosity impulse, i.e., may have been indicative of hallucinogenic effects. Several animals were observed to repeatedly grimace at the hair bundles, as if trying to elicit a fear behavior from the hair bundles. Animal 93110 of the 500 mg/kg/day group was observed to sit in one corner of the cage gazing at its own vomit while an unaffected animal (93222) appeared to attempt to rouse the interest of 93110 via backpatting, followed by vigorous backpatting. Interestingly, the sole remaining high-dose animal (93990, the diminutive male), even after the second day's dosage, still showed no symptoms. Even though this animal was the smallest in weight within the highest-dose group, it showed no symptoms. It showed no vomiting, disinterest, self-scratching, anxiety, or aggression. Also no hair loss was observed. Although no hair bundles were present (because no hair loss occurred), this animal was not seen to 'play' with inanimate objects present in the enclosure, such as its food bowl or stool or bits of rope, etc. This animal, rather, was seen only to stare fixedly at the handlers through the bars of the cage and/or to retreat rapidly when the handlers entered the enclosure with the long poking sticks to check under certain items (chairs, recreational tire) for hair bundles and or deposits of runny stool.

By the middle of Day 3, all of the animals in the 500 mg/ kg/day group had succumbed. Pre-death, these showed, in addition to the effects noted above, symptoms ranging from whimpering to performing a rolling dementia-type motion on the cage floor, sometimes accompanied by shrieking or frothing. After succumbing, all five animals were removed from the enclosure and necropsied. Renal failure was seen to be the cause of death in all cases. Interestingly, these animals did not enter a catatonic state pre-death, but instead appeared to be quite alert, manifesting labored breathing and, in some cases, bursts of energetic rope-climbing. Coordination was adjudged to be adversely affected, based on the higher-than-normal frequency of falls from the rope. Post-fall reactions ranged from no reaction to frustration reactions, with or without self-punishment behaviors (i.e., self-hitting, self-hair-pulling, rapid shakes of head).

Toward the end of Day 3, all animals in the two lowest dose groups (250 and 100 mg/kg/day) were observed to be in

27

some form of distress. Some of these had lapsed into a catatonic state; some refused to take food; many had runny brightly colored stools; some sat eating their stool while intermittently shrieking.

Animals 93852, 93881, and 93777, of the 250 mg/kg/day group, in the last hours before death, appeared to experience a brief period of invigoration and renewed activity, exhibiting symptoms of anxiety, as well as lurching, confusion, and scratching at the eyes with the fingers. These animals were seen to repeatedly walk or run into the cage bars, after which they would become agitated. Blindness or partial blindness was indicated. When brightly colored flags were waved in front of these animals, some failed to respond, while others responded by flinging stool at the handlers.

By noon on Day 4, all of the animals in the 250 mg/kg/day group had succumbed, been removed from the enclosure, and necropsied. In every case the cause of death was seen to be renal failure.

By the end of Day 4, only the five 100 mg/kg/day animals remained, along with the aforementioned very resilient diminutive male in the highest dose group (93990), who continued to manifest no symptoms whatsoever. This animal continued to show no vomiting, retching, nausea, disorientation, loss of motor skills, or any of the other symptoms described above. This animal continued to move about the enclosure normally and ingest normal amounts of food and water and in fact was seen to have experienced a slight weight gain and climbed the rope repeatedly with good authority.

On Day 5, animal 93444 of the 100 mg/kg/day group was observed to have entered the moribund state. Because of its greatly weakened condition, this animal was not redosed in the morning. Instead, it was removed from the enclosure, sacrificed moribund, and necropsied. Renal failure was seen to be the cause of death. Animal 93887 (100 mg/kg/day group) was seen to repeatedly keel over on one side while wincing. This animal succumbed at 1300 hrs on Day 5, was removed from the enclosure, and necropsied. Renal failure was seen to be the cause of death. Between 1500 hrs on Day 5 and 2000 hrs on Day 5, animals 93254 and 93006 of the 100 mg/kg/day dose group succumbed in rapid succession while huddled in the NW corner of the large enclosure. Both animals exhibited wheezing and rapid clutching and release of the genitals. These two animals were removed from the enclosure and necropsied. In both cases the cause of death was seen to be renal failure.

This left only animal 93555 of the 100 mg/kg/day dose group and animal 93990, the diminutive male of the highest-dose group. 93555 exhibited nearly all of the aforementioned symptoms, along with, toward the end of Day 5, several episodes during which it inflicted scratches and contusions on its own neck and face by attempting to spasmodically reach for something beyond the enclosure. This animal also manifested several episodes of quick spinning. Several of these quick-spinning episodes culminated in sudden hard falling. In two cases, the sudden hard fall was seen to result in tooth loss. In one of the cases of tooth loss, the animal was seen to exhibit the suite of aggressive behaviors earlier exhibited toward the hair bundles. In addition, in this case, the animal, after a prolonged period of snarling at its tooth, was observed to attack and ingest its own tooth. It was judged that, if these behaviors continued into Day 6, for humanitarian reasons, the animal would be sacrificed, but just after 2300 hrs, the animal discontinued these behaviors and only sat listlessly in its own stool with occasional writhing and therefore was not sacrificed due to this improvement in its condition.

By 1200 hrs of Day 5, the diminutive male 93990 still exhibited no symptoms. He was observed to be sitting in the SE corner of the enclosure, staring fixedly at the cage door. This condition was at first mistaken to be indicative of early catatonia but when a metal pole was inserted and a poke attempted, the animal responded by lurching away with shrieking, which was judged normal. It was also noted that 93990 occasionally seemed to be staring at and/or gesturing to the low-dose enclosure, i.e., the enclosure in which 93555 was still sitting listlessly in its own stool occasionally writhing. By the end of Day 5, 93990 still manifested no symptoms and in fact was observed to heartily eat the proffered food and weighing at midday Day 6 confirmed further weight gain. Also it climbed the rope. Also at times it seemed to implore. This imploring was judged to be, possibly, a mild hallucinogenic effect. This imploring resulted in involuntary laughter on the part of the handlers, which resulted in the animal discontinuing the imploring behavior and retreating to the NW corner where it sat for quite some time with its back to the handlers. It was decided that, in the future, handlers would refrain from laughing at the imploring, so as to be able to obtain a more objective idea of the duration of the (unimpeded) imploring.

Following dosing on the morning of Day 6, the last remaining low-dose animal (93555), the animal that earlier had attacked and ingested its own tooth, then sat for quite some time writhing in its own stool listlessly, succumbed, after an episode that included, in addition to many of the aforementioned symptoms, tearing at its own eyes and flesh and, finally, quiet heaving breathing while squatting. This animal, following a limited episode of eyes rolling back in its head, entered the moribund state, succumbed, and was necropsied. Cause of death was seen to be renal failure. As 93555 was removed from the enclosure, 93990 was seen to sit quietly, then retreat to the rear of the enclosure, that is, the portion of the enclosure furthest from the door, where it squatted on its haunches. Soon it was observed to rise and move toward its food bowl and eat heartily while continuing to look at the door.

Following dosing on Day 7, animal 93990, now the sole remaining animal, continued to show no symptoms and ate and drank vigorously.

Following dosing on Day 8, likewise, this animal continued to show no symptoms and ate and drank vigorously.

On Day 9, it was decided to test the effects of extremely high doses of Borazadine by doubling the dosage, to 20,000 mg/kg/day. This increased dosage was administered intravenously on the morning of Day 9. No acute effects were seen. The animal continued to move around its cage and eat and drink normally. It was observed to continue to stare at the door of the cage and occasionally at the other, now-empty, enclosures. Also the rope-climbing did not decrease. A brief episode of imploring was observed. No laughter on the part of the handlers occurred, and the unimpeded imploring was seen to continue for approximately 130 seconds. When, post-imploring, the stick was inserted to attempt a poke, the stick was yanked away by 93990. When a handler attempted to enter the cage to retrieve the poking stick, the handler was poked. Following this incident, the conclusion was reached to attempt no further retrievals of the poking stick, but rather to obtain a back-up poking stick available from Supply. As Supply did not at this time have a back-up poking stick, it was decided to attempt no further poking until the first poking stick could be retrieved. When it was determined that retrieving the first poking stick would be problematic, it was judged beneficial that the first poking stick was now in the possession of 93990, as observations could be made as to how 93990 was using and/or manipulating the poking stick, i.e., effect of Borazadine on motor skills.

On Day 10, on what was to have been the last day of the study, upon the observation that animal 93990 still exhibited no effects whatsoever, the decision was reached to increase the dosage to 100,000 mg/kg/day, a dosage 10 times greater than that which had proved almost immediately lethal to every other animal in the highest-dose group. This was adjudged to be scientifically defensible. This dosage was delivered at 0300 hrs on Day 10. Remarkably, no acute effects were seen other than those associated with injection (i.e., small, bright purple blisters at the injection site, coupled with elevated heart rate and extreme perspiration and limited panic gesturing) but these soon subsided and were judged to be related to the high rate of injection rather than to the Borazadine itself.

Throughout Day 10, animal 93990 continued to show no symptoms. It ate and drank normally. It moved energetically about the cage. It climbed the rope. By the end of the study period, i.e., midnight of Day 10, no symptoms whatsoever had been observed. Remarkably, the animal leapt about the cage. The animal wielded the poking stick with good dexterity, occasionally implored, shrieked energetically at the handlers. In summary, even at a dosage 10 times that which had proved almost immediately fatal to larger, heavier animals, 93990 showed no symptoms whatsoever. In all ways, even at this exceptionally high dosage, this animal appeared to be normal, healthy, unaffected, and thriving.

At approximately 0100 hrs of Day 11, 93990 was tranquilized via dart, removed from the enclosure, sacrificed, and necropsied.

No evidence of renal damage was observed. No negative effects of any kind were observed. A net weight gain of 3 kg since the beginning of the study was observed.

All carcasses were transported off-site by a certified medical waste hauler and disposed of via incineration.

The Observers

PAUL LAFARGE

'To observe is to destroy.'
— Paul Poissel

I

Let me begin by saying that when I built the observatory I had no intention of looking into the past. The truth is that I didn't intend to build the observatory at all; it grew out of a web of circumstance, the way mushrooms grow out of dimness and rain. First there was one of those March storms which strike you as a planned and personal affront, like a stalker who goes away for three weeks and then calls you in the middle of the night to let you know that you will have no lasting reprieve, now or ever. The sky turned green, then black. It spat hailstones which struck birds dead off the trees and left dents in the tin roofs of buildings downtown. The hail turned to ice when it touched the ground; snowplows plowed into parked cars and no one was allowed to drive anywhere. My girlfriend went outside to mail some letters, slipped, and broke her wrist; medics with specially ridged shoes had to rescue her from the sidewalk. The papers called it the storm of the fin de siècle, and the Weather Bureau, where I worked, hadn't seen it coming. As soon as the roads cleared, I was instructed to come up with a slogan for the Bureau's face-saving campaign. 'The message here is that no one's perfect,' said the Creative Director. 'We've got to tell them that on every life a little rain must fall.' I worked at it all day, trying to come up with something philosophical and optimistic. All I could think of were smashed cars, shattered roofs, the tiny carcasses of swallows frozen to the ground. When the Creative Director came around for my input, I shook my head.

'What have you got for us?'

I showed him the piece of paper with the only slogan I had been able to think of: These are the omens of the rites that failed.

'What is this? Is this a fucking joke?' The Director tore the page into quarters, and let them fall.

The next day the buses were blazoned with the slogan April Showers May Bring Flowers, and I was out of work. I told my girlfriend what had happened. 'You really fucked up,' she said. I tried to explain that something was actually wrong, that the storm was a sign of something being actually wrong. What I said was: 'We shouldn't pretend that we can see the future, and when we do, the future laughs at us.'

'Maybe so.' She cradled her splinted wrist. 'But what are you going to do now?'

I told her that I'd think of something. But I spent my days watching historical television and wishing that I could have been a saint, a gangster, a cowboy, or an astronaut, some profession in which my actions would have been writ large but very far away. My girlfriend, a medical transcriptionist, nursed her wrist and carried on her numerous intimate friendships by telephone, late at night. She told me that I couldn't go on like this forever, spending my savings on take-out food and televised boxing. I didn't look up. 'Did you know that the Roman Emperor Nero was only one of a series of emperors with the same name?'

On June 1st she left me for a voice at the other end of the telephone line, in an area code that had recently been created to contain the excess population of Cleveland. Without her I couldn't afford the rent on our apartment, so I packed everything up and drove north to Commonstock, where my father still lived in our old house. It was too big for him now, but he didn't want to give up the lawn, the elms, the view of Lake Commonstock, and the fish that washed up on its shores every morning, victims of the acid rain. I moved back into the room where I'd grown up. Nothing about it had changed except that, the summer after my freshman year of college, I'd taken down the poster for *Wind in the Willows* from over my bed, and put up a photograph of a veiled woman smoking a Gauloise. When I was in college I thought she looked mysterious; now she seemed, at most, cold and a little vapid, the kind of woman who said evidently when she meant yes. I took her down and put Frog and Toad in their old, iconic position, pulled my college books from the shelves and put my childhood books back in their places. For a week I lived among the glories of the last unequivocally happy period of my life, the years between twelve and fifteen, when childhood had done its worst and I, already a survivor, felt newly hatched and capable of anything. Then I found my journal from that time. On January 25th, the day I turned fifteen, I'd written: We waste our time feeling sorry for animals, whereas in fact the animals should feel sorry for us. That night I took Frog and Toad down and moved my children's books back into the attic.

*

In college I studied philosophy, because I still believed that you could understand the world by thinking about it. When that turned out not to be true I forgot most of what I'd read, but one thing stays with me, one moment: that part at the end of the *Symposium* where Socrates says, 'Starting from individual beauties, the quest for the universal beauty must find you ever mounting the heavenly ladder, stepping from rung to rung – that is, from one to two, and from two to every lovely body, from bodily beauty to the beauty of institutions,' and so on. The heavenly ladder. What a beautiful idea that was: that, just by thinking about it, you could climb away from everything familiar, from the earth to the sky and up and up and up.

My father looked around my empty room and asked me what I was going to do next.

'Why,' I said, 'I'm going to build an observatory.' I hadn't thought of doing anything like that before. In fact I'd never been much interested in the stars. I knew from camping trips and the like that you were supposed to be able to see figures in among them. I'd owned one of those illustrated books that gives you the pictures of animals and hunters and so on, and the other pictures, so dissimilar, of disjoint stars with lines between them. The analogy between the two sets of illustrations was hard enough to grasp when it was confined to the book; when it blossomed to fill the entire vastness of the night sky it became entirely unmanageable. I could never make out anything smaller than the Milky Way, the moon and its reflection in Lake Commonstock. It was the idea of the observatory that appealed to me. I would build myself a structure, small, sealed, windowless except for the telescope-slit in the roof, and entirely my own.

'Ah,' my father said.

'I want to do something with my hands. I've never built anything before.'

'Didn't you used to build model airplanes?'

He should have known. The airplanes were his idea, to engage me when, as a little boy, I seemed already to have grown tired of what life had to offer in the way of scheduled activities. 'Those were toys. This is going to be for real. A real working observatory.' I thought about what it would look like. 'It's going to have a roof that turns. So that I can see stars in different parts of the sky.'

'Why do you want to see the stars?'

'What's wrong with the stars?'

'Let me see if I understand. You want something that will challenge you.'

'There are comets and nebulas.'

'But not challenge you too much.'

'Black holes, and pulsars and quasars.'

'Why don't we go camping?' This had been another of my father's enthusiasms when I was a child. 'We'll go to Mount Head, spend a few days tooling around. The two of us. Plenty of stars up there. Hm?'

'Just the other day I read that scientists have discovered a new planet. Unlike the others, this one doesn't move.'

My father left the room, his head bowed in defeat.

Of course he had to have a hand in planning it. Together we trudged up and down the property with an old sextant which had been sitting, unused, on our mantel ever since we moved to Commonstock. My father said that it belonged to the sea captain who had lived in the house before us, but as the previous tenant was an insurance broker, I had always suspected that it was a decorator's touch, imported from a Mystic junk shop to fulfill someone's vision of a settled life in New England. My father made a show of holding one end of it to his eye and tilting the other until, from his perspective, it was level with the tops of the trees; after which he showed me the instrument and recorded its reading in degrees. Whether this is the approved use of the sextant I do not know; but in any event there was only one place on the property where the observatory could go: a sort of knoll halfway between the house and the water, from which you had an unobstructed view of the lake, the neighbors' houses, and the gentle rise of Mount Head in the background. The knoll stood at the center of our view from the house; an observatory built there would block the line of sight from the house to the water. Nonetheless my father, excited by his newfound competence with the sextant, gave me permission to build there and even required, based on his table of measurements, that I do so.

That night when the sky turned the color of blue ink I went to sit on the knoll. The moon hadn't risen and the air was still; there must have been thousands of stars visible overhead. I knew none of them by name. The stars were named by Arabs, in their desert long ago, separating with their naked eyes the numberless unnamed stars from the handful they had made their own. The stars were a pale jumble to me, but I could see the Arabs clearly enough. They sat up very straight on the sand dunes and drank cups of Arabian coffee while their horses waited patiently under the trees. The Arabs traded gold rings and drank coffee and then, almost as an afterthought, they named the stars.

*

The Commonstock Public Library had a large collection of
back issues of the relevant periodicals: *Sky*, *Telescope Making*,
Zenith and *Azimuth*. With their help I began my initiation
into the world of semi-anonymous individuals who share a
personal relation to the sky. I read about their telescopes, their
Newtonians and refractors and Cassegrains, and saw, as if with
their eyes, the heavens in blurry magnification, almost without
color but painfully evocative in their detail, as though each
celestial object were a tremendously important word uttered
just out of earshot. I read about their observatories and their
marital problems, the two equally complex and durably tied
together. I had never suspected that so many people took
refuge from the world in small rooms, alone, all night. Their
letters – '7th July. Magnificent Saturn at 2317 hours. Tried
to get my wife to come out and see it' – comforted me, and
I smiled angelically at the other inhabitants of the Commonstock Library's reading room. Not all the news in the
magazines was good: it turned out that, given the cost of
materials and my inexperience at building large structures, the
domed observatory that I'd first imagined was impracticable.
Leafing through plans for various home-grown structures, I
came across a model called the 'Rolling Ridge Observatory,'
invented by Robert E. Reisenweber of Erie, PA. It looked like
an outsized sentry box with a roof that rolled away onto an
adjacent scaffold to expose the telescope to the stars. No
specialized parts were necessary for its construction, and from
start to finish it would cost less than a thousand dollars. I
pinned a photograph of the Rolling Ridge Observatory to my
wall, and for a long time it was the only decoration in my
room.

'Have you ever worked with lumber?' asked the building-supply man. His posture implied habitual skepticism. Commonstock is a town of summer houses; he must have been tired of weekend visitors coming to him with their ever-unrealized plans for decks, gazebos, extra rooms.

'I have plenty of time,' I said. 'My father lives here.'

The building-supply man grunted. 'What kind of foundation have you got?'

'Nothing yet.'

'Well, what are you going to use?'

It hadn't occurred to me that I would need a foundation. Looking at the plans again, I saw that Robert E. Reisenweber had built his observatory on a preexisting concrete slab, presumably a relic left in his backyard by the last civilization to inhabit Erie, PA.

'I guess concrete.'

'You'll need someone to pour it, then.' The building-supply man wrote 'George' and a number on the back of a business card. 'Where are you from?'

'New York.'

'You like it there?'

'Too many streetlights,' I said. 'You can't see a damn thing, at night.'

'Ah.' The building-supply man shrugged, his suspicions about New Yorkers confirmed. 'Well, call George if you want that concrete.'

I had thought ten feet by eight for the foundation but George said it would have to be bigger. 'Wouldn't be room to swing a cat in there, otherwise.' I tried to tell him that my plans for the observatory didn't involve swinging cats. 'I'm not coming over for anything less than twelve by twelve,' he said, and so it was decided. The day before he came my father and I went out with shovels to dig the pit, like archaeologists unearthing an ancient burial mound. It felt good to be working at something again. The sun was bright and simple overhead, and the air smelled of fresh water. My father and I grunted at each other happily. George hadn't told us how deep to dig the foundation, so we outdid ourselves. It was waist-deep by the time we dropped our shovels, exhausted, and sat facing each other in the fresh earth.

'You were never a difficult child,' my father said. 'Only you were always solitary.'

My foot touched something hard. 'Is that a skull?'

My father rubbed at it. 'It's a rock,' he said. 'You kept to yourself so much we wondered if you were all right.'

'What kind of rock?'

'Just a rock. Then it seemed like you turned out all right.' He looked at me sadly. 'Did you hear Julie Eisenman got married again?'

'She was married before?'

'To a veterinary surgeon.'

'Ah.'

'Didn't you used to like her?'

'Did I?' It was possible. I had certainly liked people, even as a child. Or it might have been another of the things my father concocted for me. Dostoyevsky, in *The Brothers Karamazov*, says that the devil exists to give our lives events. But no, we have parents for that. 'When was the wedding?' My father wasn't listening to me. He had pulled a muscle in his back, and I practically had to carry him out of the excavation.

*

George, who on the telephone had sounded large and mirthful, turned out to be a scrawny man with a long neck, pigeon toes, and the face of a hawk. He laughed when he saw our pit.

'Is it too deep?'

'Depends whether you're building an observatory or a bunker.'

He walked off, laughing, and returned at the wheel of a cement truck with the words Pouliadis Construction written on the side in fading red paint. The truck left deep and muddy furrows in the grass. My father watched from a lawn chair as we poured bags and bags of cement into the pit. It soon became clear that we would not fill it; when we ran out of cement, the foundation – which would double as the floor of the observatory – was about three feet below the level of the ground. It meant installing a flight of steps down into the observatory, which was not at all in the plans. I had no instructions for building stairs; I turned to my father with a helpless look that must have been familiar to him from my model-building days. He waved at me from the lawn chair. 'Good work!' he shouted. 'Just a few feet to go!' George pointed out that the stars were already so far away that a few feet of altitude wouldn't make any difference. Which was true, but didn't make me feel any better. I had always thought of observatories as high places, but mine would be reached by stepping down. It didn't feel right.

'Beer?' George asked.

I thought he had them in the truck, but when I came over he said, 'Climb up. That's the spirit.'

He drove us to a bar in town, where I drank beer while George told me about the semi-criminal activities by which he lived. 'You hear those birds?' he asked.

'Sure.'

'Those are my birds.' Apparently the paper mill paid George to drive upstate, to the places where the air was still clean, to net birds and bring them back to Commonstock, where most of them died from the mill's yellowish exhaust. He had also, at various times, stocked the lake with fish, hauled toxic sludge down to the naval laboratory at New London, and even, he claimed, spray-painted leaves yellow and red for a busload of Japanese tourists who came to see the New England fall early in a year when the fall came late. It was as though he had been given the job of making sure that nature still looked as though it worked the way it used to. We drank beer, smoked cigarettes, and flicked the butts into the lake. The sun was warm on my shoulders and the backs of my hands. It was ridiculous for me to worry about the observatory. A few feet up or down wouldn't make any difference, or, if they did, I could fix it. I slumped in my chair, and listened to the song they were playing inside the bar, about how birds were free but two dollars wouldn't buy you a drink anymore. Which wasn't true, I thought, happily, at least not about the birds.

As the summer thickened I felt myself growing more solid, as though I was absorbing some of the durability of my construction. I went back to the building-supply man, bought wood and nails and flanged pieces of metal, screw mounts and bolts and threaded rods and wheels, casters and switches and sockets and a red-sheathed bulb to illuminate the interior. I bought glue strong enough to hold a pickup truck up in midair, an electric drill, screwdriver and screw extractor, a portable power saw, a utility belt, an apron with pockets for things I couldn't name. I stored the tools in the garage at night, but by day I carried them all with me to the building site and laid them out on the ground, in the hope that some stranger, passing by, would see their metal parts shining in the sunlight and think, What a lot of tools this family has! How practical these people are! George Pouliadis came by several times to see how I was doing, and each time his truck creaked into our driveway I felt a sense of camaraderie, as though he and I were each, in our own ways, restoring the world to a happier state.

Like anyone who invests in power tools for the first time, I thought about the end of civilization and how to prepare for it. I went to the grocery store and bought some dried fruit, instant cocoa, a camping stove, Band-Aids and a bottle of iodine. I told my father that I was preparing for minor accidents and cold nights, but in fact the darkest contingencies occupied my imagination: civil unrest, war, new plagues that would turn the bones of men to jelly and their hearts to ice. Only I would remain, safe in my observatory, with my cocoa and iodine, taking notes dispassionately on the emergence and transit of the stars. I drove in to Mystic to pick up my telescope, an eight-inch Newtonian that promised optimal magnification at a reasonable price. It had been years since I visited the old seaport, which has been restored to look as it did in the days when ships went out full of spears and came home with cargoes of blubber and ambergris, whalebone and whaleskin and stories. The three-masted ships, the wooden sidewalks, the storefronts offering salt-water taffy, chandlery, and provisions and sailcloth, impressed me with their optimism. It's not too late to turn back, said the signs for Ropes Unlimited, the Sky Shoppe, the Bit-o-Ivory, and the Cape Horn Café. I

walked to the car, whistling, carrying the telescope on my
shoulder in a vaguely military fashion.

II

George Pouliadis was right: the observatory, when I'd finished
nailing the siding to its exterior, and despite everything
promised by the good Mr Reisenweber, looked like a sort of
low fortress established to defend our house from lake-borne
invaders. I was delighted and couldn't wait until nightfall
to try a few preliminary sightings. I screwed the base of the
telescope to the metal pillar anchored in the floor, tightened
everything, and then, with a sweep of the arm, like a conductor
bringing his orchestra to life, I rolled back the roof and let
light fall for the first time on the telescope's uncovered lens.
My first discoveries, as I angled the scope low across the lake,
were as follows: one, that it was nearly impossible to focus on
anything; and, two, that everything I saw through the telescope
was upside down. Trees waved beneath the lake; below them
the mountains sank into a bottomless blue distance. I studied
the mountains first because they were the furthest away. There
was Mount David, and there Mount Redthorn, and between
them the rocky crown of Mount Head. Swinging downward,
that is, upward, the telescope brought me flying over the
autumnal forest. Then a white blur. I tightened the adjusting
screws and, by touching the knobs very gently, managed to
bring the image into focus. It was a house on the other side
of the lake, where a girl was standing on the porch. She pulled
her long brown hair back and tied it in a bun, so that I could
see her face, which was perfectly detailed, like the tiny cities

in the background of Northern Renaissance paintings. I didn't recognize the house, although it looked like it belonged in Commonstock: white clapboard with green trim and shutters, the porch probably put on by summer people, object of the building-supply man's contempt. The girl stretched her arms downward to the sky. The light had a way of finding the hollows of her body which made her seem more solid, more three-dimensional, than any of the women I had held, touched, known. She turned, and for a moment I saw, or thought I could see, the shadows on either side of her spine. Then she left the telescope's field of vision, which was not large; and by the time I had loosened the tripod's screws and adjusted the instrument, she had vanished entirely. The porch was empty and the house, from this distance, was still. I looked up from the telescope, but my mind did not return to the observatory for a long time, and when it did the place seemed strange, overlarge, and too quiet. I climbed the steps to the lawn and stood blinking in the sunlight.

That night she was in her bedroom with the curtains drawn back and the window partly open. She was playing cards by herself. From the way she moved her head, I guessed that the radio was on. Every two or three minutes she looked up at the door, as though she were waiting for someone to come in. Then she dealt her cards again, played, stopped, looked again at the door. I was afraid that I was abusing the power of the telescope, so I released the screws and let the instrument find its way among the stars. There was nothing but darkness up there. Now and then a bright object would wobble across, and I tried to fix it in my sights. Even with the telescope, though, the stars were dimensionless, colorless, less realistic even than the signs that represented them on maps. I switched on the radio, looked for music that would make what I saw more poignant. But there was no music on the air, only people talking, in pleasant voices, disturbances on the other side of the planet, and the need to be vigilant at home.

The next morning was overcast, threatening, as though the sky were looking for the words to break a difficult piece of news. I drove around the lake, past the Bendetsens', the Hoffmanns', the Rothsteins', past the deserted house of Donald Patriss, the famous animal trainer (he summers in Commonstock), the houses of various neighbors, acquaintances, friends and strangers. I couldn't find the white house with green trim. Of course I was still an amateur with the telescope. Although I might see something quite distinctly, I had no idea what it was I was looking at, or where in the unmagnified world it was to be found.

When I came back, George was showing the observatory to half a dozen children in wool sweaters and sturdy shoes.

'Not the worst piece of work I've seen around here,' he said, rubbing his chin.

'Thanks.'

'Hope you don't mind.'

The children ignored the telescope and the cleverly weighted roof, and went straight for the cocoa.

'Don't touch that stuff,' George growled at them, but I'm sure half my packets of Swiss Miss ended up in their pockets all the same.

'Sorry,' George said. 'They're German.' He explained that he'd been hired to take the children on a weekend hike in Highwash State Park. 'We're looking for fossils,' he confided.

'I didn't know there were any up there.'

'Wie viele Asteroide kennen Sie?' a child asked. 'Ich, dreißig.'

'I don't speak German, sorry.'

'It's a regular trilobite graveyard.' George winked.

I thought of him seeding the hills with prehistoric fish and ferns, purchased probably at a museum souvenir shop. The children wouldn't be disappointed. 'Bring one back for me,' I said.

'Raus, Kinder!' he hollered. 'Alle Kinder raus!'

Not long after he left for the park, it started to snow. I went to the supermarket to replace the cocoa stolen by the German children. Julie Eisenman, the veterinary surgeon's wife, was there, pushing a shopping cart of strangely forlorn produce: root vegetables and paper towels and carpet-cleaning supplies, nothing festive or indulgent or even brightly colored.

'I wondered when you'd turn up,' Julie said. 'Your father said you were back in town.'

'He tells me you're married.'

'That's right.'

'How is it?'

Julie shrugged. 'You should come over for dinner some time. Carl loves to entertain.'

She reached up to get a bottle of Windex. In that moment, her arm upstretched, her head tilted back and the collar of her blouse falling away from her throat, she looked just like the girl I'd seen through the telescope. Julie's eyes were deeper set, and she wore her hair up, but otherwise they were as alike as two frames of film, separated only by time.

'Julie,' I said, tenderly. 'You look wonderful.'

'So call me.'

'No,' I said. 'Really wonderful.'

She took my arm and pulled me to the deserted aisle where they keep the pens and paper. 'Your father is worried about you,' she murmured.

'I don't know why.'

'He thinks you should talk to someone. It might make you feel better.'

'He can think what he likes.'

'That's just what someone who was having problems would say.'

'I'm not having problems.'

'I heard about your girlfriend. I'm sorry.'

A child came up and asked if we knew where they kept the secret notebooks.

'This is all there is, sweetie,' Julie said. Then to me: 'Although I hear she wasn't much of a loss.'

The child was looking at us.

'Why don't you come tonight?' Julie asked.

'All right.'

She gave me her address: on the other side of the lake.

I drifted out of the supermarket, into a suddenly opaque world. The snow stuck in the trees, on the cars, on my eyebrows. I walked down the street, my eyes half closed and my mouth open. I tried to taste the difference between the snowflakes, to understand each one separately, and to know what all of them together added up to.

When we were fourteen, Julie Eisenman and I searched Lake Commonstock together for buried treasure. We dove down as far as we could go and extended our hands into the ropy seaweed. We pulled up shells, shoes, beer bottles older children had tossed into the water. Once, when we were coming out of the water, I gave her a white stone I'd found. She kissed me on the mouth and hugged me so that I could feel her stomach bare against my stomach. 'Do you want to come over?' she asked. 'Maybe later,' I said, afraid that she wanted something bright and terrible from me. 'Come tonight.' She waved to me from the porch and I could see her ribs move in and out with her breathing. I walked home on the side of the road, trying to make my feet hurt by pressing them against the sharp sides of stones. I didn't go that night, because I was afraid to sneak out of my house, afraid to walk the lake's edge in darkness, afraid of what would happen if I went to her.

The radio called the whiteness outside a winter storm. Schools were dismissed early, and travelers were cautioned. I made tea for my father, and told him I'd run into Julie Eisenman in town. I tried to tell him about my discovery. 'With the telescope I can see things that happened years and years ago,' I said. 'It's like everything that ever happened is happening now, somewhere very far away. Or not now, really, because everything we see in the sky is very old.' I showed him an article from *Azimuth*, the most literary of the magazines for sky enthusiasts. 'The Telescope: Window into a Lost World?' it was called. The author of the article explained how, if a large enough lens could be erected in space at a great enough distance from the earth, hypothetical beings would be able, even now, to see our planet as it was in the past. 'Through their telescopes they could watch Plato and Socrates, Michelangelo and Van Gogh, and perhaps learn more about them than we know today.'

'Why would aliens want to see Plato, though?'

'That's not the point. The point is that telescopes are always looking at the past.'

My father gave me a look which I remembered from the summers of my childhood. He used to go away for a few weeks every August to a special camp for teachers, from which he'd return, sunburned and bug-bitten, with the distant stare of a man who has climbed a real mountain to see past an imaginary horizon. While he was away, my fifteenth summer, my mother moved to Ohio. After that his stare got closer and closer, until you felt sure that it would have to take you in, but it didn't. It was as though the world of faraway things had closed in around him, displacing everything which had, until then, been close up.

'It must be something about gravity waves. Gravity waves bending light back to the earth.'

'When you were little you had everything you needed,' my father said. 'We loved you very much.'

'You don't believe me? Come and see for yourself.'

'We loved you so very much,' he said, looking past me, out the window, at the observatory. Covered in snow, it looked like an igloo. He stared at it as though he couldn't understand how this igloo, this bunker, this hermetic thing had come to be on his lawn, squarely between him and the beloved lake, which he couldn't see in any case on account of the snow.

Julie and her husband lived in an old farmhouse, which had been remodeled inside to look like a gallery where domestic life in New England was on display. Track lighting picked out a quilt, a ceramic tureen, the kitchen island where Carl stood chopping vegetables. Small and brightly scrubbed, he struck me as one of those superficially cheerful people who crush small objects in their hands when you're not watching. Julie on the other hand emitted beauty and calm. She'd let her hair down and put on a flowered summer dress despite the weather. We had a drink in the den and talked about the blizzard, as the radio called it now. Apparently it hadn't snowed this much this early in the year since 1915.

'Mythical weather,' Carl joked. 'It means we're near the end.'

'The end of what?'

'It's nothing compared to the storm we had this spring in New York.'

'Just my point. The giants are breaking out of Jotunheim,' Carl said.

'Jotunheim?'

'Carl, you're so obscure.'

'The storm we had in New York was bad, too.'

'Isn't your water boiling?'

Carl got up to check the pot. I moved closer to Julie on the sofa, and let my hand touch the side of her hand. 'I've missed you,' I said. She looked at me fondly for a moment, then moved to the other side of the sofa, and stayed there until we went in to dinner.

Carl wanted to know if the observatory had been difficult to build.

'Not really,' I said. 'All you need is some basic know-how.'

'I'll bet you need more than that.'

'I had a little help with the foundation. But I did all the rest myself.'

'And it's holding up?' Julie asked.

'Why wouldn't it hold up?'

'No one's doubting you,' Julie said. Carl assured me that he could never have done anything like it, himself.

'What do you mean, you wouldn't have done it? You don't think the observatory was a good idea?'

'Carl just means that you must have spent a lot of time on it.'

'Lots of people build their own observatories. Ordinary people, who live in Pennsylvania and states like that.'

'Sure, of course they do.'

'Are you saying something's wrong with all of us?'

'Relax, no one's saying anything.'

I asked Carl some questions about veterinary surgery. He looked puzzled and answered that he didn't know, really; his business was naming new varieties of plants which came out of a laboratory in Missouri.

I don't remember how the conversation went after that.

After dinner, when Carl went into the kitchen to do the dishes, Julie pinched my arm. 'Bastard,' she said, 'how could you?' I didn't see that I'd given any offense. In my opinion, healing sick animals is one of the noblest professions imaginable, nobler even than healing sick people, because from animals there is little hope even of gratitude.

'The veterinary surgeon,' Julie said, 'was my old husband.'

'What was his name?'

'Anselm.'

'What was wrong with him?'

'He couldn't stop talking about animals.'

'Julie,' I said, 'do you ever think about me romantically?'

'No.'

'You don't ever wish that I'd kissed you again?'

'We never kissed.'

'Yes, we did.' I told her about the stone and the lake, and how she invited me to come over. 'You played cards that night while you waited for me. But I never came.'

'You're drunk,' she said.

'That's not the point.' I explained that I was the owner of a telescope, purchased at the Sky Shoppe, in Mystic, Conn., which could see into the past. I explained to her about the age of the stars, and the giant lens in space, and told her how, by means of its manifold mirrors, its lenses and tubes and motorized mount, my telescope was capable of receiving light that had left the earth years and years ago. 'I can see you in your room when you were fourteen,' I said. 'I can see everything as if it were happening now.'

'You're completely drunk,' said Julie.

'You were beautiful,' I said.

'Carl, take him home. He can't drive.'

I don't remember the ride back around the lake. Apparently I told Carl to stop so that I could get out and vomit. Apparently – it's Carl who says so – I knelt there a long time, retching sometimes and sometimes just looking into the water.

III

After that the blinds in Julie's window were closed. I made a new discovery, though: there was a fire burning on Mount Head. Little shapes moved around it, some quickly and others quite slow. At first I couldn't make anything of them, but as I watched the shapes resolved themselves into figures, and the figures into children. They were waving and jumping up and down as they ran around the fire. What were they doing that for? I wondered if their parents knew they were up there, or if they'd snuck away and were engaged in something illicit. Probably they were drinking beer and when they'd finished dancing, they would go off into the bushes and fondle one another. I was elated. This, I thought, is how an astronomer must feel when a new comet appears in his well-mapped field of night: what an incredible glory to have, if only for a moment, sole possession, so to speak, of a celestial object. I felt the same way about the children. Because I was the only one observing them, they were mine, even more mine than they would have been if they came at that very moment into my observatory – their real proximity, in fact, would only have made a mess of all my tenderness for them, which was, in that moment, so strong that I had to wipe my eyes to keep from moistening the eyepiece.

Happy children, I thought, and closed the roof of the observatory. I made cocoa on my spirit stove, and thought about Julie young and old, and how age burns people down, so that instead of dancing around fires they go shopping and marry cinders of men with names like Carl and Anselm. Of course the same thing might be true of stars. If you could see a star as it is now, not as it was thousands of years ago, it might be a great disappointment: a great black hulk turning in the void, a lump which you would not know at all.

The next night the children were up there again, dancing with even more energy than the night before, although their fire seemed a little smaller. Were they lost? Perhaps what I mistook for dancing was actually them signaling for help, waving their arms and shouting for a grownup to come and rescue them from their unaccustomed height. But what could I do? They were lost not only in time but in space; what I saw through the telescope had taken place years before, perhaps in an altogether different place. Now one of them appeared to be waving a flag. I remembered a story I had read long ago about children who play a game on an island in the middle of a lake. It ended badly, I think. But these children seemed to be enjoying themselves. It was impossible, I know, but in the quiet of the observatory I thought I could hear their festive howling.

It snowed again on Thanksgiving, so I went to the movies in Commonstock. One of those millennial pictures was playing, about a prehistoric plague unleashed on Los Angeles when a mysterious being, possibly extraterrestrial, is exhumed from the tar pits. In the end the sexy, no-nonsense biologist and the wisecracking ex-priest save the earth by contacting friendly aliens, who arrive with the antidote and a thousand years of mysteries bundled on their tiny, reddish shoulders.

I ran into George Pouliadis on the way back to my car. He looked as though he'd aged ten years; his face was scratched and he wore the beginnings of a beard, which didn't suit him.

'Have you got fifty dollars?' he asked me.

'What for?'

'I'll pay you back the next time I see you.'

'Sure.' It was the least I could do, after all the times he'd helped me. 'How was the hike? Did you see many fossils?'

'Ssh!'

'What? I thought you liked nature.'

'Nature,' George said, 'will kick our ass every time. Every time.' He climbed into his truck and drove off, and, as far as anyone knows, he was never seen in Commonstock again.

*

My father came to see me in the observatory. He studied the pictures of the children I'd taken with my telescope's photographic attachment. In one picture you can see the children clearly, leaping up against the background of the fire. In another they seem to be holding hands, although it's possible that two of them, upright, are carrying a third, supine, between them.

'What are these?'

'Just things in the sky.'

'Are those galaxies?' He pointed to the separate tongues of the fire.

'I believe it's a nebula,' I said.

'God, a nebula. What about this?' He pointed to a child's torso.

'Dark matter.'

He whistled. 'We should show these to the astronomers. I bet they don't see pictures like this every day.'

'I'll bet they don't.'

'They're really some pictures.'

'Yes, they are.'

'By the way, have you seen George lately?'

'No. Why?'

He shook his head. 'I knew he was no good, ever since he dug that foundation too deep.'

I pointed out that the foundation was our work, not George's.

'Hm,' he said. 'These are really some pictures.'

'Yes, they are.'

'You're all right, aren't you?'

'Never better.'

*

After the Thanksgiving storm, the children were gone from the mountaintop. I looked for them night after night, on Mount Head and the neighboring hills, but their fire was burned out, their dance over. It was hard for me to get used to their absence. I spent the days on the sofa, reading magazines; after dark, sometimes, I walked a little way along the edge of the lake. One night, entirely by accident, I saw what I think was a planet, hanging over a jagged field of trees. The planet was dim, stippled, unmoving and more or less without interest, compared to the other things I'd seen, but at least it reminded me not to give up looking. We run around as if it were the end of the world, and everything were lost, when all the while, without knowing it, we have been populating heaven with our mistakes.

In January I left Commonstock and drove back to New York, where I found work at an ad agency, researching the market for a new kind of storm drain. I rented an apartment in Ozone Park, high above the scattered streetlights, and set up my telescope in a portable mount that I built myself. I don't use it often now, but some nights I sit up late, looking northeast through the eyepiece. I wonder what became of my children, and how they came down from the mountain, and when, and when, they will come to me.

Walking on the Rings of Saturn

PAUL COLLINS

LUNAR HUMANOIDS –
We were thrilled with astonishment to perceive four successive flocks
of large winged creatures, wholly unlike any kind of birds, descend
with a slow even motion from the cliffs on the western side, and
alight upon the plain. They were first noted by Dr Herschel, who
exclaimed, 'Now, gentlemen, my theories against your proofs, which
you have often found a pretty even bet, we have here something
worth looking at: I was confident that if we ever found beings in
human shape, it would be in this longitude!'
 – *New York Sun*, August 28, 1835

Life on the moon!

It seemed too good to be true – and so it was, in the end.
But for a few weeks in 1835, it was as real as the newspaper
gripped in every American's hands. Readers could thank journalist Richard Locke for the bizarre account of lunar life; but
for the even more bizarre thoughts behind them, they had to
turn to a shy, self-taught astronomer from Scotland.

Thomas Dick was not born into the contemplative life. In
1774, science was still a gentleman's profession, well out of
reach of the likes of Dick's father, a weaver. But the son of this
humble weaver had a revelation in 1782, at the age of eight,
when he saw a meteorite flash before him in the evening
sky. Soon he was spending his workdays at the loom reading

borrowed books on astronomy; at night, he ground his own lenses and constructed crude telescopes with pasteboard tubes. He fell in with academics and spent much of his early life teaching, preaching, and promoting, in his words, 'literary and philosophical societies adapted to the middling and lower ranks of society.' His youthful interest in astronomy was never lost in all this activity; on the contrary, it became the center-piece of his lifelong obsession with marrying religion and science. To Dick, the heavens – both spiritual and physical – were God's work made visible on a vast scale to earthly inhabitants.

With successful teaching and writing stints behind him, Dick decided, at the age of 53, to fully devote himself to his lifelong passion. He quit teaching and went to work building a small cottage on a hill near Dundee, fitted with its own library and observatory. Being by nature a reserved and rather sober man, the remote perch suited him just fine. By night, he watched the skies, having long since graduated from his apprenticeship of homemade lenses and pasteboard tubes. By day, he wrote books – great masses of them – expounding upon education, prison reform, fire safety, preaching, and, most of all, astronomy.

He was tremendously popular in Great Britain and in the US, in part because he could write on scientific discoveries for the common man in a way that his learned colleagues never could. But clarity alone doesn't explain his wide popularity. Dick had captured the public imagination with his belief that every single planet, moon, comet, and star was inhabited with intelligent beings. And what was more, he had a fair idea of how to reach them.

*

While walking across a field, you find a watch on the ground. All these minerals couldn't have combined together to form a watch on their own; surely this watch must have had a watchmaker. Walking further, you kick up a chunk of quartz. Examined closely, it reveals a fantastic crystalline structure. You assumed the carefully designed watch had a maker; why not the chunk of quartz?

This was the opening argument of William Paley's 1802 work *Natural Theology*, which lent its name to the entire field that arose in its wake. Though these ideas had been bubbling for some time, it was Paley who spread natural theology to the intelligentsia.

To a natural theologian, the wisdom and moral perfection of God was evidenced by the compact design and utility of every natural object. Today we might see giraffes as the evolutionary survivor of merciless natural selection, winning over dead-end mutations by virtue of being able to eat lofty edible leaves. But to a natural theologian, a giraffe was evidence of God's kindly hand – creating a plain with high trees, He provided for the giraffe's welfare by giving their necks a good stretch.

The movement came to a head in the 1830s, when the Cambridge don William Whewell's Bridgewater Treatise allowed and even encouraged the belief that a benevolent God would populate other worlds with beings intelligent enough to appreciate the beauty of his creations. This idea had also some currency in the 17th century: the theologian Giordani Bruno was burned at the stake for this belief in 1600, and both the English bishop John Wilkins and the French scientist Bernard le Bovier de Fontenelle advocated it later that century. Now, though, it was to be revived dramatically by Whewell and other scientists like Sir David Brewster. But it was Dick, the humble Scottish astronomer, who went further than anyone else dared to imagine.

To Dick, the massive workings of the skies were a means to a magnificent and inscrutable end. For it to be otherwise, a means without an end, would reveal our Maker to be a cruel existentialist (though, at the time, Dick perhaps wouldn't have used that word). The universe would be, as his book *The Sidereal Heavens* claimed, 'one wide scene of dreariness, desolation, horror, and silence, which would fill a spectator from this world with terror and dismay ... without one sentient being to cheer the horrors of the scene.' This was clearly unacceptable in a Christian God, as was the 'wild hallucination' that our own life was an accident of primordial chemistry. We did not exist as a result of fortunate material reactions – the world existed to please us, a conceit now known as the Anthropic Principle. 'Matter,' Dick insisted, 'was evidently framed for the purpose of mind.'

It also followed that having matter anywhere without a sentient being for it to serve would be pointless. Therefore, every celestial body must be inhabited. Intelligent life was more than a mere accident of our planet, or of perhaps one or two others: it was the natural state of the universe. To believe otherwise was 'impious, blasphemous, and absurd.' Writings like Dick's *Celestial Scenery* are thunderous on this point: 'Let us suppose for a moment that the vast regions on the surfaces of the planets are only immense and frightful deserts, devoid of inhabitants – wherein does the wisdom of the Creator appear in the supposition? Would this be an end worthy of INFINITE WISDOM?'

With every world being inhabited, it was natural enough for Dick to first turn his attentions on the moon. By Dick's estimate, if the moon were as crowded as England, it would have a population of 4.2 billion. And with every order of life inhabiting every world, he went on in *The Sidereal Heavens* to use this formula to calculate the population of the visible universe:

There would be the following number of inhabitants in these worlds, 60,573,000,000,000,000,000,000,000; that is, sixty quartillions, five hundred and seventy three thousand trillions, a number which transcends human conception. Among such a number of beings, what a variety of orders may exist, from the archangel and the seraph to the worm and the microscopic animaliculum!

But there is no explanation, sadly, of why a benevolent God would want to make every planet as crowded as England.

Given the magnificent intricacy of virtually any object, Dick's thinking naturally led him to believe that every celestial object was inhabited, including comets and asteroids. 'Comets may be the abodes of greater happiness than is to be found on our sublunary world,' he marveled, 'and may be peopled with intelligences of a higher order than the race of man.' These comets might be peopled with rather worldly fellows (or rather, cometary fellows), sophisticated and wizened by the vaster and more diverse prospects afforded to them by their long, irregular orbits inside the solar system. He imagined that they might be a race of astronomers, sailing through space in their icy observatory, in eternal contemplation of the planets: 'Their movable observatory, cruising from sun to sun, carries them in succession through every different point of view.' With keen enough eyes, perhaps these cometary beings could spy upon a whole other order of beings altogether – the ones, Dick proclaimed, that lived in the interior of the sun.

Dick also believed the rings of Saturn to be solid, in the mistaken belief that mere dust debris would have already been flung into space. Given their solidity, and the sublime views of the planet surface below and the heavens above, Dick thought that surely these rings must be populated with 'numerous orders of intellectual beings.'

These intelligent neighbors were not invulnerable, though. In Dick's time, the asteroid belt between Mars and Jupiter was still a relatively new discovery, and some hazarded the guess that it might be the remains of a planet. In Dick's thinking – because all planets were inhabited – this cataclysm becomes a celestial Sodom: 'The fate of the beings that inhabited the original planet must have been involved in the awful catastrophe . . . nor should we consider it inconsistent with what we know of the physical government of the Almighty.' Some scientists – then, as now – fretted over the possibility of a comet smashing into the Earth and snuffing out the human race. But however vengeful this planet-smashing God was, Dick could not imagine that this was the common moral state of the universe:

The benevolent Father of all did not intend that this moral derangement should be universal and perpetual . . . If a world which has been partly deranged by the sin of its inhabitants abounds with so many pleasures, what numerous sources of happiness must abound, and what ecstatic joys must be felt in those worlds where mortal evil has never entered, where diseases and death are unknown.

A good God meant that most, and maybe all, other worlds were still in a state of innocence. Perhaps, then, it was just as well that we couldn't corrupt them through human contact – a notion that has enjoyed currency among science-fiction writers ever since.

In fact, Dick thought that alien intellects and morals might be far more advanced than ours. The distant and irregular motion of the outer planets would demand a superhuman mind in order to make the astronomical observations needed to appreciate God's celestial workings. Comets swooped in irregular orbits, while the inhabitants of the rings of Saturn lived on multiple rings that (by his guess) all moved at confusingly different speeds:

Intelligent minds exist in the regions of Jupiter, Saturn, and Uranus ... Those minds, in all probability, are endowed with faculties superior in intellectual energy and acumen to those of our globe. For the rapidity and complexity of the [planetary] motion ... require[s] the exertion of [superhuman] intellectual faculties.

And lunar astronomers had to surmount their initially lunar-centric view of the universe to realize that their role was twice diminished: that is, circling another world that was itself circling a sun. But our moon's astronomers, favored with long nights and a thin atmosphere – for Dick refused to believe that the moon lacked any air at all – could at least take solace in crystal-clear views of their earthly brethren.

Better still, he hinted, perhaps these Lunarians didn't even need telescopes to do this. Although our weak earthly eyes might not be able to view them with the most powerful instruments, aliens might have eyes that could spy upon us unaided. Dick's mind also drifted to imagining how the night might look on other planets: 'The most splendid object in the nocturnal sky of Venus will be the Earth . . . Our moon will likewise be seen from Mars like a small star accompanying the Earth.' In fact, Dick could scarcely conceive blind or dim-eyed aliens. What else is the universe for, he asked, but contemplation by its inhabitants?

All these speculations on interplanetary vistas were easy enough to consider in the abstract, but Dick popularized a grander earthly plan. Reasoning that all alien intelligences spoke the universal language of geometry, in *Celestial Scenery* he proposed the construction of a gigantic geometrical figure on the plains of Siberia:

A correspondence with the inhabitants of the moon could only be begun by means of such mathematical contemplations and ideas which we and they must have in common. They might perhaps erect a similar one in reply. Schemes far more foolish and preposterous than the above have been contrived and acted upon in every age of the world. The millions which are now wasting in the pursuits of mad ambition and destructive warfare might, with far greater propriety, be expended in constructing a huge triangle or ellipsis of many miles in extent, in Siberia or any other country.

On a slightly more practical note, Dick envisioned a worldwide corps of thousands of astronomers, each allocated a particular part of the moon to survey for years, all in order to detect any long-term changes in vegetation or topography, either of which might indicate the urban handiwork of an intelligent race.

Even in his era, long before radio, Dick imagined that

humans might contrive some better means of reaching out into the ether. 'Man is only in the infancy of his being,' he mused, for he knew that his monumental proposals were also monumentally unwieldy means of interplanetary communication:

We may conceive that intellectual beings, to whatever portion of the material world they originally belonged, may hold the most intimate converse with one another, by modes peculiar to their economy, and which are beyond the conceptions of the physical universe; so that distance in point of space shall form no insuperable barrier to the mutual communication of sentiments and emotions.

For a few months in 1835, it seemed that Dick's vision might come true.

It began quietly enough. On August 21, 1835, the *New York Sun* reported that astronomer Sir John Herschel 'has made some astronomical discoveries of the most wonderful description, by means of an immense telescope.' Hyperbole was common to newspapers of the time, so this announcement could have meant almost anything. What it did mean was revealed a day later: in South Africa, the ingenious Herschel had built a telescope so powerful that, when the cap was left off during the day, it melted the plaster walls into blue glass, burned a hole through the observatory, and then set fire to a nearby grove of trees. This insanely powerful telescope could magnify objects by an unheard-of 42,000 times, and was promptly turned at the moon the next night to reveal . . . a field of poppies.

As if in an opium dream, the magical images unfolded:

A beach of brilliant sand, girt with wild castellated rocks, apparently
of green marble . . . with grotesque blocks of gypsum, and festooned
at the summit with the clustering foliage of unknown trees. We
were speechless with admiration . . . [Later we saw pyramids] of
monstrous amethysts, of a diluted claret color, glowing in the
intensest light of the sun!

If *Sun* readers were stunned by the news, so were the news-
agents: the issue sold out, and printers scrambled to keep up
with demand for it and the following issue. The *Sun* had
scooped every other paper in the country by obtaining the
latest copy of the *Edinburgh Journal of Sciences*, which apparently
held Dr Andrew Grant's account of the lunar discoveries.
Unable to procure a copy of the account for themselves, com-
peting papers immediately reprinted the story. But even they
couldn't have anticipated the next electrifying revelation:
animal life.

The dawn of August 25 saw New Yorkers sitting down and
rubbing their eyes in disbelief. Herschel had discovered herds
of small bison living on the moon. What was more, there was
a menagerie of bizarre lunar animals that almost defied earthly
description:

The next animal perceived would be classed on earth as a monster.
It was of a bluish lead color, about the size of a goat, with a head
and beard like him, and a single horn, slightly inclined forward from the perpendicular. The female was destitute of horn and
beard, but had a much longer tail. It was gregarious, and chiefly
abounded on the acclivitous glades of the woods. In elegance of
symmetry it rivaled the antelope, and like him it seemed an agile
sprightly creature, running with great speed, and springing from

the green turf with all the unaccountable antics of a young lamb or kitten.

Looking further across the lunar plains, they saw palm trees, islands of shimmering quartz, and herds of miniature reindeer, elk, and zebra. Animals ranged in size from mice to a bear with horns, and included – most startlingly – the biped beaver. As tall as humans, they walked upright, skating gracefully among their villages of tall huts, which all had chimneys that showed their tribes to be acquainted with the use of fire.

As adept readers may have already guessed, there was something missing from this fantastic narrative – an elusive quality that we might call reality. For the source of these articles was not Dr Andrew Grant, but a gang of merry hoaxers at the *New York Sun* led by one Richard Adams Locke.

Locke was a brash young British expatriate, and his schooling at Cambridge, in the 1820s, would have placed him in a hotbed of natural theology. The sight of Dick and his ilk being reprinted and parroted across American periodicals was just too tempting for Locke to pass up. The 1820s had already brought at least two clumsily executed claims of life on the moon. With his university training, though, Locke was able to imitate his instructors' rhetoric with perfect pitch.

Like any good hoax, Locke's began from reasonable-sounding premises. Dick and Whewell's writing had already made alien life a plausible and maybe inevitable discovery. Herschel was a respected member of a famous family of astronomers, and he had in fact recently set up shop in South Africa. Still, for all their savvy, neither Locke nor *Sun* publisher Moses Beach (the father of future *Scientific American* publisher Alfred

Beach) could have guessed at the sensational nationwide impact of their 'discovery.' The circulation of the *New York Sun* leaped fivefold overnight, and Locke's articles were reprinted by newspapers across the country. Fellow journalists clamored for more details, and enthusiastic astronomers besieged ticket agents to book passages to South Africa. To top this media mayhem would be a challenge indeed – but Locke did not disappoint.

On August 28th, the *Sun* reported the biggest scoop in the history of journalism: there were people on the moon. Or rather . . . a sort of people:

They averaged four feet in height, were covered, except on the face, with short and glossy copper-colored hair, and had wings composed of a thin membrane . . . In general symmetry of body and limbs they were infinitely superior to the orangoutang [sic] . . . Some of these creatures had crossed this water and were lying like spread eagles on the skirts of the wood. We could then perceive that they possessed wings of great expansion, and were similar in structure to that of the bat . . . We scientifically denominated them as Vespertilio-homo, or man-bat; and they are doubtless innocent and happy creatures, notwithstanding that some of their amusements would but ill comport with our terrestrial notions of decorum.

These man-bats lived in a land of towering sapphire pyramids and were accompanied by flocks of doves. In their more relaxed moments, they could be seen picnicking on cucumbers.

Locke now had the nation's ear. In a time when many lands were as yet unmapped, such fantastic claims about another planet could be easily accepted. But really, we might ask, could Locke's fellow journalists have been that gullible? This comment from the *New York Evening Post* stands on its own as a reply:

That there should be winged people in the Moon does not strike us as more wonderful than the existence of such a race of beings on Earth . . . [such as described by] Peter Wilkins, whose celebrated work not only gives an account of the general appearance of habits of a most interesting tribe of flying Indians, but also of all those more delicate and engaging traits which the author [Wilkins] was enabled to discover by reason of the conjugal relations he entered into with one of the females of the winged tribe.

Not surprisingly, at this point – if not well before – it dawned on Locke and Beach that all this attention could be worth a good deal of money. Following the distinct smell of lucre in the air, they set about printing up the articles in book form. The first printing of *Great Astronomical Discoveries Lately Made by Sir John Herschel at the Cape of Good Hope* (now reproduced as 'Moon Walk 1835' at http://users.visi.net/~cwt/moonwalk.html) quickly sold out its run of 60,000 copies; pirated editions rushed in to fill the void. The public couldn't get enough of it: congregations began taking up collections for missionaries to preach gospel to the man-bat race, and scalpers sold copies of the coveted book for tidy sums of cash.

Inevitably, Locke's time ran out. Astronomers seeking copies of his sources, met with increasingly evasive replies, began to get suspicious. Arriving ships showed no sign of the famous article by Dr Grant in the *Edinburgh Journal of Sciences*. But in the end, vanity did the hoax in. Unable to contain himself, the star journalist pulled aside a friend and revealed his grand

prank – he had fooled the whole nation! – and, of course, the
friend was sworn to utter secrecy.

Locke awoke the next day to screaming headlines. And so
on September 16 – its chutzpah intact, if not its credibility
– the *New York Sun* admitted to the hoax, but excused it on
the outrageous grounds that it had performed a public service
by 'diverting the public mind, for a while, from the bitter apple
of discord, the abolition of slavery . . .' But if they couldn't be
bothered to come up with a better excuse, perhaps it was
because Locke and Beach were too busy counting the small
fortune they'd made off the whole absurd affair.

Dick was unamused. In a footnote to *Celestial Scenery* he huffs:

The author of this deception, I understand, is a young man in the
city of New York, who makes some professions as to scientific
acquirements, and he may be perhaps disposed to congratulate himself . . . The Law of Truth ought never for a moment to be sported
with . . . For when untutored minds and the mass of the community
detect such an imposition, they are apt to call in question the real
discoveries of science . . . It is to be hoped that the author of the
deception to which I have adverted, as he advances in years and in
wisdom, will perceive the folly and immorality of such conduct.

It was a fatherly wheeze worthy of Polonius, but Dick needn't
have bothered. Locke merrily hoaxed gullible suckers well into
his golden years.

And they were suckers, as even Dick was to admit. Any
half-educated reader should have realized that a supposed telescope with a magnification power of 42,000 times would make
the moon, a quarter-million miles distant, appear about six

miles away. 'To perceive such objects [as animals],' Dick commented wryly, 'it was requisite that they should have been brought within six yards instead of six miles.'

Edgar Allan Poe, on the other hand, was quite tickled by the whole affair. Writing in the October 1846 issue of *Godey's Lady's Book*, Poe thanked Locke for having whipped up a sales frenzy that ended up financing most of New York's penny newspaper presses. Poe was no stranger to successful hoaxes, as he had at least three to his credit – his own 'Hans Pfall' moon hoax, the bizarre suspended animation of 'M Valdemar,' and the past-lives scam of 'Mesmeric Revelation.' Poe, often quick to accuse competitors of plagiarism, was warm in his praise of Locke.

Nonetheless, for a few years after the lunar hoax, Dick's ideas were quoted in popular periodicals of the day, and gained a wider (if distorted) circulation through Locke's spoof. He also made his way anonymously into the hands of many unsuspecting readers. In 1846 a chapbook of Dick's *The Solar System* was published in America by the American Sunday-School Union, one of a countless number of tract societies that flooded the American frontier and the British countryside with edifying books on science, theology, and treacly moral tales. Dick's name doesn't appear anywhere on (or in) it. Nor does it have any hint of Dick's far-out cosmology: to look at it, you'd think it was nothing more than a nice little guide to the planets put out by a nice little church press. We can only imagine some grizzled dirt farmer in Nebraska scratching his beard as he set his copy down, pondering the building of a Siberian monument to communicate with Lunarians.

Amusingly enough – though probably not to Thomas Dick, had he lived to see it – Locke's hoax stayed in print longer than the work that it spoofed. Dick went out of print not long after his death in 1857, while Locke's *Great Astronomical Discoveries* outlasted Locke himself, with a fifth edition published in 1871, the year that he died.

So why did Dick's works go out of print first? For one thing, Dick's narrative became almost less credible than Locke's. Presented with any evidence that didn't accord with his notion of a wise and kindly God, Dick would reject it out of hand. For example, an apparent glow on the moon had been attributed by some colleagues to lunar volcanoes. Impossible, Dick declared: volcanoes were the result of our fall from grace, and the presence of 'such appalling and destructive agents . . . would be to virtually admit that the inhabitants of that planet are in the same depraved condition as the inhabitants of this world.' He reacted the same way to correct evidence of screamingly high wind speeds on Jupiter. Such observations, he sniffed, simply showed our ignorance of the planet's indubitably pleasant weather: 'A West India hurricane, blowing at the rate of a hundred miles an hour, has blown heavy cannon out of a battery . . . What, then, would be the force of a gale moving at the rate of a thousand miles per hour? [It is] altogether inconsistent with the idea of a comfortable habitation either for sensitive or intellectual beings.'

Natural theology's ensuing death was slow and painful. Its vulnerability lay in its ultimate allegiance to scripture, rather than to scientific methodology. When scripture didn't accord with scientific fact, the resulting reinterpretation of scripture took it further and further away from a literal reading of the Bible, and further out of the grasp of popular understanding. After 1850, in the first glimmerings of evolutionary biology and quantum physics, the link became so tenuous that one may as well be speaking of two different subjects entirely: Nature and Theology. Most people did, and so came the end of Natural Theology.

The only other easy option, an admission that scripture might be wrong, was dismissed out of hand by theorists like Whewell: 'The results of true geology and astronomy cannot be inconsistent with the statement of true theology.' Whewell himself declined in his later years into ineffectual and pathetic attempts to have copies of Darwin removed from his university library.

Dick was spared from these sights; when he died in 1857, the first drops of Darwinism had not yet eroded public belief. Posterity has been less kind to him, though: His once-popular tracts are nearly impossible to find and have been entirely out of print for well over a century. The 1855 edition of his complete works that I found at the University of California-Berkeley still had uncut pages. As far as I could tell, I was the first person in 143 years to even open it.

The Girl with Bangs

ZADIE SMITH

I fell in love with a girl once. Some time ago, now. She had
bangs. I was twenty years old at the time and prey to the
usual rag-bag of foolish ideas. I believed, for example, that
one might meet some sweet kid and like them a lot – maybe
even marry them – while all the time allowing that kid to
sleep with other kids, and that this could be done with no
fuss at all, just a chuck under the chin, and no tears. I believed
the majority of people to be bores, however you cut them;
that the mark of their dullness was easy to spot (clothes, hair)
and impossible to avoid, running right through them like a
watermark. I had made mental notes, too, on other empty
notions – the death of certain things (socialism, certain types
of music, old people), the future of others (film, footwear,
poetry) – but no one need be bored with those now. The only
significant bit of nonsense I carried around in those days, the
only one that came from the gut, if you like, was this feeling
that a girl with soft black bangs falling into eyes the colour
of a Perrier bottle must be good news. Look at her palming
the bangs away from her face, pressing them back along her
hairline, only to have them fall forward again! I found this
combination to be good, intrinsically good in both form and
content, the same way you think of cherries (life is a bowl of;
she was a real sweet) until the very centre of one becomes
lodged in your windpipe. I believed Charlotte Greaves and

79

her bangs to be good news. But Charlotte was emphatically bad news, requiring only eight months to take me entirely apart; the kind of clinically efficient dismembering you see when a bright child gets his hand on some toy he assembled in the first place. I'd never dated a girl before, and she was bad news the way boys can never be, because with boys it's always possible to draw up a list of pros and cons, and see the matter rationally, from either side. But you could make a list of cons on Charlotte stretching to Azerbaijan, and 'her bangs' sitting solitary in the pros column would outweigh all objections. Boys are just boys after all, but sometimes girls really seem to be the turn of a pale wrist, or the sudden jut of a hip, or a clutch of very dark hair falling across a freckled forehead. I'm not saying that's what they really are. I'm just saying sometimes it seems that way, and that those details (a thigh mole, a full face flush, a scar the precise shape and size of a cashew nut) are so many hooks waiting to land you. In this case, it was those bangs, plush and dramatic; curtains opening on to a face one would queue up to see. All women have a backstage, of course, of course. Labyrinthine, many-roomed, no doubt, no doubt. But you come to see the show, that's all I'm saying.

I first set eyes on Charlotte when she was seeing a Belgian who lived across the hall from me in college. I'd see her first thing, shuffling around the communal bathroom looking a mess – undone, always, in every sense – with her T-shirt tucked in her knickers, a fag hanging out of her mouth, some kind of toothpaste or maybe mouthwash residue by her lips and those bangs in her eyes. It was hard to understand why this Belgian, Maurice, had chosen to date her. He had this great accent, Maurice, elaborately French, like you couldn't be more French, and a jaw line that seemed in fashion at the time, and you could tick all the boxes vis-à-vis personal charms; Maurice was an impressive kind of a guy. Charlotte was the kind of woman who has only two bras, both of them grey. But after a while, if you paid attention, you came to realize that she had a look about her like she just got out of a bed, no matter what time of day you collided with her (she had a stalk of a walk, never looked where she was going, so you had no choice) and this tendency, if put under the heading 'Qualities That Girls Sometimes Have,' was a kind of poor relation of 'Bedroom Eyes' or 'Looks Like She's Thinking about Sex All the Time' – and it worked. She seemed always to be stumbling away from someone else, towards you. A limping figure smiling widely, arms outstretched, dressed in rags, a smouldering city as backdrop. I had watched too many films, possibly. But still: a bundle of precious things thrown at you from a third-floor European window, wrapped loosely in a blanket, chosen frantically and at random by the well-meaning owner, slung haphazardly from a burning building; launched at you; it could hurt, this bundle; but look! You have caught it! A little chipped, but otherwise fine. Look what you have saved! (You understand me, I know. This is how it feels. What is the purpose of metaphor, anyway, if not to describe women?)

Now, it came to pass that this Maurice was offered a well-paid TV job in Thailand as a newscaster, and he agonized, and weighed Charlotte in one hand and the money in the other and found he could not leave without the promise that she would wait for him. This promise she gave him, but he was still gone, and gone is gone, and that's where I came in. Not immediately – I am no thief – but by degrees; studying near her in the library, watching her hair make reading difficult. Sitting next to her at lunch watching the bangs go hither, and, I suppose, thither, as people swished by with their food trays. Befriending her friends and then her; making as many nice noises about Maurice as I could. I became a boy for the duration. I stood under the window with my open arms. I did all the old boy tricks. These tricks are not as difficult as some boys will have you believe, but they are indeed slow, and work only by a very gradual process of accumulation. You have sad moments when you wonder if there will ever be an end to it. But then, usually without warning, the hard work pays off. With Charlotte it went like this: she came by for a herbal tea one day, and I rolled a joint and then another and soon enough she was lying across my lap, spineless as a mollusk, and I had my fingers in those bangs – teasing them, as the hairdressers say – and we had begun.

Most of the time we spent together was in her room. At the beginning of an affair you've no need to be outside. And it was like a filthy cocoon her room, ankle-deep in rubbish; it was the kind of room that took you in and held you close. With no clocks and my watch lost and buried, we passed time by the degeneration of things; the rotting of fruit, the accumulation of bacteria, the rising tideline of cigarettes in the vase we used to put them out. It was a quarter past this apple. The third Saturday in the month of that stain. These things were unpleasant and tiresome. And she was no intellectual; any book I gave her she treated like a kid treats a Christmas present – fascination for a day and then the quick pall of boredom; by the end of the week it was flung across the room and submerged; weeks later when we made love I'd find the spine of the novel sticking into the small of my back, paper cuts on my toes. There was no bed to speak of. There was just a bit of the floor that was marginally clearer than the rest of it. (But wait! Here she comes, falling in an impossible arc, and here I am by careful design in just the right spot, under the window, and here she is, landing and nothing is broken, and I cannot believe my luck. You understand me. Every time I looked at the bangs, the bad stuff went away.)

Again: I know it doesn't sound great, but let's not forget the bangs. Let us not forget that after a stand-up row, a real screaming match, she could look at me from underneath the distinct hairs, separated by sweat, and I had no more resistance. Yes, you can leave the overturned plant pot where it is. Yes, Rousseau is an idiot if you say so. So this is what it's like being a boy. The cobbled street, the hopeful arms hugging air. There is nothing you won't do.

Charlotte's exams were coming up. I begged her to look through her reading list once more, and plan some strategic line of attack, but she wanted to do it her way. Her way meant reading the same two books – Rousseau's *Social Contract* and Plato's *Republic* (her paper was to be on people, and the way they organize their lives, or the way they did, or the way they should, I don't remember; it had a technical title, I don't remember that either) – again and again, in the study room that sat in a quiet corner of the college. The study room was meant to be for everyone but since Charlotte had moved in, all others had gradually moved out. I recall one German graduate who stood his ground for a month or so, who cleared his throat regularly and pointedly picked up things that she had dropped – but she got to him, finally. Charlotte's papers all over the floor, Charlotte's old lunches on every table, Charlotte's clothes and my clothes (now indistinguishable) thrown over every chair. People would come up to me in the bar and say, 'Look, Charlotte did X. Could you please, for the love of God, stop Charlotte doing X, please?', and I would try, but Charlotte's bangs kept Charlotte in the world of Charlotte and she barely heard me. And now, please, before we go any further: tell me. Tell me if you've ever stood under a window and caught an unworthy bundle of chintz. Gold plating that came off with one rub; faked signatures, worthless trinkets. Have you? Maybe the bait was different – not bangs, but deep pockets either side of the smile or unusually vivid eye pigmentation. Or some other bodily attribute (hair, skin, curves) that recalled in you some natural phenomenon (wheat, sea, cream). Same difference. So: have you? Have you ever been out with a girl like this?

Some time after Charlotte's exams, after the 2.2 that had been stalking her for so long finally pounced, there was a knock on the door. My door – I recall now that we were in my room that morning. I hauled on a dressing-gown and went to answer it. It was Maurice, tanned and dressed like one of the Beatles when they went to see the Maharashi; a white suit with a Nehru collar, his own bangs and tousled hair, slightly long at the back. He looked terrific. He said, 'Someone in ze bar says you might 'ave an idea where Charlotte is. I need to see 'er – it is very urgent. 'Ave you seen 'er?' I had seen her. She was in my bed, about five feet from where Maurice stood, but obscured by a partition wall. 'No . . .' I said. 'No, not this morning. She'll probably be in the hall for breakfast though, she usually is. So, Maurice! When did you get back?' He said, 'All zat must come later. I 'ave to find Charlotte. I sink I am going to marry 'er.' And I thought, Christ, which bad movie am I in?

I got Charlotte up, shook her, poured her into some clothes, and told her to run around the back of the college and get to the dining hall before Maurice. I saw her in my head, the moment the door closed – no great feat of imagination, I had seen her run before; like a naturally uncoordinated animal (a panda?) that somebody has just shot – I saw her dashing incompetently past the ancient walls, catching herself on ivy, tripping up steps, and finally falling through the swing doors, looking wildly round the dining hall like those movie time-travellers who know not in which period they have just landed. But still she managed it, apparently she got there in time, though as the whole world now knows, Maurice took one look at her strands matted against her forehead, running in line with the ridge-ways of sleep left by the pillows and said, 'You're *sleeping* with her?' (Or maybe, 'You're sleeping with *her*?' – I don't know; this is all reported speech) and Charlotte, who, like a lot of low-maintenance women, cannot tell a lie, said, 'Er . . . yes. Yes,' and then made that signal of feminine relief; bottom lip out, air blown upwards; bangs all of a flutter.

Later that afternoon, Maurice came back round to my room, looking all the more noble, and seemingly determined to have a calm man-to-man 'You see, I have returned to marry her/I will not stand in your way'-type of a chat, which was very reasonable and English of him. I let him have it alone. I nodded when it seemed appropriate; sometimes I lifted my hands in protest but soon let them fall again. You can't fight it when you've been replaced; a simple side-step and here is some old/new Belgian guy standing in the cobbled street with his face upturned, and his arms wide open, judging the angles. I thought of this girl he wanted back, who had taken me apart piece by piece, causing me nothing but trouble, with her bangs and her anti-social behaviour. I was all (un)done, I realized. I sort of marvelled at the devotion he felt for her. From a thousand miles away, with a smouldering city as a backdrop, I watched him beg me to leave them both alone; tears in his eyes, the works. I agreed it was the best thing, all round. I had the impression that here was a girl who would be thrown from person to person over years, and each would think they had saved her by some miracle when in actual fact she was in no danger at all. Never. Not even for a second.

He said, 'Let us go, zen, and tell 'er the decision we 'ave come to,' and I said yes, let's, but when we got to Charlotte's room, someone else was putting his fingers through her curls. Charlotte was always one of those people for whom sex is available at all times – it just happens to her, quickly, and with a minimum of conversation. This guy was some other guy that she'd been sleeping with on the days when she wasn't with me. It had been going on for four months. This all came out later, naturally.

Would you believe he married her anyway? And not only that, he married her after she'd shaved her head that afternoon just to spite us. All of us – even the other guy no one had seen before. Maurice took a bald English woman with a strange lopsided walk, and a temper like a gorgon, back to Thailand and married her despite friends' complaints and the voluble protest of Aneepa Kapoor, who was the woman he read the news with. The anchorwoman, who had that Hitchcock style: hair tied back tight in a bun, a spiky nose and a vicious red mouth. The kind of woman who doesn't need catching. 'Maurice,' she said, 'you owe me. You can't just throw four months away like it wasn't worth a bloody thing!' He e-mailed me about it. He admitted that he'd been stringing Aneepa along for a while, and she'd been expecting something at the end of it. For in the real world, or so it seems to me, it is almost always women and not men who are waiting under windows, and they are almost always disappointed. In this matter, Charlotte was unusual.

The Hypnotist's Trailer

ANN CUMMINS

A woman, Josephine, read an ad in the advertiser one day: Addiction Therapist. Can Cure Anything. Hypnotism; Psychic Massage. Josephine smoked, and she drank a little bit, too. She decided to give the hypnotist a try. She took her daughter along.

The hypnotist lived and worked in a trailer on a paved lot at the base of Stone Mountain. He was a hairy man but his teeth were straight and his fingernails clipped. His place was sparsely furnished, a rattan couch, a tweedy chair. No little vases, no magazines.

'Let's skip the preliminaries and get right down to it,' the hypnotist said. 'Do you believe in God?'

'Yes,' Josephine said.

'What does he look like?'

This confused her.

'Does he have a beard?'

'Oh, yes.'

'I have a beard.'

'Yes you do.'

'He has long hair and brown eyes, too.'

Josephine supposed he did.

In short order, the hypnotist convinced her that she was in the presence of God.

'Do you believe that God can deliver you from your sins? Will you put your trust in the Lord?'

She did. She would.

'Give me a token of your trust, then.'

'Token?'

'Something you value. Your purse perhaps.'

The daughter – Irene was her name – laughed, and a shadow crossed the hypnotist's face. He glanced at the girl. She was pretty in a trashy way. Her face was white with makeup, and her eyes were lined with green. She wore her hair in a half-shaved, half-dyed style, which he hated. She was a skinny thing, though. He liked skinny things, and he felt a sudden urge to involve her.

'Your daughter was right to laugh,' he said. 'A purse is just a thing.'

Josephine smiled at the girl; Irene rolled her eyes.

'Give me something you truly value,' the hypnotist said. He winked at the girl. 'Give me your daughter.'

Irene laughed. 'Yeah, Mom. Give me to him.'

'My daughter?' Josephine frowned. Irene caused Josephine countless sleepless nights and tormented days. Josephine looked at the hypnotist who was stroking his beard, eyeing the girl. To her surprise, the man's face began to change – to lose its rough and flabby cheeks and nose, to smooth and tighten.

Suddenly she threw her arms around Irene. 'You can't have her!' she hissed.

The hypnotist raised his eyebrows, then looked at his feet.

'It's all my fault she's bad,' Josephine whispered.

'I can see that,' he whispered back.

Irene slipped out from her mother's grasp. She was pleased

to be noticed. But also bored. She began kicking her foot, fidgeting. The hypnotist frowned. Boredom was not good. Boredom broke the mood. He ran his tongue over his teeth, leaned forward, smiled at Josephine, and said, 'Give me your belly button.'

'What?' Josephine said.

'Give me your navel.'

The girl grinned. This she liked.

'Give it to me,' he whispered.

The woman looked down. She lifted her shirt, pushed down her skirt, and looked at it. What did he mean, give it to him? Was it like what you did with kids when you pretended to take their noses? She looked at her daughter. Irene nodded. It must be like what you did with kids. Josephine laughed. She reached down and grabbed her belly button. It came off in her hand. She stared at it. It was flat as a penny, but as she watched the ends began to curl up.

'Good,' the hypnotist said.

She pushed it against her middle, trying to reattach it. Her ears were ringing. It wouldn't stay.

'Only God can put it back,' the hypnotist said. 'You see. You didn't trust after all.'

'I didn't,' she wailed. She held the navel in her right hand. Her throat had thickened, and her temples were throbbing. She felt like crying.

'I will take good care of it because I believe you value it. Do you hear what I'm saying to you, Josephine? I believe you.'

She looked at him. 'You believe me?'

'I believe you, and I believe in you!' He said this with such conviction that her throat opened, and tears came to her eyes.

'Let me see it for a minute,' he said.

'See it?'

'Just for a minute.'

'Why?'

'To heal it. It's dying. Look at it.'

She opened her hand. The navel had curled up into a little ball. It was brown and wrinkled. Her hand began to shake violently.

'Here.' He covered her hand with both of his. 'There, there,' he said. 'Now I have it. It's okay.' And he began to stroke it.

She watched closely. At first, she could see no difference, but then she noticed that the color was changing. Was the color changing? Yes. The color was fading, and the thing was growing. It was, with each stroke, flattening out to its original shape, and it was turning a sort of peachish. She smiled. He was fixing it.

'Now,' he said. 'How's that? Better?'

'Yes,' she whispered. She held out her hand, but he did not give it back.

'I want to talk to you about something, Josephine.'

'Oh,' Josephine said. She sat back in her chair. She knew whatever he was going to say was right. She drank too much. She smoked too much. She laced her fingers over her stomach. Without her navel, she felt naked.

'Did you notice how easily this came off?' She swallowed. 'That wouldn't happen in a healthy person.' He looked at the daughter. She had her elbow on her knee, her chin in her hand; she was absorbed by something outside the window.

'In a healthy person, the center is vibrant; it's elastic. Shall I show you?' He began to wave his hand over the navel. 'Watch it,' he whispered. The little thing in the middle of his palm began to throb, and to fill with color. He touched its edges.

He licked his finger and ran it around the rim. He looked at the girl. She was really a very pretty girl. He admired the haughty turn of her head, the regal line of her ear, the curve of her jaw – the awkward neck, the long and turtleish neck that would, when she was older and fatter, lose its sinewy grace, but now turned elegantly at the clavicle. He followed the line of her neck, under the skimpy halter to the bare and pointed shoulder, down to the rose tattooed on her arm, back up to the shoulder, and down along the teenage breast which curved nicely, not too full, not too flat, there against the thin cotton. He closed his eyes and ran his finger slowly along the lip of the navel. 'Look,' he whispered. 'Watch me make it grow.'

Josephine, watching, saw her navel turn a translucent white, the color of a communion host, a shimmering world from a cold and beautiful night – God's night – and it had grown. When he held it at a certain angle, tilted slightly toward her, she saw the moon, and saw herself reflected in it. It was hers! She laughed.

The hypnotist opened his eyes. He looked at the mother, at her slack jaw and gleaming eyes, and he laughed, too. 'Look,' he said. He twirled the thing on his finger. 'Watch this.' He tossed it in the air, and it began to wobble, to redden, and smell a little like perfume. The disc was changing from orange to red to pink, undulating, and Josephine began sliding up and down in her chair, and her skirt hiked up. He stared at her thigh. It was a nasty little thigh, plump and unmuscled, just the way he liked them.

'Stand up,' he commanded. 'Turn around.'

Irene glanced from the window to see her mother dancing in slow, snaky circles, running her tongue over her lips, rubbing her hands over herself. Her mother – a reserved woman. Her mother was from a line of reserved women. Even when she was drunk, her mother would wander around the house tucking things in. But now she began catching her skirt and pulling it up, shimmying up and down, and the man's tongue was resting between his teeth. His eyes were little beads in his face. 'Bend over,' he whispered. Josephine bent at the waist, shook her head between her knees.

'Mom?' Irene said.

The hypnotist leaned back in his chair, clasped his hands behind his head, and said, 'Well, hello, Josephine.'

'Hey!' Irene said. The man glanced at the girl. Irene glared stonily at him, and he sneered. He looked her up and down, then looked into her eyes and saw his own reflection, an ugly fat man. He looked closer. Stared into the contempt of Irene's eyes and saw himself as she saw him – a flabby-skinned, dim-eyed, feeble-gummed half man, looked further then and saw the man he would become: his lips began to turn inward, and his skin to hang from his sharpened cheekbones, his eye sockets to protrude, and his eyes to sink. Irene, caught in his stare, saw his shoulders begin to bow, his chest under his shirt to sink, his hands and lips and head to shake. His aged face was a mesh of tiny broken blood vessels, blue and red, and his eyes were pupil-less pools of pain, dank, sludgy bogs oozing tears.

In spite of herself, Irene's young throat constricted, and her heart was moved to pity; she heard a bird call, and began to notice a faint odor in the room.

The hypnotist glanced out the window at the mountain with its nothing-colored surface and stone-cold center, at this scenic stupor where they'd made him park his trailer.

He looked at Josephine, whose face was red, whose eyes were mostly pupil. His heart flexed. He curled his lip.

'Okay, now,' he whispered, and the woman straightened. She smoothed her skirt, perched on the couch, put her fingers to her lips, glanced cautiously at her daughter, who seemed to be listening to something. Josephine shivered.

'Okay, now, watch it shrink.' Josephine sat back and watched. The hypnotist took down the moon which had been hovering over his head and began to fold it in triangles, each triangle smaller than the last, and when it was the size of his hand, he began to mold it into a glowing sphere. He covered it with his other hand, closed his eyes, opened them, opened his hand, and there was her navel again, a perfect little peach disc, flat as a penny, but with the little spiral in the middle. He smiled and held it out to her. She started to reach for it when he opened his fingers. 'Oops,' he said. 'I dropped it.' He laughed an ugly laugh.

'You dropped it?' Josephine said.

'Where'd it go?' he said.

'You dropped it?' she said again, and there was a tremor, something that could have been fear, or perhaps anger, in her voice.

'Where is it?' he said.

Josephine was staring at the floor. 'I don't know,' she said. She dropped to all fours. She began heaving, then hiccuping and sobbing. 'Renie, it's lost.'

'What's lost?' Irene shook herself, rubbed her eyes, saw her mother crawling around on the floor. 'What's lost?'

He picked his foot up, studied the bottom of his shoe, seemed to scrape something off the bottom, winked at Josephine. He popped the thing in his mouth. Josephine's mouth dropped open and her eyes bulged.

'What's lost?' Irene demanded.

The hypnotist shrugged. 'Everything,' he said. His right cheek poufed like a chipmunk's. 'I have eaten the plum she gave me. It was cold,' he said. 'So delicious.' He opened his mouth, fluttered his purple tongue. And then he swallowed. He sat back and licked his lips. 'Another satisfied customer.'

Irene scowled. 'Nothing's lost, Mom.'

Josephine was clutching her stomach as if she had been run through with a sword, and the hypnotist was grinning. When had he felt so good? He leaned forward, shielded his mouth with his hand, and whispered a little secret to Josephine. 'She's right, you know. It's not lost. Looky here. It's in the cuff of my pant.'

Josephine sagged against the couch. She stared miserably at the little disc he fished from the cuff.

'Let's go, Mom,' Irene said.

'Go?' Josephine said. 'We can't go.'

'She can't go,' the hypnotist agreed. 'I got her gumption.'

But Irene was tired of this. Why had she come? She didn't want to come. Josephine had begged her to come. Be my courage, Josephine had said. She was always having to be Mama's courage. That's what daughters are for, Josephine liked to say.

Irene stood. 'I'm going,' she said.

'Going?' Josephine said.

Irene, hands fisted, stood over her mother. Josephine, looking up, saw Irene poised for flight. Poised in that if-you-don't-pay-attention-to-me-right-now-you'll-regret-it stance, and Josephine frowned. Really, the girl had the attention span of a pea! And so rude!

Suddenly, Josephine wanted a drink. She couldn't talk to the girl anymore.

She wanted a smoke. She began digging around in her purse but then remembered why she was here. Wasn't he supposed to do something about this? She frowned at the man. He leered at her. Her stomach flipped.

But it was getting late, and she wanted a smoke. She stood up. Her legs wobbled, and her head spun. She clutched her purse with both hands, and walked carefully to the door. She felt as if her parts didn't quite connect.

'Go?' the hypnotist boomed.

Josephine looked back at him. The man's eyes smoldered, and she shuddered.

'Aren't you forgetting something?' he said.

Josephine moistened her lips. But Irene had her hand on the knob, and when the door opened, Josephine saw the man's eyes grow wide. How sweet, she thought. He doesn't want me to leave.

And I, a married woman.

The air in the room was rotten with perfume. The hypnotist stared at the door. White-knuckled, he gripped his chair. His lips twitched spastically into something that wanted to be, and then was, a smile. 'Go?' He threw his head back and laughed. 'Need not be present to win!' he shouted.

He looked from the door to the little hairs on his knuckles, turned his left hand over. With eyes half-closed, he gazed at the center of his palm. The skin was yellowish, thick, though as he watched it began to change, to bubble tumor-like. Gradually, the skin tightened and stretched and seemed to crack. A glowing disk, flat as a penny, worried its way to the surface.

The hypnotist held it up to his eye. There was a pinpoint hole at the center, and he stared through it at the door, and laughed again. He tossed the disk into the air, caught it. 'Heads or tails?' He slapped it hard onto the back of his hand. 'Tails. You lose.' He ground the thing into his hand, then watched it emerge on the other side.

Was that the whisper of wheels on pavement? 'Back again?' He cocked his head and smiled at the door. But he heard no humming engine. The little disk quivered.

The six-o'clock sun filtered through the blinds, scissoring the couch where the woman had sat. The trailer was quiet. He listened for the birds, but the birds never sang in the six-o'clock heat. He frowned at the door. 'Well aren't you the little flirt,' he said.

He got up, walked to the door, opened it, looked out into the cellophane waves that shimmied above the asphalt. Hot, stinky tar bubbled up through cracks at the base of his stoop. There was no one on the lot but him. There was no one in the drive.

'Gone?' he said. He shrugged. 'Oh, well.'

Really, he blamed himself. He was always going too far. A little rambunctious, that's what he was. Always had been. He chuckled at himself, at the way he was. And he was so sure he'd get lucky today – if not with the girl, then the mom. 'Just shows you never can tell,' he said.

In the palm of his hand, he held the disk over the asphalt. 'If you don't want it,' he shouted in the direction of the road, 'I don't either.' With the index finger of his left, he flicked the disk.

It jiggled.

He flicked it again.

It jiggled.

He pushed it hard with the ball of his thumb, then shook his hand vigorously.

The little peach, grown sticky in the heat, clung to him.

He stepped back into the room, closed the door. His hands were gooey with it. 'Down the drain you go,' he said, heading toward the bathroom, but stopped. It seemed, somehow, larger. Had it grown? Could it have? Irritated, the thing sat, swollen and flaming, in the ball of his hand, and it smelled! Did it stink? He put it to his nose and sniffed. An odor, surely blood, the suffocating stink of blood-laced perfume, spoiled the air, and his hand itched. He scratched. The thing throbbed. It was a throbbing itch, and his fingers – he saw with horror – were swelling. He tried to make a fist but the fingers, each of them, were red and pregnant and didn't want to close. And perhaps— His eyes weren't so good anymore.

Yes, tiny blue veins laced the crusted edges of the thing in his hand. He began to tremble. When he looked closely he saw that the veins extended beyond the thing and into— Into?

Like a small boy, he put his hand behind his back. The birds were singing again. The thing was pulsing. Into him? His ears were ringing.

'Now you see it,' he murmured. 'Now you don't.' He gasped.

It was gone. He felt it leave! He pulled his hand from behind his back. His palm was flat and yellow. He laughed, and then he hiccuped because there it was again, a slimy, pulsing, growing gob.

'Nowyouseeit, nowyoudon't!'

It jiggled, little belly laugh. The birds twittered.

This was wrong. He held it upside down, shook his hand, shook it vigorously, but the more he shook, the bigger it got. He stopped shaking. Sweat beads rolled along his fat lines. She—

Shouldn't have given it. What was she thinking? To give such a thing!

Then why'd you take it, dummy, he couldn't help but think, if you were only going to give it back? All sales final!

He slumped into his chair. He felt like crying, and he felt like laughing. Well, this was something new at least. He stared at the wad in the palm of his hand. 'Are you my little wife?' he said. He ran his finger over the thing, which was now, clearly, a translucent, pulsing membrane. He shuddered. 'Are you my love?'

Tedford and the Megalodon

JIM SHEPARD

He'd brought some books with him on the way out, but had lost the lot of them on the transfer to the smaller boat. One of the lifting pallets had upset and spilled the crate down the side of the ship. His almanac had been saved, for which he was thankful.

Among the losses had been his Simpson and his Eldredge; his *Osteology and Relationships of Chondrichthyans*; his *Boys' Book of Songs*; Balfour's *Development of Elasmobranch Fishes*; and, thrown in from his childhood, his Beadle Boys' Library, including *Wide Awake Ned: The Boy Wizard*.

Above his head, interstellar space was impossibly black. That night he wrote in his almanac, *Velvet set with piercing bits of light*. There seemed to be, spread above him, some kind of galactic cloud arrangement. Stars arced up over one horizon and down the other. The water nearest the ice seemed disturbingly calm. Little wavelets lapped the prow of the nearest kayak. The cold was like a wind from the stars.

Thirty-three-year-old Roy Henry Tedford and his little pile of provisions were braced on the lee side of a talus slope on a speck of an island at somewhere around degree of longitude 146 and degree of latitude 58, seven hundred miles from Adélie Land on the Antarctic Coast, and four hundred from the nearest landfall on any official map: the unprepossessing dot of Macquarie Island to the east. It was a fine midsummer night in 1923.

His island, one of three ice-covered rocks huddled together in a quarter-mile chain, existed only on the hand-drawn chart that had brought him here, far from those few shipping lanes and fishing waters this far south. The chart was entitled, in Heuvelmans's barbed-wire handwriting, alongside his approximation of the location, *The Islands of the Dead*. Under that Heuvelmans had printed in block letters the aboriginal word *Kadimakara*, or 'Animals of the Dreamtime.'

Tedford's provisions included twenty-one pounds of hard-tack, two tins of biscuit flour, a sack of sweets, a bag of dried fruit, a camp-stove, an oilskin wrap for his almanac, two small reading-lanterns, four jerry cans of kerosene, a waterproofed one-man tent, a bedroll, a spare coat and gloves, a spare set of Wellington boots, a knife, a small tool set, waterproofed and double-wrapped packets of matches, a box camera in a specially made mahogany case in an oilskin pouch, a revolver, and a Bland's .577 Axite Express. He'd fired the Bland's twice, and both times been knocked onto his back by the recoil. The sportsman in Melbourne who'd sold it to him had assured him that it was the closest thing to field artillery that a man could put to his shoulder.

He was now four hundred miles from sharing a wish, or a word, or a memory. If all went well, it might be two months before he again saw a friendly face. Until she'd stopped writing, his mother had informed him regularly that it took a powerful perversity of spirit to send an otherwise intelligent young man voluntarily into such a life.

His plan looked excellent on paper. He'd already left another kayak, with an accompanying supply depot, on the third or westernmost island, in the event bad weather or high seas prevented his return to this one.

He'd started as a student of J.H. Tate's in Adelaide. Tate had assured himself of volunteers for his fieldwork by making a keg of beer part of his collection kit, and had introduced Tedford to evolutionism and paleontology, enlivening the occasional dinner party by belting out, to the tune of 'It's a Long Way to Tipperary':

It's a long way from Amphioxus,
It's a long way to us;
It's a long way from Amphioxus
To the meanest human cuss.
Farewell, fins and gill slits,
Welcome, teeth and hair —
It's a long long way from Amphioxus,
But we all came from there!

Tedford had been an eager acolyte for two years and then had watched his enthusiasm stall in the face of the remoteness of the sites, the lack of monetary support, and the meagerness of the finds. Three months for an old tooth, as old Tate used to put it. Tedford had taken a job as a clerk for the local land surveyor, and his duties had exposed him to a panoply of local tales, whispered stories, and bizarre sightings. He'd found himself investigating each, in his free time, in search of animals known to local populations but not to the world at large. His mode was analysis, logical dissection, and reassembly, when it came to the stories. His tools were perseverance, an appetite for observation, a tolerance for extended discomfort, and his aunt's trust fund. He'd spent a winter month looking for bunyips, which he'd been told inhabited the deep waterholes and roamed the billabongs at night. He'd found only a few fossilized bones of some enormous marsupials. He'd been fascinated by the paringmal, the 'birds taller than the mountains,' but had uncovered them only in rock paintings. He'd spent a summer baking on a blistering hardpan awaiting the appearance of the legendary cadimurka.

All that knocking about had become focused on the day that a fisherman had shown him a tooth he'd dredged up with a deep-sea net. The thing had revealed itself to be a huge whitish triangle, thick as a scone, the root rough, the blade enamel-polished and edged with twenty or so serrations per centimeter. The heft had been remarkable: that single tooth had weighed nearly a pound.

Tedford had come across teeth like it before, in Miocene limestone beds. They belonged, Tate had assured him, to a creature science had identified as *Carcharodon Megalodon*, or Great Tooth, a recent ancestor of the Great White Shark, but nearly three times as large: a monster shark, with jaws within which a tall man could stand without stooping, and a stout, oversized head. But the tooth that Tedford held in his hand was white, which meant it came from an animal either quite recently extinct, or not extinct at all.

He'd written up the find in the *Tasmanian Journal of Natural Science*. The editor had accepted the piece but refused its inflammatory title.

A year later nearly to the day, his eye had been caught by a newspaper account of the Warrnambool Sea Monster, christened for the home port of eleven fishermen and a boy, in three tuna boats, who had refused to go to sea for several days. They'd been at work at certain far-off fishing grounds that only they had discovered, which lay beside a shelf plunging down into very deep water, when an immense shark, of unbelievable proportions, had surfaced among them, taking nets, one of the boats, and a ship's dog back down with it. The boy in the boat that had capsized had called out, 'Is that the fin of a great fish?' and then everything had gone topsyturvy. Everyone had been saved from the vortex except the dog. They'd been unanimous that the beast had been something the like of which they'd never seen. In interviews conducted in the presence of both the local Fisheries Inspector and one B. Heuvelmans, dentist and naturalist, the men had been questioned very closely, and had all agreed upon the details, even down to the creature's length, which seemed absurd: at least sixty-five feet. They'd agreed that it was at least the length of the wharf shed back at their bay. The account made clear that these were men used to the sea and to all sorts of weather, and to all sorts of sharks, besides. They had seen whale sharks and basking sharks. They recounted the way the sea had boiled over from the thing's surfacing and its subsequent submersion. This was no whale, they'd insisted; they'd seen its terrible head. They'd agreed on everything: the size of its dorsal, the creature's staggering width, its ghostly whitish color. What seemed most to their credit, in terms of their credibility, was their flat refusal to return to the sea for nearly a week, despite the loss of wages involved: a loss they could ill afford, as their wives, also present for the interviews, pointed out.

It had taken him a week to get away, and when he'd finally gotten to Warrnambool no one would speak to him. The fishermen had tired of being the local sport, and had told him only that they wished that anyone else had seen the thing rather than them.

He'd no sooner been back at his desk when other stories had appeared. For a week, there'd been a story every morning, the relevance of which only he apprehended. A small boat had been swamped south of Tasmania, in calm seas, its crew missing. A ninety-foot trawler had struck a reef in what was charted as deep water. A whale carcass, headless and bearing trenchlike gashes, had washed ashore near Hibbs Bay.

As soon as he could get away, he took the early coach back to Warrnambool and looked up B. Heuvelmans, the dentist, who turned out to be an untidy cockatoo of a man holed up in a sanctuary at the rear of his house, where he'd built himself a laboratory. As he explained impatiently to Tedford, in the afternoons he retired there, unavailable to his patients' pain and devoted to his entomological and zoological studies, many of which lined the walls. The room was oppressively dark and close. Dr Heuvelmans was secretary to the local Scientific Society. Until recently he'd been studying a tiny but monstrous-looking insect found exclusively in a certain kind of dung, but since the fishermen's news, the Sea Monster story had entirely obsessed him. He sat in a rotating chair behind a broad table covered with books, maps, and diagrams, and suggested they do what they could to curtail Tedford's visit, which could hardly be agreeable to Tedford, and was inexpressibly irksome to his host. While he talked, he chewed on the end of what he assured Tedford was a dentifricial root. He sported tiny, horn-rimmed sunglasses and a severely pointed beard.

He wanted no help and he was perfectly content to be considered a lunatic. His colleagues only confirmed his suspicion that one of the marvels of Nature was the resistance that the average human brain offered to the introduction of knowledge. When it came to ideas, his associates stuck to their ruts until forcibly ejected from them. Very well. That ejection would come about soon enough.

Had he information beyond that reported in the newspapers? Tedford wanted to know.

That information alone would have sufficed for him, Heuvelmans retorted; his interviews at least had demonstrated to his satisfaction that if he believed in the beast's existence he did so in good company. But in fact, he *did* have more. At first he would proceed no further upon that point, refusing all direct inquiry. The insect he'd been studying was apparently not eaten by birds because of a spectacularly malodorous or distasteful secretion, which began to rise faintly from the man's clothing the longer Tedford sat in the stuffy little room.

But the longer Tedford did sit, mildly refusing to stir, the more information the excitable Belgian brought forth. He talked of a fellow tooth-puller who'd befriended some aborigines up near Coward Springs and Bopeechee and who'd reported that they spoke of hidden islands to the southeast infused with the spirit of the deep upwellings, something terrible, something malevolent, something to be avoided. He'd reported that they had a word for 'shark that devours the sea.' He displayed a piece of fisherman's slate – from a boat he said had gone entirely missing – on which was written 'Please help us. Find us soon before we die.'

Finally, when Tedford apparently seemed insufficiently impressed, he'd gone into a locked cabinet with a great flourish and had produced a tooth – white – identical to the tooth Tedford had been shown. The Warrnambool fishermen had pulled it from the tatters of their net-line, he said.

Moreover, the dentist said, working the dentifricial root

around his back molars, he'd found the fishing grounds. And with them, the islands.

Tedford had been unsuccessful at concealing his shock and excitement.

The job had taken him a couple of weeks, Heuvelmans had gone on, but on the whole he was quite set up by his overall ingenuity and success. He was traveling there in a matter of days, to positively identify the thing, if not catch it. Could Tedford accompany him? Not by a long chalk.

What they were talking about, Heuvelmans mused, after they'd both had sufficient time to ponder the brutality of his refusal, would be second only to the Sperm Whale as the largest predator the planet had ever produced. He then lapsed into silence with the look of a man peering into deep space.

When Tedford finally asked what sort of weapons he intended to bring, the man quoted Job: 'He esteemeth iron as straw, and brass as rotten wood.' And when his guest responded, 'Am I to understand that you're proceeding unarmed?' Heuvelmans said only merrily, 'He maketh the deep to boil like a pot.'

Tedford had taken his leave intending to return the next day, and the next, and the next, but had come back the following morning to discover Heuvelmans already gone, on, as his housekeeper put it, 'a sea-voyage.' He never returned.

Tedford finally asked the housekeeper to notify him if there was any news, and two weeks after that the good woman wrote to say that part of the stern of the ship her master had contracted, the *Tonny*, had floated ashore on the Tasmanian coast.

He'd prevailed upon the housekeeper to give him access to

the sanctuary – in order that he might help solve the mystery of the poor man's disappearance – and there discovered, in the course of tearing the entire place apart, the man's notes, a copy of the precious map: everything. On one of the three islands there was said to be a secret opening, a hidden entry to a sort of lagoon otherwise completely encircled by rock and ice. He was to look for light blue ice along the water level, under a half-dome overhang, to paddle up to that place, and to push through what he found. That would be his private gate into the unknown.

It had reached the point at which his friends had noticed that the great majority of his expressions reflected discontent, and he'd started speaking openly about being crowded round by an oppressive world. Everything had been herded into a few narrow margins; everything had been boxed up and organized. What was zoology – or paleontology – but an obsessive reordering of the boxes? Finding what science insisted wasn't there – that was the real contribution.

He liked to believe that he was the sort of man who viewed the world with an unprejudiced eye and judged it in a reasonable way. In letters to those few undemanding correspondents who'd remained in touch, he described himself as suppliant before the mysteries of Nature.

He felt more frequently as though his only insight was his desire to be left alone. Passing mirrors, he noticed that his bearing was that of someone who'd seen his share of trouble and expected more on the way.

He didn't find himself to be particularly shy. When addressed he always responded. He had proposed to one woman, and she had visibly recoiled, and replied that their friendship had been so good and so pleasant that it would have been a pity to have spoiled it.

His first memory was of beating on the fireplace hob with a spoon. Asked by his father what he thought he was doing, he replied, 'I'm playing pretty music.'

His mother, whose family had made a fortune in shipbuilding, was prone to remarks like, 'I have upgraded my emeralds, down through the years.'

As a boy he'd felt his head to be full of pictures no one else could see. It was as if the air had been heavy-laden with strange thoughts and ideas. He'd grown up on an estate far outside of their little town, with his brother Freddy as his closest and only friend. Freddy had been two years older. They'd trapped bandicoots and potoroos in the understory of eucalyptus stands, and Freddy had taught him how to avoid getting nipped by jew lizards and scaly-foots. They'd ridden each other everywhere on the handlebars of their shared bicycle, and worked together on chores. They couldn't have been more different in their parents' eyes: tall and fair Freddy, who'd announced at the age of fourteen that he'd been called upon to minister to lost souls in the interior, once he came of age; and the diminutive Roy, with a mat of brown hair he'd never fully wrestled into order and a tendency to break jars of preserves or homemade wine just from restlessness. Freddy had helped out at the local hospital, while Roy had collected filthy old bones and left them lying around the house. Freddy's only failing, in fact, seemed to have been his inability to more fully transform his brother.

Until it all went smash, the day before Roy's fourteenth birthday, when Freddy, on an errand to the lumber mill, somehow had pitched into the circular saw and had been cut open from sternum to thigh. He'd lived for two days. His brother had visited him twice in the hospital, and each time Freddy had ignored him. Just before he had died, in Roy's presence, he had asked their mother if she could hear the angels singing. She had fallen to weeping again, and had told him she couldn't. 'What a beautiful city,' he had responded. And then he had died.

Tedford's father had never mentioned the accident again. His mother had talked about it only with her sister and a close cousin. They'd had one other child, Mina, who had caught a chill and died at the age of seven.

His father had become the kind of man who disappeared the moment attention was directed elsewhere. He seemed to leave just for the sensation of motion. He had developed a way of lingering on a word, kneading it for its sadness. His mother had evolved the belief that Providence put such people as Freddy on Earth to make everyone happy, and then to open everyone's eyes to certain virtues once they were gone.

Tedford had been found a month after the accident, asleep in the road with a mouthful of raw onion, and a paring knife in his hand.

No one had ever talked to him about his brother's refusal to see him. And until his brother had died, he would have said that his life story had been the story of a nuisance.

Dawn came like a split along the horizon. The first night had gone well, he thought, peering out of his tent flap. He'd even slept. While he pulled on his over-clothes the walls of the tent bucked and filled in the wind. His arms and back ached from the previous day's paddling. Cold damp air filled his sleeves and the back of his shirt.

The night before it had occurred to him, the moment he'd

extinguished his reading-lantern, that for the next two months he would be as far from human aid as he would be on the moon. If he ran into serious mishap, only his own qualities would save him.

Old Tate had used to remark, often after having noted some particularly odd behavior on Tedford's part, that there were as many different kinds of men in the world as there were mothers to bear them and experiences to shape them, and in the same wind, each gave out a different tune. Tedford had slowly discovered himself to be unfit for life in the land-surveyor's office as he had gradually come to understand his inability to express to anyone else the awful resiliency the image of *Carcharodon Megalodon* had taken on in his psyche.

The creature inhabited dreams that did not even feature marine settings. He'd once pronounced its name in church services. As far as *Carcharodon Megalodon* was concerned, he was still a caveman, squatting on his haunches and bewitched by the magic-conjuring representation he himself had drawn on the wall.

But if he were acting like a schoolboy, at least he'd resolved to address the problem, and see Life as it was, for its own sake, prepared to take the consequences. Lacing up his boots, he reasoned to himself that he wanted to see the animal itself, and not his fear and delight in it.

Fifteen million years ago, such monsters had been the lords of creation, the lords of time; then they'd remained nearly unchanged throughout the ages, carrying on until there were only a few stragglers hanging on the very edge of annihilation. Life had gone on around them, leaving them behind. The monsters science knew about, and the ones it didn't. The formation of the northern ice caps and the extension of the southern during the Pleistocene had resulted in the drastic lowering of the sea level, exposing the continental shelves around Australia and Antarctica and trapping all sorts of marine life in the deep pockets of isolated water. Tedford was convinced that in a few of those deep pockets – adjacent to the cold, nutrient-rich bottom current that seemed to originate along the edge of Antarctica, to flow north to all the other continents of the world – his quarry resided, surfacing every so often in the same remote feeding-zones.

What percentage of the sea's surface had been explored? (Never mind its abyssal depths.) And meanwhile, dunderheads who plowed back and forth across the same sea-lanes with their roaring engines announced with certainty that there was nothing unusual to see in the ocean. Outside of those narrow water-lanes, upon which everyone traveled, it was all darkness. He was in an unexplored area the size of Europe. He was in a region of astounding stories. And he had always lived for astounding stories.

His first day of searching came up a bust when a cresting wave swamped his kayak a few feet from camp. He spent the bulk of the afternoon shivering and beating his arms and having to disassemble and examine the camera for water damage. His second day was scotched when he slipped on an icy slope outside his tent and badly sprained an ankle. The third dawned grey and ominous and turned to an ice storm in the time it took him to outfit his kayak. The fourth dawned bright and clear and he lay in his tent, cold and wet, his ankle throbbing, unwilling to even believe that things were beginning to turn around.

He finally roused himself and hurried into his outer clothes and spent some time in the blinding sunlight chipping the glaze of ice off his kayak's control surfaces. He breakfasted on some dried fruit and tea. The sea was calm. He loaded the camera and rifle in their oilskin pouches into the storage basket on the kayak's prow, hung his compass around his neck, put his map-packet in his jacket pocket, settled into his seat, and shoved off from the ice with his paddle. His little tent seemed to be awaiting his return.

He traveled east along the lee side of the island. It was larger than he'd realized. He saw streaks of guano on some of the rocks but otherwise no sign of life. The paddling seemed to help the pain in his ankle, and the ice slipped by at a walking speed. Every so often he had to skirt what looked like submerged ice-reefs.

The easternmost island unveiled itself through a torus-shaped mist. From what he could see in his bobbing little boat, it looked to be the largest of the three. The seas around it displayed more chop, perhaps from the open ocean beyond. He spent the remainder of the day circling it twice, each time more slowly. He saw no light blue ice, no half-dome overhang, no hidden entry. Upon completion of the second full circuit, he despaired, and immediately upbraided himself for his lack of pluck.

The sun was getting low. To the south, in the far distance, ice-fields stretched from horizon to horizon, with peaks towering higher than mast-heads.

He bobbed back and forth for a bit in the gathering swell, stymied, and then paddled a hundred yards or so offshore and began his circuit again, from a different perspective.

Halfway around on the northern side he spied a bit of yellow fifty feet up on an ice-shelf. He considered various approaches to it for some minutes, trying to calm his excitement, paddling this way and that, and finally puzzled out what looked like a workable route. He lost another half-hour trying to find a secure tie-up. When he finally began climbing, he had only an hour or so of sunlight left.

Even with his ankle, it was an easier climb than he'd hoped. At the top he came upon a recent encampment sheltered in the lee of a convex wall of ice-covered rock. There were meat tins and an old bottle. It looked as if the contents of a small leather bag had been burned. Only two notebooks and a stylographic pencil were left. The notebooks were empty.

He assumed all of this was Heuvelmans's work. Perhaps he'd had the ship he'd contracted wait some distance away while he'd made the rest of the journey alone.

But what to make of it? He crouched among the tins, feeling himself maddeningly unable to concentrate. It was only when he stood, aware that the light was failing at such a rate that he had to leave without delay, that he saw the rock cairn, arranged in an arrow-shape, pointing to the west, and the island from which he'd come.

He spent the evening in his bedroll listening to his tent walls buffet madly in the wind, and trying to devise a method of measuring the salinity of his little bay. The morning revealed the interior canvas to be tapestried with thin sheets of ice crystals in fantastic designs.

Sunrise was a prismatic band in the east, violet near the water and shading to golden above. He found it difficult to conceive that along that violet line, steamers ran, and men talked about the small affairs of life.

He'd secured a packet from Hobart on the southeastern coast of Tasmania for the trip across the south Indian Ocean. In spite of the steamships and railways and motor cars, the whole place had felt close to the end of the earth, especially at night. Tedford had prowled around in his sleeplessness, and in the last hours before dawn, the hills around the docks had emanated with layers of unearthly noises. He'd spent a little time in some pubs but had found a general state of disinterest in science to be the case among the fishermen and dockhands. His ship had left in the predawn darkness of his third day in the town, and he remembered thinking as it pulled away from its moorings that he was now up to his neck in the tureen.

Three mackintoshed figures had been walking the quay alongside his ship in a thin, cold rain. He'd thought of calling out to them a last word, and had dismissed the notion. He'd seen big ships and little ships on his way out of the harbor, some with their decklights burning and some in darkness except for the riding lights upon their mainstays. He'd been able to make out the names of a few of them as his ship's light had passed over their overhanging sterns or bows. Lighters and small craft had been crowded into their darker shadows. Near a steamship's funnel, a great lamp had illuminated some coaling basins and the sides of a wharf.

Once the sun was up, he had passed the time imagining that every wave had its twin, and singling one out and searching for its mate. The islands had revealed themselves only a few miles west of Heuvelman's coordinates, and he'd arranged his pickup date, descended the ship's ladder into his heaving kayaks, at that point lashed together, had given the ship's mate a cheery wave, and had set off from the hull. He'd looked back only once, and the ship had disappeared by that point.

He opened a tin and made sure of his breakfast. While he ate he observed how the snow around his campsite organized itself into little crescents, as though its lee sides had been scooped out with tablespoons.

How he'd liked life, he wanted to think – every bit of it, the colored and the plain, the highlights and the low! He wondered whether the mere feel of things – common things, all sorts of things – gave anyone else the intensities of contentment that they provided him.

He thought he would start with the windward side before the breeze picked up. When he set off, a petrel winged past overhead, in a leisurely manner: the first sign of life. A half an hour later he noted, out to sea, the steam-puff fountains blown into the air by the exhalations of whales.

Again he circled the entire island without finding anything. This time he repeated the circle even closer to the shore, however, his kayak often bumping and scraping on rocks. In a protected hollow, he found another arrow, this one hastily carved into the rock. It pointed the way into an unpromisingly narrow backwater, which, when he maneuvered it, opened a bit into an odd kind of anteroom. The water below him seemed to drop off into infinity. The wavelet sounds were excessively magnified in the enclosed space. Way below, he could make out thick schools of dull green fish, two to four feet long, which he assumed to be rock cod.

Before him was a wall of ice thirty feet high. He bumped and nudged his kayak back and forth. The wind played tricks down the natural chimney. He could see no opening, and he sat.

But in the late morning, when the sun cleared the opposite wall above him, it illuminated, through the ice, a ridge about ten feet high, in the middle of which a six-foot-wide fissure had opened. The ice in frozen cascade over the fissure turned a pearl blue.

He hacked at it and it came away in slabs which dunked themselves and swirled off in eddies. He kept low, poled his way in with his oar, and the mouth of a great blue cavern opened on his right hand.

When he passed clear of the cavern it was as though his vision was drowned in light. The sun rebounded everywhere off snow and ice. It took him minutes, shading his eyes, to get his bearings.

He was in an ice-walled bay, square in shape, perhaps four hundred yards across. The water seemed even deeper than it had before, and suffused with a strange cerulean light. There was no beach, no ledge. At their apex, the walls looked to be seventy feet high.

The atmosphere above them seemed to have achieved a state of perfect visibility. Away from the sun, in a deep purple sky, a single star was shining. The taste of the air was exhilarating.

He waited. He circled the bay. He felt a silent and growing desire for lunch. Schools of big fish roiled and turned, every-where he looked in the depths.

He'd wait all day, if necessary. He'd wait all night. His kayak drifted to and fro, his paddle shipped and dripping from the blade, while he double-checked his rifle and his lantern. He removed his camera from its case.

The fish-schools continued to circle and chase themselves about, every so often breaking the surface. He waited. Halfway through the afternoon the detonations of an ice fall boomed off to the west. The sun started to dip. The shadows in the little bay seemed to grow cooler. He suppered on some hardtack and a sip of water.

There was a great upwelling that he rode, like a liquid dome; and then calm. He put a hand on his camera and then his rifle's stock as well. His pulse eventually steadied. A pale moon rose, not very high above the ice wall. While he watched, it acquired a halo. The temperature was dropping. His breath was pluming out before him.

He judged he'd been in the bay, floating, for six hours. His legs were stiff and his bum sore. When he rotated his foot, his ankle lanced and radiated with pain.

He'd been lucky with the weather, he knew. The South Pole was the Southern Hemisphere's brew vat of storms.

The darkness was now more complete. He switched on his lantern. As he swung it around, shadows became stones, or shards of ice. The water was as motionless as indigo glass, until he lifted his paddle and began to stroke with it, and every stroke sent more and more ripples across the shining surface.

As he paddled, he reiterated for himself what Tate had taught him regarding the cardinal features of Life: the will to live, the power to live, the intelligence to live, and the adaptiveness to overcome minor dangers. Life carried itself forward by its own momentum, while its mode was carved and shaped by its battle with its environment.

He sang a song his father had sung to him, while he paddled:

> Over his head were the maple buds
> And over the tree was the moon,
> And over the moon were the starry studs
> That dropped from the Angels' shoon.

He stopped and drifted once again, turning his bow so he could gaze at his wake. Freddy had always referred to him as Old Moony because of his daydreaming. Tedford carried in his almanac, back at his campsite, his membership card in the Melbourne Scientific Society and his only photograph of his brother: a murky rendering of a tall, sweet-looking boy with pale hair.

Above him the southern lights bloomed as green and pink curtains of a soap-bubble tenuousness. He could see the stars through them. The entire eastern sky was massed with auroral light. Draperies shimmered across it.

There in his bay, uplifted on the swell of the round earth, he could see how men had come to dream of Gardens of Eden and Ages of Gold. He wondered more things about *Carcharodon Megalodon* than he could have found out in a lifetime of observation; more than he had tools to measure. All that he could attend to now was a kind of dream noise, huge and muted, that the bay seemed to be generating, resonant on the very lowest frequencies. That, and a kind of emotional mirage of himself as the dying man taking his leave. He considered the picture as if from high on the ramparts of ice, and found it to be oddly affecting. The cold was insistent and he felt his every fiber absorbed in it, his consciousness taken up in some sort of ecstasy of endeavor. The air felt alive with its innumerable infinitesimal crystallizations. His ankle throbbed.

He fancied he heard submarine sounds. Then, more distinctly, the stroke of something on the surface. His lantern revealed only the after-turbulence.

He paddled over. In the moonlight, splashes made silvery rings. He would have said he was moving through a pool of quicksilver.

The moon disappeared and left him in darkness. He glided through it, close enough to whatever had surfaced to taste a mephitic odor upon the air.

For the first time he was frightened. He kept his lantern between his legs and shipped his paddle and pulled his Bland's to him by the stock. This thing was the very figure of the terrifying world around him, of the awfulness of nature.

The surface of the bay began to undulate. His little craft rocked and bobbed accordingly, in the darkness. He was very near the end but he had not, and would not, lose good cheer. Things had come out against him, but he had no cause for complaint.

Why had his brother refused to see him? Why had his brother refused to see him? Tears sprang to his eyes, making what little light there was sparkle.

The moonlight reemerged like a curtain raised upon the bay. Above it, the stars appeared to rise and fall on a canopy inflated by wind. But there was no wind, and everything was perfectly still. Everything was silent. His heart started beating in his ears.

The water alone dipped and swirled. Just below the surface, shoals of fish panicked, scattering like handfuls of thrown darts.

He caught sight of a faint illumination in the depths. As it rose, it took the shape of a fish. The illumination was like phosphorescence, and the glimmer gave it obscure, wavering outlines.

There was a turbulence where the moon's reflection was concentrated and then a rush of water like a breaking wave as the shark surged forward and up. The body towered over Tedford's head. He lost sight of the ice wall behind it in the spray.

It was as if the bottom itself had heaved surfaceward. The run-up of its splash as it dove sent his kayak six or seven feet up the opposite wall, and he was barely able to keep his seat. He lost both his rifle and his lantern.

The backwash carried him to the middle of the bay. He was soaked, and shaking. Seawater and ice slurried around his legs. He experienced electric spikes of panic. His camera bobbed and tipped nearby in its oilskin pouch, and then sank. A wake, a movement started circling him. The dorsal emerged, its little collar of foam at its base, and flexed and dripped, itself as tall as a man. The entire animal went by like a horrible parade. He estimated its length at fifty feet. Its thickness at twelve. It was a trolley car with fins.

It turned on its side, regarding him as well, its eye remarkable for its size and its blackness against the whiteness of the head, hobgoblin-like. It sank, dwindling away to darkness, and then, deep below, reemerged as a vast and gaping circle of teeth coming up out of the gloom.

Where would Tedford have taken his find, had he been able to bring it back? Who understood such a creature's importance? Who understood loss? Who understood separation? Who understood the terrors of inadequacy laid bare? The shark's jaws erupted on either side of Tedford's bow and stern, curtains of spray shattering outwards, turning him topsy-turvy, spinning him to face the moon, leaving him with a flash of Jonah-thought, and arresting him an instant short of all for which he had hoped, and more.

Three Meditations on Death

WILLIAM T. VOLLMANN

I

Catacomb Thoughts

Death is ordinary. Behold it, subtract its patterns and lessons from those of the death that weapons bring, and maybe the residue will show what violence is. With this in mind, I walked the long tunnels of the Paris catacombs. Walls of earth and stone encompassed walls of mortality a femur's-length thick: long yellow and brown bones all stacked in parallels, their sockets pointing outward like melted bricks whose ends dragged down, like downturned bony smiles, like stale yellow snails of macaroni – joints of bones, heads of bones, promiscuously touching, darkness in the center of each, between those twin knucklespurs which had once helped another bone to pivot, thereby guiding and supporting flesh in its passionate and sometimes intelligent motion toward the death it inevitably found – femurs in rows, then, and humerii, bones upon bones, and every few rows there'd be a shelf of bone to shore death up, a line of humerii and femurs laid down laterally to achieve an almost pleasing masonry effect, indeed, done by masonry's maxims, as interpreted by Napoleon's engineers and brickmen of death, who at the nouveau-royal command had elaborated and organized death's jetsam according to a sanitary aesthetic. (Did the Emperor ever visit that place? He was not afraid of death – not even of causing it.) Then there were side-chambers walled with bones likewise crossed upon bone-beams; from these the occasional skull looked uselessly out; and every now and then some spiritual types had ornamented the facade with a cross made of femurs. There had been laid down in that place, I was told, the remains of about six million persons – our conventional total for the number of Jews who died in the Holocaust. The crime which the Nazis accomplished with immense effort in half a dozen years, nature had done here without effort or recourse, and was doing.

I had paid my money aboveground; I had come to look upon my future. But when after walking the long arid angles of prior underground alleys I first encountered my brothers and sisters, calcified appurtenances of human beings now otherwise gone to be dirt, and rat-flesh, and root-flesh, and green leaves soon to die again, I felt nothing but a mildly melancholy curiosity. One expects to die; one has seen skeletons and death's heads on Halloween masks, in anatomy halls, cartoons, warning signs, forensic photographs, photographs of old SS insignia, and meanwhile the skulls bulged and gleamed from walls like wet river-boulders, until curiosity became, as usual, numbness. But one did not come out of the ground then. Bone-walls curled around wells, drainage sockets in those tunnels; sometimes water dripped from the ceiling and struck the tourists' foreheads – water which had probably leached out of corpses. A choking, sickening dust irritated our eyes and throats, for in no way except in the abstract, and perhaps not even then, is the presence of the dead salutary to the living. Some skulls dated to 1792. Darkened, but still not decayed, they oppressed me with their continued existence. The engineers would have done better to let them transubstantiate. They might have been part of majestic trees by now, or delicious vegetables made over into young children's blood and growing bones. Instead they were as stale and stubborn as old arguments, molds for long-dissolved souls, churlish hoardings of useless matter. Thus, I believed, the reason for my resentment. The real sore point was that, in Eliot's phrase, 'I had not thought death had undone so many'; numbness was giving way to qualmishness, to a nauseated, claustrophobic realization of my biological entrapment. Yes, of course I'd known that I must die, and a number of times had had my nose rubbed in the fact; this was one of them, and in between those episodes my tongue glibly admitted what my heart secretly denied; for why should life ought to bear in its flesh the dissolving, poisonous faith of its own inescapable defeat? Atop bony driftwood, skulls slept, eyeholes downwards, like the shells of dead hermit crabs amidst those wracked corpse-timbers. This was the necrophile's beach, but there was no ocean except the ocean of earth overhead from which those clammy drops oozed and dripped. Another cross of bone, and then the inscription – SILENCE, MORTAL BEINGS – VAIN GRANDEURS, SILENCE – words even more imperious in French than I have given them here, but no more necessary, for the calcified myriads said that better than all poets or commanders. In superstition the carcass is something to be feared, dreaded and hated; in fact it deserves no emotion whatsoever in and of itself, unless it happens to comprise a souvenir of somebody other than a stranger; but time spent in the company of death is time wasted. Life trickles away, like the water falling down into the catacombs, and in the end we will be silent as our ancestors are silent, so better to indulge our vain grandeurs while we can. Moment by moment, our time bleeds away. Shout, scream, or run, it makes no difference, so why not forget what can't be avoided? On and on twisted death's alleys. Sometimes there was a smell, a cheesy, vinegary smell which I knew from having visited a field-morgue or two; there was no getting away from it, and the dust of death dried out my throat. I came to a sort of cavern piled up to my neck with heaps of bones not used in construction: pelvic bones and ribs (the vertebrae and other small bones must have all gone to discard or decay). These relics were almost translucent, like seashells, so thin had death nibbled them. That smell, that vinegar-vomit smell, burned my throat, but perhaps I was more sensitive to it than I should have been, for the other tourists did not appear to be disgusted; indeed, some were laughing, either out of bravado or because to them it was as unreal as a horror movie; they didn't believe that they'd feature in the next act, which must have been why one nasty fellow seemed to be considering whether or not to steal a bone – didn't he have bones enough inside his living meat? He must not have been the only one, for when we came to the end and ascended to street level we met a gainfully employed man behind a table which already had two skulls on it, seized from thieves that day; he checked our backpacks. I was happy when I got past him and saw sunlight – almost overjoyed, in fact, for since becoming a part-time journalist of armed politics I am not titillated by death. I try to understand it, to make friends with it, and I never learn anything except the lesson of my own powerlessness. Death stinks in my nostrils as it did that chilly sunny autumn afternoon in Paris when I wanted to be happy.

*

In the bakeries, the baguettes and pale, starchy mini-ficelles, the croissants and pains-aux-chocolats all reminded me of bones. Bone-colored cheese stank from other shops. All around me, the steel worms of the Metro bored through other catacombs, rushing still living bones from hole to hole. In one of the book-shops on the Rue de Seine I found a demonically bound volume of Poe whose endpapers were marbled like flames; the plates, of course, hand-colored by the artist, depicted gruesomely menacing skeletons whose finger-bones snatched and clawed. I spied a wedding at the Place Saint-Germain, whose church was tanned and smoked by time to the color of cheesy bones; I saw the white-clad bride – soon to become yellow bones. The pale narrow concrete sleepers of railroads, metallic or wooden fence-rails, the model of the spinal column in the window of an anatomical bookshop, then even sticks, tree trunks, all lines inscribed or implied, the world itself in all its segments, rays, and dis-membered categories became hideously cadaverous. I saw and inhaled death. I tasted death on my teeth. I exhaled, and the feeble puffs of breath could not push my nausea away. Only time did that – a night and a day, to be exact – after which I forgot again until I was writing these very words that I must die. I believed but for a moment. Thus I became one with those skulls which no longer knew their death. Even writing this, picking my letters from the alphabet's boneyard, my o's like death's-heads, my i's and l's like ribs, my b's, q's, p's and d's like ball-ended humerii broken in half, I believed only by fits. The smell came back into my nose, but I was in Vienna by then – whose catacombs, by the way, I decided not to visit – so I went out and smelled espresso heaped with fresh cream. The writing became, as writing ought to be, informed by choreographies and paradigms which mediated that smell into something more than its revolting emptiness. I take my meaning where I can find it; when I can't find it, I invent it. And when I do that, I deny meaninglessness, and when I do that I am lying to myself. Experience does not necessarily lie, but that smell is not an experience to the matter which emits it. Death cannot be experienced either by the dead or the living. The project of the Parisian workmen, to aestheticize, to arrange, and thus somehow to transform the objects of which they themselves were composed, was a bizarre success, but it could have been done with stale loaves of bread. It affected bones; it could not affect death. It meant as little, it said as little, as this little story of mine. It spoke of them as I must speak of me. I can read their meaning. Death's meaning I cannot read. To me death is above all things a smell, a very bad smell, and that, like the skeletons which terrify children, is not death at all. If I had to smell it more often, if I had to work in the catacombs, I would think nothing of it. And a few years or decades from now, I will think nothing about everything.

II

Autopsy Thoughts

It shall be the duty of the coroner to inquire into and determine the circumstances, manner, and cause of all violent, sudden or unusual deaths . . .

California state code, sec. 274911

Aldous Huxley once wrote that 'if most of us remain ignorant of ourselves, it is because self-knowledge is painful and we prefer the pleasures of illusion.' That is why one brushes off the unpleasantly personal lesson of the catacombs. But we can extend the principle. Not only self-knowledge hurts. Consider the black girl whom an investigator pulled from a dumpster one night. Her mouth was bloody, which wasn't so strange; she could have been a homeless alcoholic with variceal bleeding. But, shining the flashlight into that buccal darkness, the investigator caught sight of a glint – neither blood nor spittle sparkling like metal, but metal itself – a broken-off blade. In her mouth, which could no longer speak, lay the truth of her death. The investigator couldn't give her her life back, but by this double unearthing – the knife from the corpse, the corpse from the stinking bin – he'd resurrected something else, an imperishable quantity which the murderer in his fear or fury or cold selfishness meant to entomb – namely, the fact of murder, the reality which would have been no less real had it never become known, but which, until it was known and proved, remained powerless to do good. – What good? Quite simply, determining the cause of death is the prerequisite for some kind of justice, although justice, like other sonorous concepts, can produce anything from healing to acceptance to compensation to revenge to hypocritical clichés. At the chief medical examiner's office they knew this good – knowing also that the job of turning evidence into justice lay not with them but with the twelve citizens in the jury box: – what coroners and medical examiners do is necessary but not sufficient. Probably the black woman's family had figured that out, if there was any family, if they cared, if they weren't too stupefied with grief. The morgue would be but the first of their Stations of the Cross. (Afterward: the funeral parlor, the graveyard, perhaps the courtroom, and always the empty house.) Dealing with them was both the saddest and the most important part of the truth-seeker's job: as I said, knowledge hurts. Dr Boyd Stephens, the Chief Medical Examiner of San Francisco, would later say to me: 'One of the things I hoped you'd see was a family coming in here grieving. And when it is a crime of violence, when someone has her son shot during a holdup, that makes it very hard; that's a tremendous emotional blow.' I myself am very glad that I didn't see this. I have seen it enough. In the catacombs death felt senseless, and for the investigator who found the black woman, the moral of death remained equally empty, as it must whether the case is suicide, homicide, accident, or what we resignedly call 'natural causes.' Twenty-six years after the event, a kind woman who had been there wrote me about the death of my little sister. I was nine years old, and my sister was six. The woman wrote: 'I remember you, very thin, very pale, your shoulders hunched together, your hair all wet and streaming sideways. You said, "I can't find Julie."' She wrote to me many other things that she remembered. When I read her letter, I cried. Then she went on: 'I am tempted to say that Julie's drowning was a "senseless death" but that's not true. I learned the day she died that there are realms of life in which the measure of sense and nonsense don't apply. Julie's death exists on a plane where there is no crime and no punishment, no cause and effect, no action and reaction. It just happened.' Fair enough. Call it morally or ethically senseless, at least. (I don't think I ever wrote back; I felt too sad.) Only when justice itself condemns someone to death, as when a murderer gets hanged or we bombard Hitler's Berlin or an attacker meets his victim's lethal self-defense, can we even admit the possibility that the perishing had a point. Principled suicides also mean something:

Cato's self-disembowelment indicts the conquering Caesar who would have granted clemency, and whose patronizing power now falls helpless before a mere corpse. But most people (including many suicides, and most who die the deaths of malicious judicial injustice) die the death of accident, meaninglessly and ultimately anonymously discorporating like unknown skulls in catacombs – and likewise the black woman in the dumpster. No matter that her murderer had a reason – she died for nothing; and all the toxicology and blood spatter analyses in the world, even if they lead to his conviction, cannot change that. The murderer's execution might mean something; his victim's killing almost certainly will not.

FROM THE WHITE HEARSE TO THE VIEWING ROOM

In fiscal year 1994–95, slightly more than eight thousand people died in San Francisco County. Half of these deaths could be considered in some sense questionable, and reports on them accordingly traveled to Dr Stephens's office, but in three thousand cases the doubts, being merely pro forma, were eventually cleared, signed off by physicians – that is, explained circumstantially if not ontologically. The remaining 1,549 deaths became Dr Stephens's problem. His findings for that year were: 919 natural deaths, 296 non-vehicular accidents, 124 suicides, ninety-four homicides, thirty mysterious cases, six sudden infant death syndromes, and eighty vehicular fatalities, most of which involved pedestrians, and most of which were accidents (there were six homicides and one suicide). And now I'm going to tell you what his people did to reach those findings. In San Francisco they had a white ambulance, or hearse as I might better say, which was partitioned between the driver's seat and the cargo hold, and the cargo hold could quickly be loaded or unloaded by means of the white double doors, the inside of which bore an inevitable reddish-brown stain: anything that touches flesh for years must get corrupted. It smelled like death in there, of course, which in my experience is sometimes similar to the smell of sour milk, or vomit and vinegar, or of garbage, which is to say of the dumpster in which the murdered girl had been clumsily secreted. A horizontal partition subdivided battered old stainless-steel stretchers into two and two. Because San Francisco is hilly, the stretchers, custom-welded years before by a shop just down the street, were made to be stood upright, the bodies strapped in, and rolled along on two wheels. 'Kind of like a wheelbarrow in a way,' one stretcher man said. This might be the last time that the dead would ever again be vertical, as they serenely traveled, strapped and sheeted, down steep stairs and sidewalks. The ambulance pulled up behind Dr Stephens's office, in a parking lot that said ambulance only. Out came each stretcher. Each stretcher went through the door marked no admittance, the door which for those of us whose hearts still beat might better read no admittance yet. Inside, the body was weighed upon a freight-sized scale, then wheeled into the center of that bleak back room for a preliminary examination, and fingerprinted three times (if it still had fingers and skin), with special black ink almost as thick as taffy. Finally it was zipped into a white plastic bag to go into the fridge overnight. If the death might be homicide, the investigators waited longer – at least twenty-four hours, in case any new bruises showed up like last-minute images on a pale sheet of photographic paper floating in the developer, as might happen when deep blood vessels had been ruptured. Bruises were very important. If the body of a man who seemed to have hanged himself showed contusions on the face or hands, the investigators would have to consider homicide.

By now perhaps the family had been told. In the big front room that said absolutely no admittance I heard a man say, 'Yes, we have Dave. I'm so sorry about what happened to Dave.' If the family came, they would be led down a narrow corridor to a door that said viewing room. The viewing room was private and secret, like the projectionist's booth in a movie theater. It had a long window that looked out onto another very bright and narrow room where the movie would take place, the real movie whose story had already ended before the attendant wheeled in the former actor. The movie was over; Dr Stephens needed the family to verify the screen credits. They only saw the face. There was a door between the viewing room and the bright and narrow room, but someone made sure to lock it before the family came, because they might have tried to embrace this thing which had once been someone they loved, and because the thing might not be fresh anymore or because it might have been slammed out of personhood in some hideous way whose sight or smell or touch would have made the family scream, it was better to respect the love they probably still felt for this thing which could no longer love them, to respect that love by respecting its clothes of ignorance. The people who worked in Dr Stephens's office had lost their ignorance a long time ago. They blunted themselves with habit, science and grim jokes – above all, with necessity: if the death had been strange or suspicious, they had to cut the thing open and look inside, no matter how much it stank.

*

A Solomonic parable: Dr Stephens told me that once three different mothers were led into the viewing room one by one to identify a dead girl, and each mother claimed the girl as hers, with a desperate relief, as I would suppose. I know someone whose sister was kidnapped. It's been years now and they've never found her. They found her car at the side of the road. My friend used to live with her sister. Now she lives with her sister's clothes. From time to time the family's private detective will show her photographs of still another female body partially skeletonized or not, raped or not, and she'll say, 'That's not my sister.' I know it would give her peace to be able to go into a viewing room and say (and believe), 'Yes, that's Shirley.' Those three mothers must all have given up hoping that their daughters would ever speak to them or smile at them again. They wanted to stop dreading and start grieving. They didn't want to go into viewing rooms anymore. And maybe the glass window was dirty, and maybe their eyes were old or full of tears. It was a natural mistake. But one mother was lucky. The dead girl was really her daughter.

THE INNOCENT METER MAID

To confirm that identification, someone at Dr Stephens's office had already looked inside the dead woman's mouth, incidentally discovering or not discovering the gleam of a knife-blade, observed her dental work, and matched it to a dentist's files. Somebody had fingerprinted her and found a match; somebody had sorted through her death-stained clothes and come up with a match. Starting with flesh and cloth, they had to learn what the mothers didn't know. The meter maid didn't know, either, and I am sure she didn't want to know. A young man eased some heroin into his arm – maybe too much, or maybe it was too pure (heroin just keeps getting better and better these days). He died and fell forward, his face swelling and purpling with lividity. The meter maid didn't know, I said. Even after he began to decompose, she kept putting parking tickets on his windshield.

'I'M A HAPPY CUSTOMER'

A stinking corpse, pink and green and yellow, lay naked on one of many parallel downsloping porcelain tables each of which drained into a porcelain sink. The man's back had hurt. Surgery didn't help, so he took painkillers until he became addicted. The painkillers proving insufficiently kind, he started mixing them with alcohol. When the white ambulance came, there were bottles of other people's pills beside his head. He was not quite forty.

'Everything's possible,' said one morgue attendant to another, leaning against a gurney, while the doctor in mask and scrubs began to cut the dead man open. 'You're limited only by your imagination.' I think he was talking about special effects photography. He had loaned his colleague a mail-order camera catalog.

Meanwhile the dagger tattooed on the dead man's bicep trembled and shimmered as the doctor's scalpel made the standard Y-shaped incision, left shoulder to chest, right shoulder to chest, then straight down the belly to the pubis. The doctor was very good at what he did, like an old Eskimo who I once saw cutting up a dying walrus. The scalpel made crisp sucking sounds. He peeled back the chest-flesh like a shirt, then crackled the racks of ribs, which could almost have been pork. His yellow-gloved hands grubbed in the scarlet hole, hauling out fistfuls of sausage-links – that is, loops of intestine.

Then he stuck a hose in and left it there until the outflow faded to pinkish clear. Beset by brilliant lavender, scarlet, and yellow, the twin red walls of rib-meat stood high and fragile, now protecting nothing, neatly split into halves.

The dead man still had a face.

The doctor syringed out a blood sample from the cavity, sponged blood off the table, and then it was time to weigh the dead man's organs on a hanging balance, the doctor calling out the numbers and the pretty young pathology resident chalking them onto the blackboard. The lungs, already somewhat decomposed, were indistinct masses which kept oozing away from the doctor's scalpel. 'Just like jello,' he said sourly.

The right lung was larger than the left, as is often the case with right-handed people. Another possible cause: the dead man had been found lying on his right side, a position which could have increased congestion in that lung. Either way, his death was meaningless.

His heart weighed 290 grams. The doctor began to cut it into slices.

'This vessel was almost.entirely occluded with atherosclerosis,' explained the resident. 'He used a lot of drugs. Cocaine hastens the onset of atherosclerosis. We get lots of young people with old people's diseases.'

That was interesting to know and it meant something, I thought. In a sense, the investigators understood the dead man. I wondered how well he'd been understood before he died.

'God, his pancreas!' exclaimed the doctor suddenly. 'That's why he died.' He lifted out a purple pudding which spattered blood onto the table.

'What happened?' I asked.

'Basically, all these enzymes there digest blood. This guy was hemorrhagic. The chemicals washed into his blood vessels and he bled. Very common with alcoholics.'

Out came the liver now, yellow with fatty infiltrations from too much alcohol. 'See the blood inside?' said the doctor. 'But the pancreas is a sweetbread. The pancreas is a bloody pulp. Blood in his belly. Sudden death. We got lucky with him – he's an easy one. This is a sure winner.'

Quickly he diced sections of the man's organs and let them ooze off his bloody yellow-gloved fingers into amber jars. The pathology and toxicology people would freeze them, slice them thinner, stain them and drop them onto microscope slides, just to make sure that he hadn't overdosed on something while he bled. Meanwhile the doctor's knowledge-seeking scalpel dissected the neck, to rule out any possibility of secret strangulation. Many subtle homicides are misdiagnosed as accidents by untrained people, and some accidents look like murders. The doctor didn't want that to happen. Even though he'd seen the pancreas, he wanted to be as thorough as he could to verify that there was no knife-blade in the mouth, that all the meaning had come out. – 'Okay, very good,' he grunted. Then the attendant, who I should really call a forensic technician, sewed the dead man up, with the garbage bag of guts already stuck back inside his belly. His brain, putrefying, liquescent, had already been removed; his face had hidden beneath its crimson blanket of scalp. The attendant sewed that up, too, and the man had a face again.

'I'm a happy customer,' said the doctor.

OF JOKES AND OTHER SHIELDS

If the doctor's wisecracks seem callous to you, ask yourself whether you wouldn't want to be armored against year after year of such sights and smells. Early the next morning I watched another doctor open up an old Filipino man who, sick and despondent, had hanged himself with an electric cord. I have seen a few autopsies and battlefields before, but the man's stern, stubborn stare, his eyes glistening like black glass while the doctor, puffing, dictated case notes and slashed his guts (the yellow twist of strangle-cord lying on an adjacent table) gave me a nightmare that evening. This doctor, like his colleague, the happy customer, was doing a good thing. Both were proving that neither one of these dead men had been murdered, and that neither one had carried some contagious disease. Like soldiers, they worked amidst death. Green-stained buttocks and swollen faces comprised their routine. They had every right to joke, to dull themselves. Those who can't do that don't last.

Strangely enough, even their job could be for some souls a shelter from sadder things. Dr Stephens himself used to be a pediatric oncologist before he became coroner in 1968. 'At that time, we lost seventy-five percent of the children,' he said. 'Emotionally, that was an extremely hard thing to do. I'd be dead if I stayed in that profession.'

The thought of Dr Stephens ending up on one of his own steel tables bemused me. As it happens, I am married to an oncologist. She goes to the funerals of her child patients. Meanwhile she rushes about her life. Embracing her, I cherish her body's softness which I know comprises crimson guts.

EVIDENCE

The little cubes of meat in the amber jars went across the hall to pathology and to toxicology: underbudgeted realms making do with old instruments and machines which printed out cocaine-spikes or heroin-spikes on the slowly moving graph paper which had been state of the art in the 1960s. But after all, how much does death change? Ladies in blue gowns tested the urine samples of motorists suspected of driving while intoxicated, and with equal equanimity checked the urine of the dead. Had they, or had they not died drunk? The drunken motorist who died in a crash, the drunken suicide who'd finally overcome his fear of guns (in 17th-century Germany, the authorities encouraged condemned criminals to drink beer or wine before the execution), the drunken homicide victim who'd felt sufficiently invincible to provoke his murder – such descriptors helped attach reason to the death. Meanwhile, the blue-gowned ladies inspected the tissue samples that the doctors across the hall had sent them. I saw a woman bent over a cutting board, probing a granular mass of somebody's tumor, remarking casually on the stench. If the stomach was cancerous, if the liver was full of Tylenol or secobarb, that comprised a story, and Dr Stephens's people were all the closer to signing off that particular death certificate.

In her gloved hands, a lady twirled a long, black-bulbed tube of somebody's crimson blood. On a table stood a stack of floppy disks marked police cases. Here was evidence, information, which might someday give birth to meaning. Kidneys floated in large translucent white plastic jars. They too had their secret knives-in-the-mouth – or not. They might explain a sudden collapse – or rationalize the toxic white concentration of barbiturates in the duodenum, if the decedent's last words did not. In San Francisco one out of four suicides left a note. Some of the laconic ones might leave unwitting messages in their vital organs. 'I would say that about twenty-five percent of the suicides we have here are justified by real physical illness,' Dr Stephens told me. 'We had one gentleman recently who flew in from another state, took a taxi to the Golden Gate Bridge, and jumped off. Well, he had inoperable liver cancer. Those are logical decisions. As for the others, they have transient emotional causes. A girl tells a boy she doesn't want to see him anymore, so he goes and hangs himself. No one talked to him and got him over to the realization that there are other women in the world.'

Look in the liver then. Find the cancer – or not. That tells us something.

'And homicide?' I asked. 'Does that ever show good reason?'

'Well I've seen only a few justified homicides,' Dr Stephens replied. 'We handle a hundred homicides a year, and very few are justified. They're saving their family or their own lives. But the vast majority of homicides are just a waste, just senseless violent crimes to effect punishment.'

And accident? And heart attack, and renal failure? No reason even to ask. From the perspective of the viewing room, it is all senseless.

DEATH CAN NEVER HURT YOU UNTIL YOU DIE

On that Saturday morning while the doctor was running the hanged man's intestines through his fingers like a fisherman unkinking line, and the forensic tech, a Ukrainian blonde who told me about her native Odessa, was busily taking the top of his head off with a power saw, I asked: 'When bodies decompose, are you at more or less of a risk for infection?'

'Oh, the TB bacillus and the AIDS virus degrade pretty quickly,' said the doctor. 'They have a hard time in dead bodies. Not enough oxygen. But staph and fungus grow . . . The dead you have nothing to fear from. It's the living. It's when you ask a dead man's roommate what happened, and the dead man wakes up and coughs on you.'

He finished his job and went out. After thanking the tech and changing out of my scrubs, so did I. I went back into the bright hot world where my death awaited me. If I died in San Francisco, there was one chance in five that they would wheel me into Dr Stephens's office. Although my surroundings did not seem to loom and reek with death as they had when I came out of the catacombs – I think because the deaths I saw on the autopsy slabs were so grotesquely singular that I could refuse to see myself in them, whereas the sheer mass and multiplicity of the catacomb skulls had worn down my un-belief – still I wondered who would cough on me, or what car would hit me, or which cancer might already be subdivid-ing and stinking inside my belly. The doctor was right: I would not be able to hurt him then, because he'd be ready for me. Nor would his scalpel cause me pain. And I walked down Bryant Street wondering at the strange absurdity of my soul, which had felt most menaced by death when I was prob-ably safest – how could those corpses rise up against me? – and which gloried in removing my disposable mask and inhaling the fresh air, letting myself dissolve into the city with its deadly automobiles and pathogen-breathers, its sail-boats and bookstores; above all, its remorseless futurity.

III

Siege Thoughts

And now, closing my eyes, I reglimpse tangents of atrocities and of wars. I see a wall of skulls in the Paris catacombs. Likewise I see the skulls on the glass shelves at Choeung Ek Killing Field. In place of the tight wall of catacomb skulls gazing straight on at me, sometimes arranged in beautiful arches, I see skulls stacked loosely, laid out on the glass display shelves in heaps, not patterns – although it would give a deficient impression to omit the famous 'genocide map' a few kilometers away in Phnom Penh; this is a cartographic representation of all Cambodia, comprised of murdered skulls. At Choeung Ek, they lie canted upon each other, peering and grinning, gaping and screaming, categorized by age, sex and even by race (for a few Europeans also died at the hands of the Khmer Rouge). Some bear cracks where the Khmer Rouge smashed those once-living heads with iron bars. But to my uneducated eye there is nothing else to differentiate them from the skulls of Paris. The Angel of Death flies overhead, descends and kills, and then he goes. The relics of his work become indistinguishable, except to specialists such as Dr Stephens, and to those who were there. (I remember once seeing a movie on the Holocaust. When the lights came on, I felt bitter and depressed. It seemed that the movie had 'reached' me. And then I saw a man I knew, and his face was very pale and he was sweating. He was a Jew. He was really there. The Nazis had killed most of his family.) Before the Angel strikes, of course, the doomed remain equally indistinguishable from the lucky or unlucky ones who will survive a little longer. Death becomes apprehensible, perhaps, only at the moment of dying.

To apprehend it, then, let's approach the present moment, the fearful time when they're shooting at you and, forgetting that your life is not perfect, you crave only to live, sweat and thirst a little longer; you promise that you'll cherish your life always, if you can only keep it. Thus near-death, whose violence or not makes no difference. A woman I loved who died of cancer once wrote me: 'You will not be aware of this but it is the anniversary of my mastectomy and I am supposed to be happy that I survived and all that. Actually it has been a terrible day.' She'd forgotten, like me; she'd shrugged death off again, not being godlike enough to treasure every minute after all. The first time I survived being shot at (maybe they weren't shooting at me; maybe they didn't even see me), I pledged to be happier, to be grateful for my life, and in this I have succeeded, but I still have days when the catacombs and Dr Stephens's autopsy slabs sink too far below my memory, and I despise and despair at life. Another fright, another horror, and I return to gratitude. The slabs rise up and stink to remind me of my happiness. A year before her terrible day, the one I'd loved had written: 'They had to use four needles, four veins last time. I cried as they put the fourth needle in. My veins are not holding up. I vomited even before leaving the doctor's office and then spent four days semi-conscious, vomiting. I thought very seriously about immediate death. Could I overdose on the sleeping pills, I wondered . . . My choices aren't that many and I would like to be there to hate my daughter's boyfriends.' I remember the letter before that on pink paper that began, 'I know I said I wouldn't write. I lied. I've just been told this weekend that I have invasive breast cancer and will have a mastectomy and removal of the lymph nodes within the week. I am scared to death. I have three small kids . . . I am not vain. I do not care about my chest but I do want to live . . . So, tell me. This fear – I can smell it – is it like being in a war?' – Yes, darling. I have never been terminally ill, but I am sure that it is the same.

In one of her last letters she wrote me: 'There was definitely a time when I thought I might die sooner rather than later – it took me awhile to believe that I would probably be okay. It still doesn't feel truly believable but more and more I want it to be the case – mostly because I want to raise my interesting and beautiful children and because I want to enjoy myself . . . My hair grew back to the point that I no longer use the wig.'

In another letter she wrote me: 'Here are the recent events in my life. I am not unhappy with them but they do not compare with being shot at and losing a friend and perhaps they will amuse you. I set up a fish tank in my study . . . I got the kids four fish. They named only one. I told them once they had learned to clean and change the tank and feed the fish and explain how gills work, then they could get a guinea pig. I am not into pets, preferring children. The one catfish in the tank is in great distress and swims around madly looking for a way to die.'

When I close my eyes, I can see her as she looked at seventeen, and I can see her the way she was when she was thirty-four, much older, thanks in part to the cancer – bonier-faced, with sparse hair, perhaps a wig, sitting on the steps beside her children. I never had to see her in Dr Stephens's viewing room. I never saw her body rotting. I'll never see her de-personalized skull mortared into a catacomb's wall. Does that mean I cannot envision death, her death? The six million death's-heads under Paris weigh on me much less than her face, which you might call too gaunt to be beautiful, but which was still beautiful to me, which only in a photograph will I ever see again.

But – again I return to this – her death was meaningless, an accident of genetics or environment. No evil soul murdered her. I am sad when I think about her. I am not bitter.

I am sad when I think about my two colleagues in Bosnia who drove into a land-mine trap. Their names were Will and Francis. I will write about them later. At the time, because there were two distinct reports and holes appeared in the windshield and in the two dying men, I believed that they were shot, and when armed men approached I believed that I was looking at their killers. Will I had known only for two days, but I liked what I knew of him. Francis was my friend, off and on, for nineteen years. I loved Francis. But I was never angry, even when the supposed snipers came, for their actions could not have been personally intended. We were crossing from the Croatian to the Muslim side; the Muslims were sorry, and such incidents are common enough in war.

But now I open a letter from my Serbian friend Vineta, who often had expressed to me her dislike of Francis (whom she never met) on the grounds of his Croatian blood, and who after commenting in considerable helpful and businesslike detail on my journalistic objectives in Serbia, then responded to my plans for the Muslim and Croatian sides of the story (my items seven and eight) as follows: 'You see, dear Billy, it's very nice of you to let me know about your plans. But, i don't give a shit for both croats and muslims!' At the end of her long note she added this postscript: 'The last "personal letter" I got was two years ago, from my late boyfriend. The

Croats cut his body into pieces in the town of B—— near Vukovar. His name was M——.' Then she wrote one more postscript: 'No one has a chance to open my heart ever again.'

This is what violence does. This is what violence is. It is not enough that death reeks and stinks in the world, but now it takes on inimical human forms, prompting the self-defending survivors to strike and to hate, rightly or wrongly. Too simple to argue that nonviolent death is always preferable from the survivors' point of view! I've heard plenty of doctors' stories about the families of dying cancer patients who rage against 'fate.' Like Hitler, they'd rather have someone to blame. 'Everybody's angry when a loved one dies,' one doctor insisted. 'The only distinction is between directed and undirected anger.' Maybe so. But it is a distinction. Leaving behind Dr Stephens's tables, on which, for the most part, lie only the 'naturally' dead with their bleeding pancreases, the accidentally dead, and the occasional suicide, let us fly to besieged Sarajevo and look in on the morgue at Kosevo Hospital, a place I'll never forget, whose stench stayed on my clothes for two days afterwards. Here lay the homicides. I saw children with their bellies blown open, women shot in the head while they crossed the street, men hit by some well-heeled sniper's anti-tank round. Death joked and drank and vulgarly farted in the mountains all around us, aiming its weapons out of hateful fun, making the besieged counter-hateful. Every morning I woke up to chittering bullets and crashing mortar rounds. I hated the snipers I couldn't see because they might kill me and because they were killing the people of this city, ruining the city in every terrible physical and psychic way that it could be ruined, smashing it, murdering wantonly, frightening and crushing.

But their wickedness too had become normal: this was Sarajevo in the fourteenth month of the siege. Needs lived on; people did business amidst their terror, a terror which could not be sustained, rising up only when it was needed, when one had to run. As for the forensic doctor at Kosevo Hospital, he went home stinking of death, and, like me, sometimes slept in his clothes; he was used to the smell, and his wife must have gotten used to it, too, when she embraced him. (Meanwhile, of course, some people had insomnia, got ulcers or menstrual disturbances, went prematurely grey. Here, too, undirected anger might surface. Political death, cancer death, it's all the same.)

The night after Will and Francis were killed, a UN interpreter from Sarajevo told me how she lost friends almost every week. 'You become a little cold,' she said very quietly. 'You have to.' This woman was sympathetic, immensely kind; in saying this she meant neither to dismiss my grief nor to tell me how I ought to be. She merely did the best thing that can be done for any bereaved person, which was to show me her own sadness, so that my sadness would feel less lonely; but hers had wearied and congealed; thus she told me what she had become. Like Dr Stephens and his crew, or the backpack inspector at the catacombs, like my friend Thion who ferries tourists to Choeung Ek on his motorcycle, I had already begun to become that way. Sarajevo wasn't the first war zone I'd been to, nor the first where I'd seen death, but I'll never forget it. The morgue at Kosevo Hospital, like the rest of Sarajevo, had had to make do without electricity, which was why, as I keep saying, it stank. I remember the cheesy smell of the Paris catacombs, the sour-milk smell of Dr Stephens's white hearse; after that visit to Kosevo Hospital my clothes smelled like vomit, vinegar, and rotting bowels. I returned to the place where I was staying, which got its share of machine gun and missile attacks, and gathered together my concerns, which did not consist of sadness for the dead, but only of being scared and wondering if I would eat any more that day because they'd shot down the UN flight and so the airport was closed and I'd already given my food away. Death was on my skin and on the other side of the wall – maybe my death, maybe not; trying to live wisely and carefully, I granted no time to my death, although it sometimes snarled at me. Ascending from the catacombs I'd had all day, so I'd given death all day; no one wanted to hurt me. But in Sarajevo I simply ran; it was all death, death, and death, so meaningless and accidental to me.

I wore a bulletproof vest in Mostar, which did get struck with a splinter of something which rang on its ceramic trauma plate, so to an extent I had made my own luck, but Will, who was driving, discovered that his allotted death was one which entered the face now, diagonally from the chin. His dying took forever (I think about five minutes). Vineta said that I had been cowardly or stupid not to end his misery. I told her that journalists don't carry guns. Anyhow, had I been in his seat, my bulletproof vest would have done me no good.

The woman I loved simply had the wrong cells in her breast; Vineta's boyfriend had fought in the wrong place at the wrong time, and perhaps he'd fought against the Croats too ferociously or even just too well. For the woman I loved, and for me in Sarajevo, the Angel of Death was faceless, but Vineta's tormenting Angel of Death had a Croatian face; she hated 'those Croatian bastards.' Vineta, if I could send the Angel of Death away from you, I would. Maybe someone who knows

you and loves you better than I can at least persuade your
Angel to veil his face again so that he becomes mere darkness
like the Faceless One of Iroquois legends, mere evil chance,
'an act of war,' like my drowned sister's Angel; and then your
anger can die down to sadness. Vineta, if you ever see this
book of mine, don't think me presumptuous; don't think I
would ever stand between you and your right to mourn and
rage against the Angel. But he is not Francis. Francis was
good. I don't like to see him stealing Francis's face when he
comes to hurt you.

The Angel is in the white hearse. Can't we please proceed
like Dr Stephens's employees, weighing, fingerprinting, cutting open all this sad and stinking dross of violence, trying
to learn what causes what? And when the malignity or the
sadness or the unpleasantness of the thing on the table threat-
ens to craze us, can't we tell a callous joke or two? If I can
contribute to understanding how and why the Angel kills,
then I'll be, in the words of that doctor who swilled coffee
out of one bloody-gloved hand while he sliced a dead body
with the other, 'a happy customer.' Hence this essay, and the
larger work from which this is extracted. For its many failures
I ask forgiveness from all.

Up the Mountain Coming Down Slowly

DAVE EGGERS

She lies, she lies, Rita lies on the bed, looking up, in the room that is so loud so early in Tanzania. She is in Moshi. She arrived the night before, in a jeep driven by a man named Godwill. It is so bright this morning but was so madly, impossibly dark last night.

Her flight had arrived late, and customs was slow. There was a young American couple trying to clear a large box of soccer balls. For an orphanage, they said. The customs agent, in khaki head to toe, removed and bounced each ball on the clean reflective floor, as if inspecting their viability. Finally the American man was taken to a side room, and in a few minutes returned, rolling his eyes to his wife, rubbing his forefinger and thumb together in a way meaning money. The soccer balls were cleared, and the couple went on their way. Outside it was not humid, it was open and clear, the air cool and light, and Rita was greeted soundlessly by an old man, black and white-haired and thin and neat in shirtsleeves and a brown tie. He was Godwill, and he had been sent by the hotel to pick her up. It was midnight and she was very awake as they drove and they had driven, on the British side of the road, in silence through rural Tanzania, just their headlights and the occasional jacaranda, and the constant long grass lining the way.

At the hotel she wanted a drink. She went to the hotel bar

alone, something she'd never done, and sat at the bar with a stenographer from Brussels. The stenographer, whose name she did not catch and couldn't ask for again, wore a short inky bob of black coarse hair, and was wringing her napkin into tortured shapes, tiny twisted mummies. The stenographer: face curvy and shapeless like a child's, voice melodious, accent soothing. They talked about capital punishment, comparing the stonings common to some Muslim regions with America's lethal injections and electric chairs; somehow the conversation was cheerful and relaxed. They had both seen the same documentary about people who had witnessed executions, and had been amazed at how little it had seemed to affect any of them, the watchers; they were sullen and unmoved. To witness a death! Rita could never do it. Even if they made her sit there, behind the partition, she would close her eyes.

Rita was tipsy and warm when she said good night to the Brussels stenographer, who held her hand too long with her cold slender fingers. Through the French doors and Rita was outside, and walked past the pool toward her hut, one of twelve behind the hotel. She passed a man in a plain and green uniform with a gun strapped to his back, an automatic rifle of some kind, the barrel poking over his shoulder and in the dim light seeming aimed at the base of his skull. She didn't know why the man was there, and didn't know if he would shoot her in the back when she walked past him, but she did, she walked past him, because she trusted him, trusted this country and the hotel – that together they would know why it was necessary to have a heavily armed guard standing alone by the pool, still and clean, the surface dotted with leaves. She smiled at him and he did not smile back and she only felt safe again when she had closed the hut's door and closed the door to the bathroom and was sitting on the cool toilet with her palms caressing her toes.

Morning comes like a scream through a pinhole. Rita is staring at the concentric circles of bamboo that comprise the hut's round conical roof. She is lying still, hands crossed on her chest – she woke up that way – and through the mosquito net, too tight, terrifying, suffocating in a small way when she thinks too much about it, she can see the concentric circles of the roof above and the circles are twenty-two in number, because she has counted and recounted. She counted while lying awake, listening to someone, outside the hut, fill bucket after bucket with water.

Her name is Rita. Her hair is red like a Romanian's and her hands are large. Eyes large and mouth lipless and she hates, has always hated, her lipless mouth. As a girl she waited for her lips to appear, to fill out, but it did not happen. Every year since her sixteenth birthday her lips have not grown but receded. The circles make up the roof but the circles never touch. Her father had been a pastor.

Last night she thought, intermittently, she knew why she was in Tanzania, in Moshi, at the base of Kilimanjaro. But this morning she has no clue. She knows she is supposed to begin hiking up the mountain today, in two hours, but now that she has come here, through Amsterdam and through the cool night from the airport, sitting silently alone the whole drive, an hour or so at midnight, next to Godwill – really his name was Godwill, an old man who was sent by the hotel to pick her up, and it made her so happy because Godwill was such a . . . Tanzanian-sounding name – now that she has come here and is awake she cannot find the reason why she is here. She cannot recall the source of her motivation to spend four

days hiking up this mountain, so blindingly white at the top
– a hike some had told her was brutalizing and often fatal and
others had claimed was, well, just a walk in the park. She was
not sure she was fit enough, and was not sure she would not
be bored to insanity. She was most concerned about the altitude
sickness. The young were more susceptible, she'd heard, and
at 38 she was not sure she was that anymore – young – but
she felt that for some reason she in particular was always
susceptible and she would have to know when to turn back.
If the pressure in her head became too great, she would have
to turn back. The mountain was almost 20,000 feet high and
every month someone died of a cerebral edema and there were
ways to prevent this. Breathing deeply would bring more
oxygen into the blood, into the brain, and if that didn't work
and the pain persisted, there was Diamox, which thinned the
blood and accomplished the same objective but more quickly.
But she hated to take pills and had vowed not to use them,
to simply go down if the pain grew intolerable – but how
would she know when to go down? What were the phases
before death? And what if she decided too late? She might at
some point realize that it was time to turn and walk down
the mountain, but what if it was already too late? It was
possible that she would decide to leave, be ready to live at a
lower level again, but by then the mountain would have had
its way and there, on a path or in a tent, she would die.

She could stay in the hut. She could go to Zanzibar and
drink in the sun. She liked nothing better than to drink in
the sun. With strangers. To drink in the sun! To feel the
numbing of her tongue and limbs while her skin cooked
slowly, and her feet dug deeper into the powdery sand!

*

Her hands are still crossed on her chest, and the filling of the buckets continues outside her hut, so loud, so constant. Is someone taking the water meant for her shower? At home, in St Louis, her landlord was always taking her water – so why shouldn't it be the same here, in a hut in Moshi, with a gecko, almost translucent, darting across her conical ceiling, its ever-smaller circles never interlocking?

She has bought new boots, expensive, and has borrowed a backpack, huge, and a thermarest, and sleeping bag, and cup and a dozen other things. Everything made of plastic and Gore-Tex. The items were light individually but together very heavy and all of it is packed in a large tall purple pack in the corner of the round hut and she doesn't want to carry the pack and wonders why she's come. She is not a mountain climber, and not an avid hiker, and not someone who needs to prove her fitness by hiking mountains and afterward casually mentioning it to friends and colleagues. She likes racquetball.

She has come because her younger sister, Gwen, had wanted to come, and they had bought the tickets together, thinking it would be the perfect trip to take before Gwen began making a family with her husband, Brad. But she'd gone ahead and gotten pregnant anyway, early, six months ahead of schedule and she could not make the climb. She could not make the climb but that did not preclude – Gwen used the word liberally and randomly, like some use curry – her, Rita, from going. The trip was not refundable, so why not go?

Rita slides her hands from her chest to her thighs and holds them, her thin thighs, as if to steady them. Who is filling the bucket? She imagines it's someone from the shanty behind the hotel, stealing the hot water from the heater. She'd seen a bunch of teenage boys back there. Maybe they're stealing Rita's shower water. This country is so poor. Is poorer than any place she's been. Is it poorer than Jamaica? She is not sure. Jamaica she expected to be like Florida, a healthy place benefiting from generations of heavy tourism and the constant and irrational flow of America money. But Jamaica was desperately poor almost everywhere and she understood nothing.

Maybe Tanzania is less poor. Around her hotel are shanties and also well-built homes with gardens and gates. There is a law here, Godwill had said in strained English, that all the men are required to have jobs. Maybe people chose to live in spartan simplicity. She doesn't know enough to judge one way or the other. The unemployed go to jail! Godwill had said, and seemed to like this law. The idle are like the devil! he said and then laughed and laughed.

In the morning the sun is as clear and forthright as a spotlight and Rita wants to avoid walking past the men. She has already walked past the men twice and she has nothing to say to them. Soon the bus will come to take her and the others to the base of the mountain, and since finally leaving her bed she has been doing the necessary things – eating, packing, calling Gwen – and for each task she has had to walk from her hut to the hotel, has had to walk past the men sitting and standing along the steps into the lobby. Eight to ten of them, young men, sitting, waiting without speaking. Godwill had talked about this – that the men list their occupations as guide, porter, salesperson – anything that will satisfy their government and didn't require them to be accounted for in one constant place, because there really wasn't much work at all. She had seen two of the men scuffle briefly over another American's bag, for a $1 tip. When Rita walked past them she tried to smile faintly, without looking too friendly, or rich, or sexy, or happy, or vulnerable, or guilty, or proud, or contented, or healthy, or interested – she did not want them to think she was any of those things. She walked by almost cross-eyed with casual concentration.

Rita's face is wide and almost square, her jaw just short of masculine. People have said she looks like a Kennedy, one of the female Kennedys. But she is not beautiful like that woman; she is instead almost plain, with or without makeup, plain in any light. This she knows, though her friends and Gwen tell her otherwise. She is unmarried and was for a time a foster parent to siblings, a girl of nine and boy of seven, beaten by their birth mother, and Rita had contemplated adopting them herself – had thought her life through, every year she imagined and planned with those kids, she could definitely do it – but then Rita's mother and father had beaten her to it. Her parents loved those kids, too, and had oceans of time and plenty of room in their home, and there were discussions and it had quickly been settled. There was a long weekend they all spent together in the house where Rita and Gwen were raised, Rita and her parents there with J.J. and Frederick, the kids arranging their trophies in their new rooms, and on Sunday evening, Rita said goodbye, and the kids stayed there. It was easy and painless for everyone, and Rita spent a week of vacation time in bed shaking.

Now, when she works two Saturdays a month and can't see them as often, Rita misses the two of them in a way that's too visceral. She misses having them both in her bed, the two little people, seven and nine years old, when the crickets were too loud and they were scared of them growing, the crickets, and of them together carrying away the house to devour it and everyone inside. This is a story they had heard, about the giant crickets carrying away the house, from their birth mother.

Rita is asleep on the bus but wakes up when the road inclines. The vehicle, white and square with rounded edges – it reminds her vaguely of something that would descend, backward, from a rocket ship and onto the moon – whinnies and shakes over the potholes of the muddy road and good Christ it's raining! – raining steadily on the way to the gate of Kilimanjaro. Godwill is driving, and this gives her some peace, even though he's driving much too fast, and is not slowing down around tight curves, or for pedestrians carrying possessions on their heads, or for schoolchildren, who seem to be everywhere, in uniforms of white above and blue below. Disaster at every moment seems probable, but Rita is so tired she can't imagine raising an objection if the bus were sailing over a cliff.

'She's awake!' a man says. She looks to find Frank smiling at her, cheerful in an almost insane way. Maybe he is insane. Frank is the American guide, a sturdy and energetic man, from Oregon, medium-sized in every way, with a short-shorn blond beard that wraps his face as a bandage would a man, decades ago, suffering from a toothache. 'We thought we'd have to carry you up. You're one of those people who can sleep through anything, I bet.' Then he laughs a shrill, girlish laugh, forced and mirthless.

They pass a large school, its sign posted along the road. The top half: Drive Refreshed: Coca Cola; below: Marangu Sec. School. A group of women are walking on the roadside, babies in slings. They pass the Samange Social Club, which

looks like a construction company trailer. Further up the road,
a small pink building, the K&J Hot Fashion Shop, bearing
an enormous spray-painted rendering of Angela Bassett. A boy
of six is leading a donkey. Two tiny girls in school uniforms
are carrying a bag of potatoes. A driveway leads to the Tropical
Pesticides Research Institute. The rain intensifies as they pass
another school – Coca Cola: Drive Refreshed; St Margaret's
Catholic Sec. School.

That morning, at the hotel, Rita had overheard a conversation between a British woman and the hotel concierge.

'There are so many Catholic schools!' the tourist had said.
She'd just gotten back from a trip to a local waterfall.

'Are you Catholic?' the concierge had said. She was stout,
with a clear nasal voice, a kind of clarinet.

'I am,' the tourist said. 'And you?'

'Yes please. Did you see my town? Marangu?'

'I did. On the hill?'

'Yes please.'

'It was very beautiful.'

And the concierge had smiled.

The van passes a FEMA dispensary, a YMCA, another social
club called Millennium, a line of teenage girls in uniforms,
plum-purple sweaters and skirts of sportcoat blue. They all
wave. The rain is now real rain. The people they pass are
soaked.

'Look at Patrick,' Frank says, pointing at a handsome Tanzanian man on the bus, sitting across the aisle from him. 'He's
just sitting there smiling, wondering why the hell anyone
would pay to be subjected to this.'

Patrick smiles and nods and says nothing.

*

There are five paying hikers on the trip and they are introducing themselves. There are Mike and Jerry, a son and father in matching jackets. Mike is in his late twenties and his father is maybe sixty. Jerry has an accent that sounds British but possesses the round vowels of an Australian. Jerry owns a chain of restaurants, while the son is an automotive engineer, specializing in ambulances. They are tall men, barrel-chested and thin-legged, though Mike is heavier, with a loose paunch he carries with some effort. They wear matching red jackets, scarred everywhere with zippers, their initials embroidered on the left-breast pockets. Mike is quiet and seems to be getting sick from the bus's jerking movements and constant turns. Jerry is smiling broadly, as if to make up for his son's reticence – a grin meant to introduce them both as happy and ready men, as gamers.

The rain continues, the cold unseasonable. There is a low fog that rises between the trees, giving the green a dead, faded look, like most of the forest's color had leaked into the soil.

'The rain should clear away in an hour or so,' Frank announces, as the bus continues up the hills, bouncing through the mud. The foliage everywhere around is tangled and sloppy. 'What do you think, Patrick?' Frank says. 'This rain gonna burn off?'

Patrick hasn't spoken yet and now just shrugs and smiles. There is something in his eyes, Rita thinks, that is assessing. Assessing Frank, and the paying hikers, guessing at the possibility that he will make it up and down this mountain, this time, without losing his mind.

Grant is at the back of the bus, watching the land pass through the windows, sitting in the middle of the bus's backseat, like some kind of human rudder. He is shorter than the other two men but his legs are enormous, like a power lifter's, his calves thick and hairy. He is wearing cutoff jean shorts, though the temperature has everyone else adding layers. His hair is black and short-shorn, his eyes are small and water-cooler blue.

He is watching the land pass through the window near his right cheek, and the air of outside waters his small blue eyes.

Shelly is in her late forties and looks precisely her age. She is slim, fit, almost wiry. Her hair, long, ponytailed, once blond, is fading to gray and she is not fighting it. She has the air of a lion, Rita thinks, though she doesn't know why she thinks of this animal, a lion, when she sees this small woman sitting two seats before her, in an anorak of the most lucid and expectant yellow. She watches Shelly tie a bandanna around her neck, quickly and with a certain offhand ferocity. Shelly's features are the features Rita would like for herself: a small thin nose with a flawless upward curve, her lips with the correct and voluptuous lines, lips that must have been effort-lessly sexual and life-giving as a younger woman.

'It's really miserable out there,' Shelly says.

Rita nods.

The bus stops in front of a clapboard building, crooked, frowning, like a general store in a Western. There are signs and farm instruments attached to its side, and on the porch, out of the rain, there are two middle-aged women feeding fabric through sewing machines, side by side. Their eyes briefly sweep over the bus and its passengers, and then return to their work as the bus begins again.

Frank is talking about the porters. Porters, he says, will be accompanying the group, carrying the duffel bags, and the tents, and the tables to eat upon, and the food, and propane tanks, and coolers, and silverware, and water, among other things. Their group is five hikers and two guides, and there will be thirty-two porters coming along.

'I had no idea,' Rita says to Grant, behind her. 'I pictured a few guides and maybe two porters.' She has a sudden vision of servants carrying kings aboard gilt thrones, elephants following, trumpets announcing their progress.

'That's nothing,' Frank says. Frank has been listening to everyone's conversations and inserting himself when he sees fit. 'Last time I did Everest, there were six of us and we had eighty Sherpas.' He holds his hand horizontally, demonstrating the height of the Sherpas, which seems to be about four feet or so. 'Little guys,' he says, 'but bad-asses. Tougher than these guys down here. No offense, Patrick.'

Patrick isn't listening. The primary Tanzanian guide, he's in his early thirties and is dressed in new gear – a blueberry anorak, snowboarding pants, wraparound sunglasses. He's watching the side of the road, where a group of boys is keeping pace with the bus, each in a school uniform and each carrying what looks to be a small sickle. They run alongside, four of them, waving their sickles, yelling things Rita can't hear through the windows and over the whinnies of the van going up and up through the wet dirt. Their mouths are going, their eyes angry and their teeth are so small, but by the time Rita gets her window open to hear what they're saying the van is far beyond them, and they have run off the road with their sickles. They've dropped down the hillside, following some narrow path of their own making.

There is a wide black parking lot. MACHAME GATE reads a sign over the entrance. In the parking lot, about a hundred

Tanzanian men are standing. They watch the bus enter the lot and park and immediately twenty of them converge upon it, unloading the backpacks and duffel bags from the bus. Before Rita and the rest of the hikers are off, all of the bags are stacked in a pile nearby, and the rain is falling upon them.

Rita is last off the bus, and when she arrives at the door, Godwill has closed it, not realizing she is still aboard.

'Sorry please,' he says, yanking the lever, trying to get the door open again.

'Don't worry, I'm in no hurry,' she says, giving him a little laugh.

She sees a man between the parking lot and the gate to the park, a man like the man at her hotel, in a plain green uniform, automatic rifle on his back.

'Is the gun for the animals, or the people?' she asks.

'People,' Godwill says, with a small laugh. 'People much more dangerous than animals!' Then he laughs and laughs and laughs.

It's about forty-five degrees, Rita guesses, though it could be fifty. And the rain. It's raining steadily, and the rain is cold. Rita hadn't thought about rain. When she had pictured the hike she had not thought about cold, cold, steady rain.

'Looks like we've got ourselves some rain,' Frank says.

The paying hikers look at him.

'No two ways about it,' he says.

Everything is moving rapidly. Bags are being grabbed, duffels hoisted. There are so many porters! Everyone is already wet. Patrick is talking with a group of the porters. They are dressed in bright colors, like the paying hikers, but their clothes – simple pants and sweatshirts – are already dirty, and

163

their shoes are not large and complicated boots, as Rita is wearing, but instead sneakers, or track shoes, or loafers. None wear rain gear, but all wear hats.

Now there is animated discussion, and some pointing and shrugging. One porter jumps to the ground and then lies still, as if pretending to be dead. The men around him roar.

Rita ducks into her poncho and pulls it over her torso and backpack. The poncho was a piece of equipment the organizers listed as optional; no one, it seems, expected this rain. Now she is thrilled she bought it – $4.99 at Target on the way to the airport. She sees a few of the porters poking holes in garbage bags and fitting themselves within. Grant is doing the same. He catches Rita looking at him.

'Forgot the poncho,' he says. 'Can't believe I forgot the poncho.'

'Sorry,' she says. There is nothing else to say. He's going to get soaked.

'It's okay,' he says. 'Good enough for them, good enough for me.'

Rita tightens the laces on her boots and readjusts her gaiters. She helps Shelly with her poncho, spreading it over her backpack, and arranges her hood around her leonine hair, frayed and thick, blond and white. As she pulls the plastic close to Shelly's face, they stare into each other's eyes and Rita has a sharp pain in her stomach, or her head, somewhere. She wants them here. They are her children and she allowed them to be taken. People were always quietly taking things from her, always with the understanding that everyone would be better off if Rita's life were kept simplified. But she was ready for complication, wasn't she? For a certain period of time, she was, she knows. It was the condominium that concerned everyone; she had almost bought one, in anticipation of adopting the kids, and she had backed out – but why? – just before closing. The place wasn't right; it wasn't big enough. She wanted it to be more right; she wanted to be more ready. It wasn't right, and they would know it, and they would think she would always be insolvent, and they would always have to share a room. Gwen had offered to co-sign on the other place, the place they looked at with the yard and the three bedrooms, but that wouldn't be right, having Gwen on the mortgage. So she had given up and the kids were now in her old room, with her parents. She wants them walking next to her asking her advice. She wants to arrange their hoods around their faces, wants to pull the drawstrings so their faces shrink from view and stay dry. Shelly's face is old and lined and she grins at Rita and clears her throat.

'Thank you, hon,' she says.

They are both waterproof now and the rain tick-ticks onto the plastic covering them everywhere. The paying hikers are standing in the parking lot in the rain.

'Porters have dropped out,' says Frank, speaking to the group. 'They gotta replace the porters who won't go up. It'll take a few minutes.'

'Are there replacements close by?' Grant asks.

'Probably get some younger guys,' Frank says. 'The younger guys are hungry.'

'Like the B-team, right?' Jerry says. 'We're getting the B-team!' He looks around for laughs but no one's wet cold face will smile. 'Minor leaguers, right?' he says, then gives up.

It is much too late to go home now, Rita knows. Still, she can't suppress the thought of running all the way, ten miles or so, mostly downhill, back to the hotel, at which point she would – no matter what the cost – fly to warm and flat Zanzibar, to drink and drink until half-blind in the sun.

Nearby in the parking lot, Patrick seems to settle something with the man he's speaking to, and approaches the group.

'Very wet,' he says, with a grimace. 'Long day.'

The group is going to the peak, a four-day trip up, two down, along the Machame Route. There are at least five paths up the mountain, depending on what a hiker wants to see and how quickly they want to reach the peak, and Gwen had promised that this route was within their abilities and by far the most scenic. The group's members each signed up through a website, EcoHeaven Tours, dedicated to adventure travel. The site promised small group tours of a dozen places – the Scottish Highlands, the Indonesian lowlands, the rivers of upper Russia. The trip up this mountain was, oddly enough, the least exotic-sounding. Rita has never known anyone who had climbed Kilimanjaro, but she knew people who knew people who had, and this made it just that small bit less intriguing. Now, standing below the gate, this trip seems irrelevant, irrational, indefensible. She's walking the same way thousands have before, and she will be cold and wet while doing so.

'Okay, let's saddle up,' Frank says, and begins to walk up a wide dirt path. Rita and the four others walk with him. They are all in ponchos, Grant in his garbage back, all with backpacks beneath, resembling hunchbacks, or soldiers. She pictures the Korean War Memorial, all those young men, cast in bronze, eyes wide, waiting to be shot.

Rita is glad, at least, to be moving, because moving will make her warm.

*

But Frank is walking very slowly. Rita is behind him; his pace is elephantine. Such measured movements, such lumbering effort. Frank is leading the five of them, with Patrick at the back of the group, and the porters are now distantly behind them, still in the parking lot, gathering the duffels and propane tanks and tents. They will catch up, Patrick said.

Rita is sure that this pace will drive her mad. She is a racquetball player because racquetball involves movement, and scoring, and noise, and the possibility of getting struck in the head with a ball moving at the pace of an airplane. And so she had worried that this hike would drive her mad with boredom. And now it is boring; here in Tanzania, she is bored. She will die of a crushing monotony before she even has a chance at a high-altitude cerebral edema.

After ten minutes, the group has traveled about two hundred yards, and it is time to stop. Mike is complaining of shoulder pain. His pack's straps need to be adjusted. Frank stops to help Mike, and while Frank is doing that, and Jerry and Shelly are waiting with Patrick, Grant continues up the trail. He does not stop. He goes around a bend in the path and he is out of view. The rain and the jungle make possible quick disappearances and before she knows why, Rita follows him.

Soon they are up two turns and can no longer see the group. Rita is elated. Grant walks quickly and she walks with him. They are almost running. They are moving at a pace she finds more fitting, an athletic pace, a pace appropriate for people who are not yet old. Rita is not yet old. She quit that 10k Fun Run last year but that didn't mean she couldn't do it if it wasn't so boring. She had started biking to work but then had decided against it; at the end of the day, when she's done as much as she could before 5:30, she was just too tired.

They tramp through the mud and soon the path narrows and bends upward, more vertical, brushed by trees, the banana leaves huge, sloppy and serrated. The trail is soaked, the mud deep and grabbing, but everywhere the path is crosshatched with roots, and the roots become footholds. They jump from one root to the next and Grant is relentless. He does not stop. He does not use his hands to steady himself. He is the most balanced person Rita has ever known, and she quickly attributes this to his small stature and wide and powerful legs. He is close to the ground.

They talk very little. She knows he is a telephone-systems programmer of some kind, connects 'groups of users' somehow. She knows he comes from Montana, and knows his voice is like an older man's, weaker than it should be, wheezy and prone to cracking. He is not handsome; his nose is almost piggish and his teeth are chipped in front, leaving a triangular gap, as if he'd tried to bite a tiny pyramid. He's not attractive in any kind of way she would call sexual, but she still wants to be with him and not the others.

The rainforest is dense and twisted and drenched. Mist obviates vision past twenty yards in any given direction. The rain comes down steadily, but the forest canopy slows and a hundred times redirects the water before it comes to Rita.

She is warmer now, sweating under her poncho and fleece, and she likes sweating and feels strong. Her pants, plastic pants she bought for nothing and used twice before while skiing, are loud, the legs scraping against each other with a constant, violent swiping sound. She wishes she were wearing shorts, like Grant. She wants to ask him to stop, so she can remove her pants, but worries he won't want to stop, and that anyway if he does and they do, the other hikers will catch up, and she and Grant will no longer be alone, ahead of the others, making good time. She says nothing.

There are no animals. Rita has not heard a bird, or a monkey, or seen even a frog. There had been geckos in her hut, and larger lizards scurrying outside the hotel, but on this mountain there is nothing. Her guidebook had promised blue monkeys, colobus monkeys, galagos, olive baboons, bushbacks, duikers, hornbills, turacos. But the forest is quiet and empty.

Now a porter is walking down the path, in jeans, a sweater and tennis shoes. Rita and Grant stop and step to one side to allow him to pass.

'Jambo,' Grant says.

'Jambo,' the man says, and continues down the trail.

The exchange was quick but extraordinary. Grant had lowered his voice to a basso profundo, stretching the second syllable for a few seconds in an almost musical way. The porter had said the word back with identical inflection. It was like a greeting between teammates, doubles partners – simple, warm, understated but understood.

'What does that mean?' Rita asks. 'Is that Swahili?'

'It is,' Grant says, leaping over a puddle. 'It's . . . well, it means "Hello."'

He says this in a polite way that nevertheless betrays his concern. Rita's face burns. She's traveled to Tanzania without learning any Swahili; she didn't even learn hello. She knows that Grant considers her a slothful and timid tourist. She wants Grant to like her, and to feel that she is more like him –

quick, learned, seasoned – at least more so than the others, who are all so delicate, needy, and slow.

They walk upward in silence for an hour. The walking is meditative to an extent she thought impossible. Rita had worried that she would either have to talk to the same few people – people she did not know and might not like – for hundreds of hours, or that, if the hikers were not so closely grouped, that she would be alone, with no one to talk to, alone with her thoughts. But already she knows that this will not be a problem. They have been hiking for two hours and she has not thought of anything. Too much of her faculties have been devoted to deciding where to step, where to place her left foot, then her right, and her hands, which sometimes grip trees for balance, sometimes touch the wet earth when a fall is likely. The calculations necessary make unlikely almost any other thinking – certainly nothing of any depth or complexity. And for this she is grateful. It is expansive and well-fenced, her landscape, the quiet acres of her mind, and with a soundtrack: the tapping of the rain, the swipping of her poncho against the branches, the tinny jangle of the carabiners swinging from her backpack. All of it is musical in a minimal and calming way, and she breathes in and out with the un-complicated and mechanical strength of a bear – plodding, powerful, robust.

'Poly poly,' says a descending porter. He is wearing tasseled loafers.

'Poly poly,' Grant says.

'I got here a few days before the rest of you,' Grant says, by way of explanation and apology, once the porter has passed.

He feels that he's shamed Rita and has allowed her to suffer long enough. 'I spent some time in Moshi, picked up some things.'

'"Jambo" is "Hello,"' he says. '"Poly poly" means "Step by step."'

A porter comes up behind them.

'Jambo,' he says.

'Jambo,' Grant says, with the same inflection, the same stretching of the second syllable, as if delivering a sacred incantation. Jaaaahmmmboooow. The porter smiles and continues up. He is carrying a propane tank above his head, and a large backpack sits between his shoulders, from which dangle two bags of potatoes. His load is easily eighty pounds.

He passes and Grant begins behind him. Rita asks Grant about his backpack, which is enormous, twice the size of hers, and contains poles and a pan and a bedroll. Rita had been told to pack only some food and a change of clothes, and to let the porters take the rest.

'I guess it is a little bigger,' he says.

'Is that your tent in there, too?' she asks, talking to his back.

'It is,' he says, stopping. He shakes out from under his pack and zippers open a compartment on the top.

'You're not having a porter carry it? How heavy is that thing?'

'Well, I guess . . . it's just a matter of choice, really. I'm . . . well, I guess I wanted to see if I could carry my own gear up. It's just a personal choice.' He's sorry for carrying his things, sorry for knowing 'Hello.' He spits a stream of brown liquid onto the ground.

'You dip?'

'I do. It's gross, isn't it?'

'You're not putting that sucker in there, too.'

Grant is unwrapping a Charms lollipop.

'I'm afraid so. It's something I do. Want one?'

Rita wants something like the Charms lollipop, but now she can't separate the clean lollipops in his Ziploc bag – there are at least ten in there – from the one in his mouth, presumably covered in tobacco juice.

Minutes later, the trail turns and under a tree there is what looks like a hospital gurney crossed with a handcart. It's sturdy and wide, but with just two large wheels, set in the middle, on either side of a taut canvas cot. There are handles on the end, so it can be pulled like a rickshaw. Grant and Rita make shallow jokes about the contraption, about who might be coming down on that, but being near it any longer, because it's rusty and terrifying and looks like it's been used before and often, is unpleasant, so they walk on.

When they arrive at a clearing, they've been hiking, quickly, for six hours. They are at what they assume to be their camp, and they are alone. The trees have cleared – they are above treeline – and they are now standing on a hillside, covered in fog, with high grass, thin like hair, everywhere. The rain has not subsided and the temperature has dropped. They have not seen any of the other hikers or guides for hours, nor have they seen any porters. Rita and Grant were hiking quickly and beat everyone up the trail, and were not passed by anyone, and she feels so strong and proud about this. She can tell that in some way Grant is also proud, but she knows he will not say so.

Within minutes she is shaking. It's no more than forty

degrees and the rain is harder here; there are no trees diverting its impact. And there are no tents assembled, because they have beaten the porters to the camp. Even Grant seems to see the poor reasoning involved in their strategy. The one thing Grant doesn't have is a tarp, and without it there is no point in pitching his tent on earth this wet. They will have to wait, alone in the rain, until the porters arrive.

'It'll be at least an hour,' Grant says.

'Maybe sooner for the porters?' Rita suggests.

'We sure didn't think this one through,' he says, then spits a brown stream onto a clean green banana leaf.

Under a shrub no more than four feet tall, offering little protection, they sit together on a horizontal and wet log and let the rain come down on them. Rita tries not to shiver, because shivering is the first step, she remembers, to hypothermia. She slows her breathing, stills her body, and brings her arms from her sleeves and onto her naked skin.

Frank is furious. His eyes are wild. He feels compromised. The paying hikers are all in a cold canvas tent, sitting around a table no bigger than one meant for poker, and they are eating dinner – rice, plain noodles, potatoes, tea, orange slices.

'I know a few of you think you're hotshots,' Frank says, blowing into his tea to cool it, 'but this is no cakewalk up here. Today you're a speed demon, tomorrow you're sore and sick, full of blisters and malaria and God knows what.'

Grant is looking straight at him, very serious, neither mocking nor confronting.

'Or you get an aneurysm. There's a reason you have a guide, people. I've been up and down this mountain twelve times, and there's a reason for that.'

He blows into his tea again. 'There's a reason for that, you . . . people.'

He shakes his head as if suddenly chilled. 'I need to know you're gonna act like adults, not like . . . yahoos!' And with that he burrows his thumb and forefinger into his eye sockets, a man with too much on his mind.

The food before the group has ostensibly been cooked, by the porters, but within the time it took to carry it from the tent where it was heated to this, their makeshift dining tent, the food has gone cold, as cold as if it had been refrigerated. Everyone eats what they can, though without cheer. The day was long and each hiker has an injury, or an issue of some sort. Mike's stomach is already feeling wrong, and at some point Shelly slipped and cut her hand open on a sharp stick. Jerry is having the first twinges of an altitude headache. Only Rita and Grant are, for the time being, problem-free. Rita makes the mistake of announcing this, and it seems only to get Frank angrier.

'Well, it'll happen sooner or later, ma'am. Something will. You're probably better off being sick now, because in a few days, it'll hit you harder and deeper. So pray to get sick tonight, you two.'

'You sit over there, you'll get dead,' Jerry says, pointing to a corner of the tent where a hole is allowing a drizzle to pour onto the floor. 'What kinda equipment you providing here anyway, Frank?' Jerry's tone is gregarious, but the message is plain.

'Are you dry?' Frank asks. Jerry nods. 'Then you're fine.'

They're sitting on small canvas folding stools, and the paying hikers have to hunch over to eat; there is no room for elbows. When they first sat down they had passed around and used the clear hand-sanitizing fluid provided – like soft soap but cool and stinging lightly. Rita had rubbed her hands and tried to clear the dirt from her palms, but afterward found her hands no cleaner. She looks at her palms now, after two applications of the sanitizer, and though they're dry their every crevice is brown.

The man who brought the platters of rice and potatoes – Steven – pokes his head into the tent again, his smile preceding him. He's in a purple fleece pullover with a matching stocking cap. He announces the coming of soup and everyone cheers. Soon there is soup finally and everyone devours the soup. The heat of the bodies of the paying hikers slowly warms the canvas tent and the candles on the table create the appearance of comfort. But they know that outside this tent the air is approaching freezing, and in the arc of night will dip below.

'Why are there no campfires?'

It's the first thing Mike has said at dinner.

'Honey collectors,' Frank says. 'Burned half the mountain.'

Mike looks confused.

'They try to smoke out the bees to get the honey,' Frank explains, 'but it gets out of control. That's the theory anyway. Might have been a lot of things, but the mountain burned and now they won't allow fires.'

'Also the firewood,' Patrick says.

'Right, right,' Frank says, nodding into his soup. 'The porters were cutting down the trees for firewood. They were supposed to bring the firewood from below, but then they'd run out and start cutting whatever was handy. You're right, Patrick. I forgot about that. Now they're not even allowed to have firewood on the mountain. Illegal.'

'So how do clothes get dry?' This from Jerry, who in the

candlelight looks younger, and, Rita suddenly thinks, like a man who would be cast in a soap opera, as the patriarch of a powerful family. His hair is white and full, straight and smooth, riding away from his forehead like the back of a cresting wave.

'If there's sun tomorrow, they get dry,' Frank says. 'If there's no sun, they stay wet,' he says, then sits back and waits for someone to complain. No one does, so he softens. 'Put the wet clothes in your sleeping bag. Somewhere where you don't have to feel 'em. The heat in there will dry 'em out, usually. Otherwise work around the wet clothes till we get some sun.'

'This is why those porters dropped out,' Jerry says, with certainty.

'Listen,' Frank says, 'porters drop out all the time. Some of them are superstitious. Some just don't like rain. Doesn't mean a thing. We'll be fine.'

Rita cannot get a grip on how this will work. She doesn't see how they can continue up the mountain, facing more rain, as it also becomes colder, the air thinner, and without their having any chance of drying the clothes that are surely too wet to wear. Is this not how people get sick or die? By getting wet and cold and staying wet and cold? Her concern, though, is a dull and almost distant one, because almost immediately after the plates are taken away, she feels exhausted beyond all measure. Her vision is blurry and her limbs tingle.

'I guess we're bunking together,' Shelly says, suddenly behind her, above her. Everyone is standing up. Rita rises and follows Shelly outside, where it is still drizzling the coldest rain. The hikers all say good night, Mike and Jerry heading toward the toilet tent, just assembled – a triangular structure, three poles with a tarp wrapped around, a zipper for entry and a three-foot hole dug below. Father and son are each carrying a small roll of toilet paper, protecting it from the rain with their plastic baggies containing their toothbrushes and paste. Their silhouettes are smudges scratched by the gray lines of the cold rain.

Shelly and Rita's tent is small and quickly becomes warm. Inside they crawl around, arranging their things, using their headlamps – a pair of miners looking for a lost contact lens.

'One day down,' Shelly says.

Rita grunts her assent.

'Not much fun so far,' Shelly says.

'No, not yet.'

'But it's not supposed to be, I suppose. The point is getting up, right?'

'I guess.'

'At all costs, right?'

'Right,' Rita says, though she has no idea what Shelly is talking about.

Shelly soon settles into her sleeping bag, and turns toward Rita, closing her eyes. Shelly is asleep in seconds, and her breathing is loud. She breathes in through her nose and out through her nose, the exhalations in quick effortful bursts. Shelly is a yoga person and while Rita thought this was interesting an hour ago, now she hates yoga and everyone who might foster its dissemination. Yoga people are loud breathers and loud breathers are selfish and wicked.

The rain continues, tattering all night, almost rhythmic but not rhythmic enough, and Rita is awake for an hour, listening to Shelly's breathing and the rain, which comes in bursts, as if deposited by planes sweeping overhead. She cannot help but concentrate on Shelly's breathing. She worries that she will never sleep, and that she will be too tired tomorrow, that this will weaken her system and she will succumb to the cerebral edema that is ready, she knows, to leap. She sees the aneurysm in the form of a huge red troll, like a kewpie doll, the hair aflame, though with a pair of enormous scissors, like those used to open malls and car dealerships – that the troll will jump from the mountain and, with its great circus scissors, sever Rita's medulla oblongata and her ties to this world.

Gwen is to blame. Gwen had wanted, she guesses, to help Rita do something great. Gwen had been ruthlessly supportive for decades now, sending money, making phone calls on her behalf, setting Rita up with job interviews and divorced men who on the first date wanted to hold hands after an Olive Garden dinner. Their hands were rough and fat always, and Rita wanted no more of Gwen's help. Rita loved Gwen in an objective way, in an admiring way totally separate from her obligations to sibling affection. Gwen was so tall, so narrow, could not wear heels without looking like some kind of heron in black leggings, but her laugh was round and rolling, and it came out of her, as everything did, with its arms wide and embracing. She could be president if she'd wanted that job, but she hadn't – she'd chosen instead to torment Rita with her thoughtfulness. Baskets of cheese, thank-you notes, that long weekend in Puerto Vallarta when they'd rented the convertible Beetle. She even bought Rita a new mailbox and installed it, with cement and a shovel, when it was stolen in the night. This is what Gwen did, this and humor Brad, and await her baby, and run a small business, as fruitful as she could hope, that provided closet-reorganization plans to very wealthy people in Santa Fe.

Rita knows she can't ask Shelly to share her sleeping bag but she wants a body close to her. She hasn't slept well since J.J. and Frederick went away because she has not been warm. No one ever said so but they didn't think it appropriate that the kids slept in her bed. Gwen had found it odd when Rita had bought a larger bed, but Rita knew that having those two bodies near her, never touching anywhere but a calf or ankle, her body calming their fears, was the only indispensable experience of her life or anyone else's.

As her heart blinks rapidly, Rita promises herself that the next day will be less punishing, less severe. The morning will be clear and dry and when the fog burns off, it will be so warm, maybe even hot, with the sun coming all over and drying their wet things. They will walk upward in the morning wearing shorts and sunglasses, upward toward the sun.

The morning is wet and foggy and there is no sun and everything that was wet the night before is now wetter. Rita's mood is a slashing despair; she does not want to leave her sleeping bag or her tent, she wants all these filthy people gone, and wants her things dry and clean. She wants to be alone, for a few minutes at least. She knows she can't, because outside the tent are the other hikers, and there are twenty porters, and now, a small group of German hikers, and at the far side of the camp, three Canadians and a crew of twelve – they must have arrived after dark. Everyone is waking up. She hears the pouring of water, the rattle of pots, the thrufting of tents. Rita is so tired and so awake and she comes close to crying. She wants to be in this sleeping bag, not awake but still sleeping, for two and a half hours more. In two and a half hours she could regather her strength, all of it. She would have a running start at this day, and could then leap past anyone.

There is conversation from the next tent. The voices are not whispering, not even attempting to whisper.

'You're kidding me,' one voice says. 'You know how much we paid for these tickets? How long did we plan to come here, how long did I save?'

It's Jerry.

'You know you didn't have to save, Dad.'

'But Michael. We planned this for years. I talked to you about this when you were ten. Remember? When Uncle Mark came back? Christ!'

'Dad, I just –'

'And here you're going down after one freaking day!'

'Listen. I have never felt so weak, Dad. It's just so much harder than –'

'Michael. Yesterday was the hardest day – the rest will be nothing. You heard what's-his-face . . . Frank. This was the hard one. I can see why you're a little concerned, but you gotta buck up now, son. Yesterday was bad but –'

'Shhh.'

'No one can hear us, Michael. For heaven's sake. Everyone's asleep.'

'Shh!'

'I will not have you shushing me! And I won't have you –'

There is the sound of a sleeping bag being adjusted, and then the voices become lower and softer.

'I will not have you leaving this –'

And the voice dips below audibility.

Shelly is awake now, too. She has been listening, and gives Rita a raised eyebrow. Rita reciprocates, and begins searching through her duffel bag for what to wear today. She has brought three pairs of pants, two shorts, five shirts, two fleece sweat-shirts and her parka. Putting on her socks, wool and shaped like her foot, the ankle area reinforced and double-lined, she wonders if Mike will actually be going down so soon. There is a spare garbage bag into which she shoves her dirty socks, yesterday's shirt, and her jogging bra, which she can smell — rain and trees and her.

'You'd have to break my leg,' Shelly whispers. She is still in her sleeping bag, only her face visible. Rita suddenly thinks she looks like someone. An actress. Jill Clayburgh. Jane Curtain? Kathleen Turner.

'Break my leg and cut my tendons. You'd have to. I'm doing this climb.'

Rita nods and heads toward the tent's door flaps.

'If you're going outside,' Shelly says, 'give me a weather report.'

Rita pokes her head through the flaps and is facing fifteen porters. They are all standing in the fog, just across the camp-site, under the drizzle, some holding cups, all in the clothes they were wearing yesterday. They are outside the cooking tent, and they are all staring at her face through the flaps. She quickly pulls it back into the tent.

'What's it like?' Shelly asks.

'Same,' Rita says.

Breakfast is porridge and tea and orange slices that have been left in the open air too long and are now dry, almost brown. There is toast, cold and hard and with hard butter needing to be applied with great force. Again the five paying hikers are hunched over the small card table, and they eat everything they can. They pass the brown sugar and dump it into their porridge, and they pass the milk for their coffee, and they worry that the caffeine will give them the runs and they'll have to make excessive trips to the toilet tent, which now everyone dreads. Rita had wondered if the trip might be too soft, too easy, but now, so soon after getting here, she knows that she is somewhere else. It's something very different.

'How was that tent of yours?' Frank asks, directing his chin toward Grant. 'Not too warm, eh?'

'It was a little cool, you're right, Frank.' Grant is pouring himself a third cup of tea.

'Grant thinks his dad's old canvas army tent was the way to go,' Frank says. 'But he didn't count on this rain, didja, Grant? Your dad could dry his out next to the fire, but that ain't happening up here, friend.'

Grant's hands are clasped in front of him, as if arm-wrestling with himself. He is listening and looking at Frank without any sort of emotion.

'That thing ain't dry tonight, you're gonna be bunking with me or someone else, Grant.' Frank is scratching his beard in a way that looks painful. 'Otherwise the rain and wind will make an icebox of that tent. You'll freeze in your sleep, and you won't even know it. You'll wake up dead.'

The trail winds like a narrow river up through an hour of rainforest, drier today, and then cuts through a hillside cleared by fire. Everyone is walking together now, the ground is bare and black. There are twisted remnants of trees straining from the soil, their extremities gone but their roots almost intact.

'There's your forest fire,' Frank says.

The fog is finally clearing. Though the pace is slow, around a field of round rocks knee-high, it is not as slow as the day before, and because Rita is tired and her legs are sore in every place, from ankle to upper thigh, she accepts the reduced speed. Grant is behind her and also seems resigned.

But Mike is far more ill today. The five paying hikers know this because it has become the habit of all to monitor the health of everyone else. The words 'How are you?' on this mountain do not form an innocuous or rhetorical question. The words in each case, from each hiker, give way to a distinct and complicated answer, involving the appearance or avoidance of blisters, of burgeoning headaches, of sore ankles and quads, shoulders that still, even with the straps adjusted, feel pinched. Mike's stomach feels, he is telling everyone, like there is actually a large tapeworm inside him. Its movements are trackable, relentless, he claims, and he's given it a name: Ashley, after an ex-girlfriend. He looks desperate for a moment of contentment; he looks like a sick child, lying on the bathroom floor, bent around the toilet, exhausted and defeated, who only wants the vomiting to stop.

Today the porters are passing the paying hikers. Every few minutes another goes by, or a group of them. The porters walk alone, or in packs of three. When they come through they do one of two things: if there is room around the hikers, when the path is wide or there is space to walk through the dirt or rocks beside them, they will jog around them; when the path is narrow they will wait for the hikers to step aside.

Rita and Grant are stepping aside.

'Jambo,' Grant says.

'Jambo,' the first porter says. He is about twenty, wearing a CBS News T-shirt, khaki pants and cream-colored Timberland hiking shoes, almost new. He is carrying two duffel bags on his head. One of them is Rita's. She almost tells him this but then catches herself.

'Habari,' Grant says.

'Imara,' the porter says.

And he and the two others walk past. Rita asks Grant what he's just said. Habari, Grant explains, means 'How are you,' and Imara means 'strong.'

'Blue!' Jerry yells, pointing to a small spot of sky that the fog has left uncovered. It's the first swatch of blue the sky has allowed since the trip began, and it elicits an unnatural spasm of joy in Rita. She wants to climb through the gap and spread herself out above the cloudline, as you would a ladder leading to a treefort. Soon the blue hole grows and the sun, still obscured but now directly above, gives heat through a thin layer of cloud cover. The air around them warms almost immediately and Rita, along with the other paying hikers, stops to remove layers and put on sunglasses. Frank takes a pair of wet pants from his bag and ties them to a carabiner; they hang to his heels, filthy.

Mike now has the perpetual look of someone disarming a bomb. His forehead is never without sweat beaded along the ridges of the three distinct lines on his forehead. He is sucking on a silver tube, like a ketchup container but larger.

'It's a kind of energy food,' he explains.

They are all eating the snacks they've brought. Every day Steven gives the paying hikers a sack lunch of eggs and crackers, which none of them eat. Rita is eating peanuts and raisins and chocolate. Jerry is gnawing on his beef jerky. They are all sharing food and needed articles of clothing and medical aid. Shelly loans Mike her Ace bandage, to wrap around his ankle, which he thinks is swollen. Jerry loans Rita a pair of Thinsulate gloves.

Fifteen porters pass while the paying hikers are eating and changing. One porter, more muscular than the others, who are uniformly thin, is carrying a radio playing American country music. The porter is affecting a nonchalant pride in this music, a certain casual ownership of it. To each porter Grant says Jambo and most say Jambo in return, eliciting more greetings from Jerry – who now likes to say the word, loudly.

'Jahm-BO!' he roars, in a way that seems intended to frighten.

Shelly steps over to Frank.

'What do the porters eat?' she asks.

'Eat? The porters? Well, they eat what you eat, pretty much,' Frank says, then reaches for Shelly's hips and pats one. 'Maybe without the snacking,' he says, and winks.

There is a boom like a jetplane backfiring. Or artillery fire. Everyone looks up, then down the mountain. No one knows where to look. The porters, further up the trail but still within view, stop briefly. Rita sees one mime the shooting of a rifle. Then they continue.

Now Rita is walking alone. She has talked to most of the paying hikers and feels caught up. She knows about Shelly's marriages, her PhD in philosophy, her son living in a group home in Indiana after going off his medication and using a pizza cutter to threaten the life of a co-worker. She knows Jerry, knows that Jerry feels his restaurants bring their communities together, knows that he fashioned them after Greek meeting places more than any contemporary dining model – he wants great ideas to be born over his food – and when he was expanding on the subject, gesturing with a stick he carried for three hours, she feared he would use the word *peripatetic*, and soon enough he did. She knew she would wince and she did. And she knows that Mike is unwell and is getting sicker and has begun to make jokes about how funny it would be for a designer of ambulances to lie dying on a mountain without any real way of getting to one.

The terrain is varied and Rita is happy; the route seems as if planned by hikers with short attention spans. There has been rainforest, then savannah, then more forest, then forest charred, and now the path cuts through a rocky hillside covered in ice-green groundcover, an ocean floor drained, the boulders everywhere huge and dripping with lichen of a seemingly synthetic orange.

The porters are passing her regularly now, not just the porters from her group but about a hundred more, from the Canadian camp, the German camp, other camps. She passes a tiny Japanese woman sitting on a round rock, flanked by a guide and a porter, waiting.

The porters are laboring more now. On the first day, they seemed almost cavalier, and walked so quickly that now she is surprised to see them straining, plodding and unamused. A small porter, older, approaches her back and she stops to allow him through.

'Jambo,' she says.

'Jambo,' he says.

He is carrying a large duffel with Jerry's name on it, atop his head, held there with the bag's thick strap, with cuts across his forehead. Below the strap, perspiration flows down the bridge of his nose.

'Habari?' she says.

'Imara,' he says.

'Water?' she asks. He stops.

She removes her bottle from her backpack holster and holds it out to him. He stops and takes it, smiling. He takes a long drink from the wide mouth of the clear plastic container, and then continues walking.

'Wait!' she says, laughing. He is walking off with the water bottle. 'Just a sip,' she says, gesturing to him that she would like the container back. He stops and takes another drink, then hands it to her, bowing his head slightly while wiping his mouth with the back of his hand.

'Thank you,' he says. He continues up the trail.

They have made camp. It's three in the afternoon and the fog has returned. It hangs lightly over the land, which is brown and wide and bare. The campground looks, with the fog, like a medieval battleground, desolate and ready to host the deaths of men.

Rita sits with Jerry on rocks the size and shape of beanbags while their tents are assembled. Mike is lying on the ground, on his backpack, and he looks to Rita much like what a dead person would look like. Mike is almost blue, and is breathing in a hollow way that she hasn't heard before. His walking stick extends from his armpit in a way that looks like he's been lanced from behind.

'Oh, Ashley!' he says to his tapeworm, or whatever it is. 'Why're you doing this to me, Ashley?'

Far off into the mist, there is a song being sung. The words sound German, and soon they break apart into laughter. Closer to where she's sitting, Rita can hear an erratic and small sound, a tocking sound, punctuated periodically by low cheers.

The mist soon lifts and Rita sees Grant, who has already assembled his tent, surrounded by porters. He and a very young man, the youngest and thinnest she's seen, are playing a tennis-like game, using thin wooden paddles to keep a small blue ball in the air. Grant is barefoot and is grinning.

'There he is,' says Jerry. 'Saint Grant of the porters!'

At dinner the food is the same – cold noodles, white rice, potatoes, but tonight, instead of orange slices there is water-melon, sliced into neat thin triangles, small green boats with red sails on a silver round lake.

'Someone carried a watermelon up,' Mike notes.

No one comments.

'Well, it didn't fly up,' Frank says.

No one eats the watermelon, because the paying hikers have been instructed to avoid fruit, for fear of malaria in the water. Steven, the porter who serves the meals and whose smile pre-cedes him always, soon returns and takes the watermelon back to the mess tent. He doesn't say a word.

'What happens to the guy who carried up the watermelon?' Jerry asks, grinning.

'Probably goes down,' Frank says. 'A lot of them are going down already – the guys who were carrying food that we've eaten. A lot of these guys you'll see one day and they're gone.'

'Back to the banana fields,' Jerry says.

Rita has been guessing at why Jerry looks familiar to her, and now she knows. He looks like a man she saw at Target, a portly man trying on robes who liked one so much he wore it around the store for almost an hour – she passed him twice.

As with Jerry, she's both appalled by and in awe of their obliviousness to context, to taste.

The paying hikers talk about their dreams. They are all taking Maladrone, an anti-malarial drug that for most fosters disturbing and hallucinogenic dreams. Rita's attention wanes, because she's never interested in people's dreams and has had none of her own this trip.

Frank tells a story of a trip he took up Puncak Jaya, tallest peak in Indonesia, a mountain of 16,500 feet and very cold. They were looking for a climber who had died there in 1934, a British explorer who a dozen groups had tried to locate in the decades since. Frank's group, though, had the benefit of a journal of the climber's partner, recently found a few thousand feet below. Knowing the approximate route Frankon had taken, Frank's group, once at the elevation believed to be where Frankon expired, found the man within fifteen minutes. 'There he is,' one of the climbers had said, without a trace of doubt, because the body was so well preserved that he looked precisely as he did in the last photograph of him. He'd fallen at least two hundred feet; his legs were broken but he had somehow survived, was trying to crawl when he'd frozen.

'And did you bury him?' Shelly asks.

'Bury him?' Frank says, with theatrical confusion. 'How the heck we gonna bury the guy? It's eleven feet of snow there, and rock beneath that –'

'So you what – left him there?'

'Course we left him there! He's still there today, I bet in the same damned spot.'

'So that's the way –'

'Yep, that's the way things are on the mountain.'

*

Somewhere past midnight Rita's bladder makes demands. She tries to quietly extricate herself from the tent, though the sound of the inner zipper, and then the outer, is too loud. Rita knows Shelly is awake by the time her head makes its way outside of the tent.

Her breath is visible in compact gusts and in the air everything is blue. The moon is alive now and it has cast everything in blue. Everything is underwater but with impossible black shadows. Every rock has under it a black hole. Every tree has under it a black hole. She steps out of the tent and into the cold cold air. She jumps. There is a figure next to her, standing still.

'Rita,' the figure says. 'Sorry.'

It's Grant. He is standing, arms crossed over his chest, facing the moon and also – now she sees it – the entire crest of Kilimanjaro. She gasps.

'It's incredible, isn't it?' he whispers.

'I had no idea –'

It's enormous. It's white-blue and huge and flat-topped. The clarity is startling. It is indeed blindingly white, even now, at 1 a.m. The moon gives its white top the look of china under candlelight. And it seems so close! It's a mountain but they're going to the top. Already they are almost halfway up its elevation and this fills Rita with a sense of clear unmitigated accomplishment. This cannot be taken away.

'The clouds just passed,' Grant says. 'I was brushing my teeth.'

Rita looks out on the field of tents and sees other figures, alone and in pairs, also standing, facing the mountain.

Now she is determined to make it to its peak. It is very much, she thinks, like looking at the moon and knowing one could make it there, too. It is only time and breath that stand between her and the top. She is young. She'll do it and have done it.

She turns to Grant but he is gone.

Rita wakes up strong. She doesn't know why but she now feels, with her eyes opening quickly and her body rested, that she belongs on this mountain. She is ready to attack. She will run up the path today, barefoot. She will carry her own duffel. She will carry Shelly on her back. She has slept twice on this mountain but it seems like months. She feels sure that if she were left here alone, she would survive, would blend in like the hardiest of plants – her skin would turn ice-green and her feet would grow sturdy and gnarled, hard and crafty like roots.

She exits the tent and still the air is gray with mist, and everything is frozen – her boots covered in frost. The peak is no longer visible. She puts on her shoes and runs from the camp to pee. She decides en route that she will run until she finds the stream and there she will wash her hands. Now that this mountain is hers she can wash her hands in its streams, drink from them if she sees fit, live in its caves, run up its sheer rock faces.

It's fifteen minutes before she locates the stream. She was tracking and being led by the sound of the running water, without success, and finally just followed the zebra-pattern shirt of a porter carrying two empty water containers.

'Jambo,' she says to the man, in the precise way Grant does.

'Jambo,' the porter repeats, and smiles at her.

He is young, probably the youngest porter she's seen, maybe eighteen. He has a scar bisecting his mouth, from just below his nose to just above the dimple on his chin. The containers are the size and shape of those used to carry gasoline. He lowers one under a small waterfall and it begins to fill, making precisely the same sound she heard from her bed, in her Moshi hut. She and the porter are crouching a few feet apart, his sweatshirt lashed with a zebra pattern in pink and black.

'You like zebras?' she asks.

He smiles and nods. She touches his sweatshirt and gives him a thumbs-up. He smiles nervously.

She dips her hands into the water. Exactly the temperature she expected – cold but not bracing. She uses her fingernails to scrape the dirt from her palms, and with each trowel-like movement, she seems to free soil from her hand's lines. She then lets the water run over her palm, and her sense of accomplishment is great. Without soap she will clean these filthy hands! But when she is finished, when she has dried her hands on her shorts, they look exactly the same, filthy.

The sun has come through while she was staring at them, and she turns to face the sun, which is low but strong. The sun convinces her that she belongs here more than the other hikers, more than the porters. She is still not wearing socks! And now the sun is warming her, telling her not to worry that she cannot get her hands clean.

'Sun,' she says to the porter, and smiles.

He nods while twisting the cap on the second container.

'What is your name?' she asks.

'Kassim,' he says.

She asks him to spell it. He does. She tries to say it and he smiles.

'You think we're crazy to pay to hike up this hill?' she asks. She is nodding, hoping he will agree with her. He smiles and shakes his head, not understanding.

'Crazy?' Rita says, pointing to her chest. 'To pay to hike up this hill?' She is walking her index and middle fingers up an imaginary mountain in the air. She points to the peak of Kilimanjaro, ringed by clouds, curved blades guarding the final thousand feet.

He doesn't understand, or pretends not to. Rita decides that Kassim is her favorite porter and that she'll look out for him. She'll give him her lunch. When they reach the bottom, she'll give him her boots. She glances at his feet, inside ancient faux-leather basketball shoes, and knows that his feet are much too big. Maybe he has kids. He can give the shoes to the kids. It occurs to Rita then that he's at work. That his family is at home while he is on the mountain. This is what she misses so much, coming home to those kids. They would just start in, a million things they had to talk about. She wants to sign more field trip permission slips. She wants to quietly curse their gym teacher for upsetting them. She wants to clean the gum out of J.J.'s backpack or wash Frederick's urine-soaked sheets.

Kassim finishes, his vessels full, and so he stands, waves goodbye and jogs back to the camp.

In the sun the hikers and porters lay their wet clothes out on the rocks, hang them from the bare limbs of the trees. The temperature rises from freezing to sixty in an hour and everyone is delirious with warmth, with the idea of being dry, of everything being dry. The campsite, now visible for hundreds of yards, is wretched with people – maybe four hundred of them – and the things they're bringing up the mountain. There are colors ragged everywhere, dripping from the trees, bleeding into the earth. In every direction hikers are walking, toilet paper in hand, to find a private spot to deposit their waste.

Rita devours her porridge and she knows that she is feeling strong just as a few of the others are fading. They are cramped around the card table, in the tent, and the flaps are open for the first time during a meal, and it is now too warm, too sunny. Those facing the sun are wearing sunglasses.

'Lordy that feels good,' Jerry says.

'It's like being at the beach,' Shelly says, and they laugh.

'I don't want to spoil the mood,' Frank says, 'but I have an announcement. I wanted to make clear that you're not allowed to give porters stuff. This morning, Mike thought it was a good idea to give a porter his sunglasses, and what happened, Mike?'

'Some other guy was wearing them.'

'How long did it take before the sunglasses were on this other guy?'

'Fifteen minutes.'

'Why's that, Mike?'

'Because you're supposed to give stuff to Patrick first.'

'Right. Listen, people. There's a pecking order here, and Patrick knows the score. If you have a wave of generosity come over you and wanna give someone your lunch or your shoelaces or something, you give it to Patrick. He'll distribute whatever it is. That's the only way it's fair. That understood? You're here to walk and they're here to work.'

Everyone nods.

'Why you giving your sunglasses away anyway, Mike? You're sure as hell gonna need 'em these next couple days. You get to the top and you're –'

'I'm going down,' Mike says.

'What?'

'I have to go down,' Mike says, staring at Frank, the sun lightening his blue eyes until they're sweater-grey, almost colorless. 'I don't have the desire anymore.'

'The desire, eh?'

Frank pauses for a second, and seems to move from wanting to joke with Mike, to wanting to talk him out of it, to accepting the decision. It's clear he wants Jerry to say something, but Jerry is silent. Jerry will speak to Mike in private.

'Well,' Frank says, 'you know it when you know it, I guess. Patrick'll get a porter to walk you down.'

Mike and Frank talk about how it will work. All the way down in one day? That's best, Frank says. That way you won't need provisions. Who brings my stuff? You carry your pack, a porter will carry the duffel. Get in by nightfall, probably, and Godwill will be there to meet you. Who's Godwill? The driver. Oh, the older man. Yes. Godwill. He'll come up to get you. If the park rangers think it's an emergency, they'll let him drive about half the way up. So how much of a hike will we make down? Six hours. I think I can do that. You can, Mike, you can. You'll have to. No problem. Thanks for playing. Better luck next time.

Jerry still hasn't said anything. He is eating his porridge quickly, listening. He is now chewing his porridge, his face pinched, his eyes planning.

After breakfast Rita is walking to the toilet tent and passes the cooking tent. There are six porters inside, and a small tight group outside – younger porters, mostly, each holding a small cup, standing around a large plastic tub, like those used to bus dishes and silverware. Kassim is there; she recognizes him immediately because he, like all of the porters, wears the same clothes each day. There is another sweatshirt she knows, with a white torso and orange sleeves, a florid Hello Kitty logo on the chest. Rita tries to catch Kassim's eye but he's concentrating on the cooking tent. Steven steps through the flaps with a silver bowl, and overturns it into the tub. The young porters descend upon it, stabbing their cups into the small mound of porridge until it's gone in seconds.

The trail makes its way gradually upward and winds around the mountain, and Mike, groaning with every leaden step, is still with them. Rita doesn't know why he is still with the group. He is lagging behind, with Patrick, and looks stripped of all blood and hope. He is pale, and he is listing to one side, and is using hiking poles as an elderly man would use a cane, unsure and relying too heavily on that point at the end of a stick.

The clouds are following the group up the mountain. They should stay ahead of the clouds, Frank told them, if they want to keep warm today. There has been talk of more rain, but Frank and Patrick believe that it won't rain at the next camp – it's too high. They are hiking in a high desert area called the Saddle, between the peaks of Mawenzi, a mile away and jagged, and Kibo above. The vegetation is now sparse, the trees long gone. Directly above the trail stands the mountain, though the peak is still obscured by cloud cover. She and Grant are still the only ones who have seen it, at midnight under the bright small moon.

Two hours into the day, Rita's head begins to throb. They are at 11,200 feet and the pain comes suddenly. It is at the back of her skull, where she was told the pain would begin and grow before one suffered from a cerebral edema. She begins to breathe with more effort, trying to bring more oxygen into her blood, her brain. Her breathing works for small periods of time, the pain receding, though it comes back with ferocity. She breathes quickly, and loudly, and the pain moves away when she is walking faster, and climbing steeper, so she knows she must keep going up.

She walks with a trio of South Africans who have driven to Tanzania from Johannesburg. She asks them how long it took, the drive, and guesses at sixteen, eighteen hours. They laugh, no, no – three weeks, friend, they say. There are no superhighways in East Africa! they say. They walk along an easy path, a C-shape around the mountain, through a field of shale. The rocks are the color of rust and whales, shards that tinkle and clink, loudly, under their feet.

The path cuts through the most desolate side of Kilimanjaro, an area that looks like the volcano had spewed not lava but rusted steel. There is a wind-swept look about it, the slices of shale angled away from the mountaintop as if still trying to get away from the center, from the fire.

They descend into a valley, through a sparse forest of lobelia trees, all of them ridiculous, each with the gray trunk of a coconut tree topped by an exuberant burst of green, a wild head of spiky verdant hair. A stream runs along the path, in a narrow and shallow crack in the valley wall, and they stop to fill their water bottles. The four of them squat like gargoyles and share a small vial of purification pills. They drop two of the pills, tiny and the color of steel, into the bottles and shake. They wait, still squatting like gargoyles, until the pills have dissolved, then they drop in small white tablets, meant to improve the water's taste. They stand.

She decides she will jog ahead of the South Africans, down the path. Weighing the appeal of learning more about the economic situation in sub-Saharan Africa against the prospect of running down this trail and making it to camp sooner, she chooses to run. She tells them she'll see them at the bottom and when she begins jogging, she immediately feels better. Her breathing is denser and her head clears within minutes. Exertion, she realizes, must be intense and constant.

There is a man lying in the path just ahead, as it bends under a thicket of lobelias. She runs faster, toward him. The body is crumpled as if it had been dropped. It's Mike. She is upon him and his skin is almost blue. He is asleep. He is lying on the path, his pack still strapped to his back. She dumps her pack and kneels beside him. He is breathing. His pulse seems slow but not desperate.

'Rita.'

'You okay? What's wrong?'

'Tired. Sick. Want to go home.'

'Well, I'm sure you'll get your wish now. You're a mess.'

He smiles.

Rita helps him stand and they walk slowly down the valley to the camp. It is spread out in a wide valley, the tents on the edge of a cliff – the camp this third day is stunning. It's late afternoon when they arrive and the sun is out and every-where. This is the Great Barranco Valley, sitting high above the clouds, which lie like an ocean beyond the valley's mouth, as if being kept at bay behind glass.

The tents are assembled and she helps him inside one, his head on a pillow of clothes, the sun making the interior pink and alarming. When Jerry, already at camp and washing his socks in the stream, notices that his son is present, he enters the tent, asks Rita to leave, and when she does, zips the tent closed.

In her own tent Rita is wrecked. Now that she's not moving the pain in her head is a living thing. It is a rat-sized and prickly animal living, with great soaring breaths and a restless tail, in her frontal lobe. But there is no room for this animal in her frontal lobe, and thus there is great strain in her skull. The pain reaches to the corners of her eyes. At the corners of her brow someone is slowly pushing a pen or pencil, just behind her eyes and through, into the center of her head. When she places her first and second fingers on the base of her skull, she can feel a pulsing.

The tent is yellow. The sun makes the tent seem alive; she's inside a lemon. The air seems to be yellow, and everything that she knows about yellow is here – its glory and its anemia. It gets hotter, the sun reigning throughout the day, giving and giving, though with the heaviest heart.

The night goes cold. They are at 14,500 feet and the air is thin and when the sun disappears the wind is cruel, profane. The rain comes again. Frank and Patrick are amazed by the rain, because they say it is rare in this valley, but it begins just when the sun descends, a drizzle, and by dinner is steady. The temperature is plunging.

At dinner, tomorrow's hike – the final ascent – is mapped out. They will rise at 6 a.m., walk for eight hours and stop at the high camp, where they'll eat and then sleep until 11 p.m. At 11, the group will get up, get packed, and make the final six-hour leg in the dark. They will reach the peak of Kibo at sunrise, take pictures and dawdle for an hour before making the descent, eight hours to the final camp, halfway down the mountain, the path shooting through a different side this time, less scenic, quicker, straighter.

Shelly asks if all the porters go up with the group.

'What, up to the top? No, no,' Frank says. About five do, just as guides, basically, he says. They come with the group, in case someone needs help with a pack or needs to go down. The rest of the porters stay at camp, then break it down and head out to meet the group at the final camp, on the long hike down.

After she's eaten, very little, Rita exits the tent and bumps her head against the ear of a porter. It's the man with the water by the stream.

'Jambo,' she says.

'Hello,' he says. He is holding a small backpack. There are about twenty porters around the dining tent, though only three are carrying dishes away. With the tent empty, two more are breaking down the card table and chairs. The tent is soon empty and the porters begin filing in, intending, Rita assumes, to clean it before disassembling it.

Rita lies down. She lies down slowly, resting her head so slowly onto the pillow Shelly has created for her from a garbage bag full of soft clothes. But even the small crinkling sound of the garbage bag is thunderously loud. Rita is scared. She sees the gravestone of the young man who died here six months before – they had a picture of it, and him – a beautiful young man grinning from below a blue bandanna – at the hotel, laminated on the front desk, to warn guests about pushing themselves too far. She sees her body being taken down by porters. Would they be careful with her corpse? She doesn't trust that they would be careful. They would want to get down quickly. They will carry her until they got to the rickshaw gurney and then they would run.

She listens as the paying hikers get ready for bed. She is in her sleeping bag and is still cold – she is wearing three layers but she feels flayed. She shivers but the shivering hurts her head so she forces her body to rest; she pours her own calm over her skin, coating it as if with warm oil, and she breathes slower. Something is eating her legs. She is awake when a panther comes and begins gnawing on her legs. She is watching the panther gnawing and can feel it, can feel it as if she were having her toes licked by a puppy, only there is blood, and bone, and marrow visible; the puppy is sucking the marrow from her bones, while looking up at her, smiling, asking What's your name? Do you like zebras?

She wakes up when she hears the rain going louder. She shakes free of the dream and succeeds in forgetting it almost immediately. The rain overwhelms her mind. The rain is strong and hard, like the knocking of a door, the knocking getting louder, and it won't end, the knocking – sweet Jesus will someone please answer that knocking? She is freezing all night. She awakens every hour and puts on another article of clothing, until she can barely move. She briefly considers staying at this camp with the porters, not making the final climb. There are photographs. There is an IMAX movie. Maybe she will survive without summitting.

But she does not want to be grouped with Mike. She is better than Mike. There is a reason to finish this hike. She must finish it because Shelly is finishing it, and Grant is finishing it. She is as good as these people. She is tired of admitting that she cannot continue. For so many years she has been doing everything within her power to finish but again and again she has pulled up short, and has been content for having tried. She found comfort in the nuances between success and failure, between a goal finished, accomplished, and a goal adjusted.

She puts on another T-shirt and another pair of socks. She falls back to sleep. She wakes up at dawn and Shelly is holding her, spooning. She falls to sleep.

The light through the vent is like a crack into a world uninterrupted by shape or definition. There is only white. White against white. She squints and reaches for her sunglasses, reaches around to no avail, feels only the rocks beneath the tent, and every rock beneath her fingers somehow makes its way into her head, every rock beneath her fingers is knocking against her head. She is breathing as deeply as she can but it has no effect. She knows her head is not getting enough blood. Her faculties are slipping away. She tries to do simple mental tasks, testing herself – the alphabet, states of the Union, Latin conjugations – and finds her thoughts scattered. She inhales so deeply the air feels coarse, and exhales with such force her chest goes concave. Shelly is still asleep.

It's the first light of morning. If there is sun the rain must have passed. It will not be so cold today – there is sun. Already she is warmer, the tent heating quickly, but the wind is still strong and the tent ripples loudly.

What is that? There is a commotion outside the tent. The porters are yelling. She hears Frank, his tent so close, unzip and rezip his tent's door, and then can hear his steps move toward the voices. The voices rise and fall on the wind, fractured by the flapping of the tent.

There is someone trying to enter the tent.

'Shelly,' Rita says.

'Yes, hon.'

'Who is that?'

'That's me, dear.'

Hours or seconds pass. Shelly is back. When did she leave? Shelly has entered the tent, and is now slowly rezipping the doorflap, trying not to bother her. Hours or seconds?

'Rita, honey.'

Rita wants to answer but can't find her tongue. The light has swept into her, the light is filling her, like something liquid pushing its way into the corners of a mold, and soon she's fading back to sleep.

'Rita, honey, something's happened.'

Rita is now riding on a horse, and she's on a battlefield of some kind. She is riding side-saddle, dodging bullets. She is invincible, and her horse seems to be flying. She pats her horse and the horse looks up at her, without warmth, bites her wrist and keeps running, yanking on its reins.

And then it's hours later. She opens her eyes and it doesn't hurt. Something has changed. Her head is lighter, the pain is diminished. Shelly is gone. Rita doesn't know what time it is. It's still bright. Is it the same day? She doesn't know. Everyone could be gone. She has been left here.

She rises. She opens the tent door. There is a crowd around two men zipping up a large duffel bag. The zipper is stuck on something pink, fabric or something, a striped pattern. Now they have the duffel over their shoulders, the duffel connecting their left shoulders, and there are men around them arguing. Patrick is pushing someone away, and pointing the porters with the duffel down the path. Then there is another huge duffel, carried by two more porters, and they descend the trail. Grant is there. Grant is now helping lift another duffel bag. He hoists his half onto his shoulder while another porter lifts the other side, and they begin walking, down the trail, away from the summit.

Rita closes her eyes again and flies off. There are bits of conversation that make their way into her head, through vents in her consciousness. 'What were they wearing?' 'Well think about it like the cabbies again. It's a job, right? There are risks . . .' 'Are you bringing the peanuts, too?' 'Sleeping through it all isn't going to make it go away, honey.'

J.J. and Frederick are in electric chairs. The Brussels stenographer is there, standing next to Rita, and they are smiling at the children. It is apparent in the logic of the dream that J.J. and Frederick are to be executed for losing a bet of some kind. Or because they were just born to be in the chair and Rita and the Brussels stenographer were born to hold their hands. J.J. and Frederick turn their eyes up to her and sing. They are singing to her in unison, their voices falsettos, cool and strong:

> One two
> We always knew
> Three four
> You'd never give us more

Rita is holding their hands as the vibrations start. She is resigned, knowing that there are rules and she is not the person to challenge them. But their teeth begin to chatter, and their eyes rise to her and she wonders if she should do something to stop it.

'How you feel, sweetie?'

Her head is clear and without weight. It again feels like part of her.

'You just needed time to acclimate, I bet.'

Rita raises her head and there is no pain. Lifting her head is not difficult. She is amazed at the lightness of her head.

'Well, if you're coming, I think you'll have to be ready in a few minutes. We're already very late. We gotta get a move on.'

Rita doesn't want to be in the tent anymore. She can finish this and have done it, whatever it is.

The terrain is rocky, loose with scree, and it is steep, but otherwise it is not the most difficult of hikes, she is told. They will simply go up until they are done. It will be something she can tell herself and others she has done, and being able to say yes when asked if she summitted will make a difference, will save her from explaining why she went down when two hikers over fifty years old went up.

Rita packs her parka and food, and stuffs the rest into her duffel bag for the porters to bring down to the next camp. The wind picks up and ripples the tent and she is struck quickly by panic. Something has happened. She remembers that Shelly had said something happened while she was asleep – but what? What was –

Mike. Oh Christ. Her stomach liquifies.

'Is Mike okay?' she asks.

She knows the answer will be no. She looks at Shelly's back.

'Mike? Mike's fine, hon. He's fine. I don't think he'll be joining us today, but he's feeling a little better.'

Rita remembers Grant going down the trail. What happened to Grant?

'I'm honestly not sure why he left,' Shelly says, applying a strip of white sunblock to her nose. 'He's not the most normal guy, though, is he?'

The sky is clear and though the air is still cold, maybe forty-five or so, the sun is warm to Rita's face. She is standing now, and almost can't believe she is standing. She steps over the shale to the meal tent, the thin shards of rock clinking like the closing of iron gates.

Mike is at breakfast. It's 8 a.m., and they are two hours behind schedule. They quickly eat a breakfast of porridge and hard-boiled eggs and tea. Everyone is exhausted and quiet. Grant has gone down the mountain and Mike is not going up. She smiles to Mike as he bites into an egg.

The remaining paying hikers – Rita, Jerry, Shelly – and Frank and Patrick say goodbye. They will see him again in about twelve hours, they say, and he'll feel better. They'll bring him some snow from Kibo, they say. They want to go and drag their bodies to the top, from which they can look down to him.

From the peak Rita can see a hundred miles of Tanzania, green and extending until a low line of clouds intercepts and swallows the land. She can see Moshi, tiny windows reflecting the sun, like flecks of gold seen beneath a shallow stream. Everyone is taking pictures in front of a sign boasting the altitude at the top, and its status as the highest peak in Africa, the tallest free-standing mountain in the world. Behind the signs is the cavity of Kibo, a great volcanic crater, flat, paisleyed with snow.

On the Moshi side of the mountain, the glaciers are low and wide, white at the top and striped from her viewpoint, above. She sees the great teeth of a white whale. Icicles twenty feet tall extend down and drip onto the bare rock below.

'They're disappearing,' Jerry says. He is standing behind Rita, looking through binoculars. 'They melt every year a few feet. Coming down slowly but steadily. They'll be gone in twenty years.'

Rita shields her eyes and looks where Jerry is looking.

'No more snows of Kilimanjaro, eh?' he says, and sighs in a theatrical way.

There are others at the top of Kibo, a large group of Chinese hikers, all in their fifties, and a dozen Italians in light packs and with sleek black gear. The hikers who have made it here nod as they pass each other. They hand their cameras to strangers to take their pictures. The wind comes over the mountain in gusts, like ghosts.

The hike up had been slow and steep and savagely cold. They rested ten minutes every hour and while sitting or standing, eating granola and drinking water, their bodies cooled and the wind whipped them. After four hours Shelly was faltering and said she would turn back. 'Get that pack off!' Frank yelled, tearing it off her as if it were aflame. 'Don't be a hero,' he'd said, giving the pack to one of the porters. Shelly had continued, refreshed without the weight. The last five hundred yards, when they could see the crest of the mountain just above, had taken almost two hours. They'd reached the summit as the sun crested through a band of violet clouds.

Now Rita is breathing as fast and as deeply as she can – her headache is fighting for dominion over her skull, and she is panting to keep it at bay. But she is happy that she walked up this mountain, and cannot believe she almost stopped before the peak. Now, she thinks, seeing these views in every direction, and knowing the communion with the others who have made it here, she would not have let anything stop her ascent. She knows now why a young man would continue up until crippled with edema, why his feet would have carried him while his head drained of blood and reason. Rita is proud of herself, and loves her companions, and now feels more connected to Shelly, and Jerry, Patrick and even Frank, than to Mike, or even Grant. Especially not to Grant, who chose to go down, though he was strong enough to make it. Grant is already blurry to her, someone she never really knew, a friend she knew as a child but who moved away before they could grow up together.

Rita finds Shelly, who is sitting on a small metal box chained to one of the signs.

'Well, I'm happy anyway,' Shelly says. 'I know I shouldn't be, but I am.'

Rita sits next to her, panting to keep her head clear.

'Why shouldn't you be happy?' Rita asks.

'I feel guilty, I guess. Everyone does. But I just don't know how our quitting would have brought those three porters back to life.'

Last night, Shelly says. Or the night before last. The last night we slept, when you were sick, Rita. Remember? The rain? It was so cold, and they were sleeping in the mess tent, and there was the hole, and the tent was so wet. They just didn't wake up, Rita. You didn't know? I know you were asleep but, really, you didn't know? I think part of you knew. Who do you think they were carrying down? Oh lord, look at the way the glaciers sort of radiate under the sun. They are so huge and still but they seem to pulse, don't they, honey? Where are you going?

All the way down Rita expects to fall. The mountain is steep for the first hour, the rock everywhere loose. None of this was her idea. She was put here, in this place, by her sister, who was keeping score. Rita had never wanted this. She dislikes mountains and peaks mean nothing to her. She's a boat person; she likes to sit on boats in the sun, or in the sun with her feet in the powdery sand! As the mountain is still steep she runs and then jumps and runs and then jumps, flying for twenty feet with each leap, and when she lands, hundreds of stones are unleashed and go rolling down, gathering more as they descend. She never would have come this far had she known it would be like this, all wrong, so cold and with the rain coming through the tents on those men. She makes it down to the high camp, where the porters made her dinner and went to sleep and did not wake up. This cannot be her fault. Patrick is responsible first, and Frank after him, and then Jerry and Shelly, both of whom are older, who have experience and should have known something was wrong. Rita is the last one who could be blamed; but then there is Grant, who had gone down and hadn't told her. Grant knew everything, didn't he? How could she be responsible for this kind of thing? Maybe she is not here now, running down this mountain, and was never here. This is something she can forget. She can be not-here – she was never here. Yesterday she found herself wanting something she never wanted, and she became something else and why go up when everything is wrong? Every day the porters walked ahead, helping them to get to some frigid place with a view and a savage wind, carrying watermelons and coffee for Christ's sake, and it felt wrong and she was hollow and shamed. She wanted to be able to tell Gwen that she'd done it, and she wanted to bring J.J. and Frederick a rock or something from up there, because then they'd think she was capable of anything finally and some day they would come back to her and – oh God, it was a mess and she keeps running, sending scree down in front of her, throwing rocks down the mountain, because she cannot stop running and she cannot stop bringing the mountain down with her.

At the bottom, ten hours later, she is newly barefoot. The young boy who now has her boots, who she gave them to after he offered to wash them, directed her into a round hut of corrugated steel, and she ducked into its cool darkness. Behind a desk, flanked by maps, is a Tanzanian forest ranger. He is very serious.

'Did you make it to the top?' he asks.

She nods.

'Sign here.'

He opens a log. He is turning the pages, looking for the last names entered. There are thousands of names in the book, with each name's nationality, age, and a place for comments. He finds a spot for her, on one of the last pages, at the bottom, and after all the names before her she adds her own.

The Days Here

KELLY FEENEY

I

The hotel is called the Longacre. It is not the kind of place where people introduce themselves. The only way to learn anyone's name is to listen when they are called to the telephone. The announcements are infrequent; they jangle the hollow quiet of the all-beige dining room.

I eat dinner, alone, while it is still light, with a view of the tennis courts where no one ever plays. Some nights I take a sleeping pill at dinner. It makes me feel benevolent. I love the waiter. He brings water to the table – room temperature, no ice – in a perfect clear cylinder.

Some nights I eat in my room, at my desk. I get nervous waiting for room service. I straighten up the room, making sure I have something to give as a tip. I stare at the door and look at my watch. I am afraid I will look like an amateur, even though I have some experience being waited upon in this way.

The rooms here are pleasant but inert, with worn wooden furniture in streamlined silhouettes, net-like curtains affording little privacy, and slightly faded bedspreads in yellow and turquoise. The palette emulates the decor of the famous sanitarium in Paimio, Finland, and is intended to promote respiratory health. Cleanliness used to be a big part of the rest-cure.

I read about it in the 'Legendary Longacre' brochure. Another hallmark of the 'cheerful-punitive style' is the relentless use of tatami floor mats. They torture my feet with excessive tickling.

The brochure also discusses the difference between the invalid and the convalescent diet (different kinds of broths), warns against improper food combinations, and plaintively observes that 'Crumbs in the bed are the greatest enemy to the patient's comfort.' The mineral springs dried up a long time ago, and then the movie stars stopped coming in their private planes. These days the overgrown airstrip is mostly a field of red-tipped grass.

In the spirit of the history of the place, I take two baths a day and eat crackers in bed at night.

II

I tried everything. I tried concentrating on a single far-off object, I tried writing my name in the air until I could do it forward and backward. I tried seminars and haircuts, I even tried looking myself up in the phone book. The more earnestly I sought a cure, the worse it became. I waited for her to die for so long I do not know what else to wait for. I cannot look at pictures of her or read things she wrote. I am no good at making adjustments.

It began in February; it always does. Someone would forget my birthday, and then I'd vow to improve myself.

I started drinking a kind of tea made from boiled sticks that cost eighteen dollars a pound. I pressure-cooked grains. I ate difficult, blood-cleansing vegetables. 'Sing a happy song each day,' the brochure said.

Or it wasn't February. It might have been spring or fall. I couldn't look at anything anymore, not cars or buildings or sunsets, couldn't say anything funny about the things I hated. Bad taste was everywhere and had to be put down. Whole continents shoved into the ocean, everything must go.

After breakfast, I'd move casually up the attic stairs, checking for squirrels. Often there would be a big, red-eyed, smelly thing in the trap. The trap was called Hav-a-hart, my personal motto. I'd put the thing in the trunk of my car and drive to work. One morning my boss arrived as I was teetering on a snow bank along the edge of the driveway with my captive. Jumping out of his Saab, he complimented me on an unremarkable aspect of my attire. He seemed bewildered by the sight of me. I released the squirrel, who actually spat on me before skittering out of the cage. Something saintly overcame me atop that snow bank, in spite of my dislike of bosses and rodents. For a moment I felt kind and unafraid, twelve miles from my attic. Maybe it was the diet.

At lunchtime, five days a week, I drove to town in a big hurry, trying to make every light. I'd read back issues of *Opera News* in the waiting area of the Child Study Center. I tried to care about opera. Will I ever be too old to see a shrink at the Child Study Center, I'd wonder.

After my appointment, it always seemed that I had to buy a baby gift. The woman at the store smiled at me, because of the seventeen baby gifts I bought there in three years. Did she know about the special burden of the childless? One day I bought a tiny velour hooded tunic with matching pants. Something fit for a small pasha, I mused. I also got a votive candle for myself, one with a picture of a ladder ('La Escalera') in colored glitter. I had been told to burn candles and breathe a lot.

I was on a new regime involving ornate food combinations and oriental pickles. There were foods to enjoy, foods to enjoy occasionally, and foods to avoid. Besides the regimen, there was nothing to do. Nothing to do but engage in soulless avoidance: of caffeine, alcohol, nightshades, subtropical fruits, and electricity. I was hoping for health. A clear, voiceless way of thinking.

III

Returning to the room after a morning walk around the old resort, I find the bed made. It is crisp-looking, fiercely tucked in. How thrilling to be cared for. In order to get into bed I must pry open the covers and wedge myself in, careful to lie flat as possible between the pressed linens, taking shallow breaths. A little confinement is probably good. Didn't the Puritans torture suspected witches and adulteresses by laying boards on their chests and piling heavy stones until they extracted a confession? Adding stones and asking questions, gradually crushing ribs and lungs.

IV

My boss's marriage was complicated, he told me. Difficult. I didn't want to know about it, didn't want to hear precisely how difficult or complicated it was. But since I possess a naturally watery and sympathetic manner, I listened. He was in a churlish mood because he had bumped his head on the copier. His monogrammed cuff peeked out from beneath his sport coat. This was a yellow-tie day. (I kept a private tally of how many he wore in a month.) I slouched in my chair, hoping to appear more intelligent than I felt. His lips were puffy, his eyes bulged well past their sockets. His neck looked as if it might burst open any moment. I listened as long as I thought appropriate, really thinking about office supplies.

At the office I waited for all kinds of things. I waited for FedEx and UPS, I waited for the mail, for 11 o'clock and then 3 o'clock and the excuse of going home at the end of the day. But mostly I waited for Mrs Albrecht to die.

V

The decaying hotel reminds me of the things I can't see, of the things I don't know to want. I pace around the vacant swimming pool, weaving a path among the disused cabanas. A rose branch scratches my arm; the hotel preys upon my nervous torpor. The light is sometimes perfect in the late afternoons, sweet and pink and solemn. It is the familiar light of lost opportunity.

I came here, decided to come here, as a bet, a kind of joke with myself. My back was hurting and I wanted to go some place where I could lie very still all day. No one believed I had an actual pain. No one thought it warranted room service.

The people at the front desk perhaps do not believe that I am a good person, someone who wants to be healthy. They see me check for messages nearly every hour, trying to feel that I belong in this hotel.

The clerk looks over his reading glasses at me. He does not approve of how I linger in the common room every Saturday, stuck to the celery-colored ottoman, becoming overly involved in the secrets being revealed by the famous chefs on PBS. Puffed pastry has 729 layers, I learned.

One night in my room I am startled by headlights bending their tracks across the bed. The refracted angles of light span my chest and the right side of my face. Is this company? But the car drives past. The lights slip back through the window as carelessly as they came.

VI

I think about what the office must be like when I'm not there. Does everyone still dash into their offices, slamming doors behind them? Do they stay in there a long time, bending and unbending paper clips?

The office, the Foundation, it's called, is in a suburban raised-ranch. When you open the door you see straight upstairs into the kitchen and right down to the office at the same time. The house displays its cheapness unself-consciously. That quality, and the yellow Dead End sign across the street, always seemed unlucky. Another piece of bad luck is that I worked there thirteen years and some people said I look just like my boss's wife, only thinner.

Now that I'm not there I float up the stairs, above the flimsy metal railing, and peer around the hall corner to see who's there. Mrs Albrecht's bedroom is now the new person's office. A desk is where her bed once was. I pass into the kitchen where the chrome tea kettle reflects in convex miniature the paintings on the wall behind me. An entire world of yellow squares. I move quietly, cloudlike, down the hall, into what used to be the nurse's room and is now my boss's office. It has been abandoned for an afternoon tennis date. The mail teeters in tall piles. The computer screen burns with the text of an essay he's writing. After Mrs Albrecht's husband died, a Polish nurse named Yadwiga ran screaming from this room, never to return, because of a ghost.

The phone lights up; downstairs someone is making a call.

VII

Mrs Albrecht, the woman who kept her husband's foundation going, refused to die for a long time. The year before, the second or third time we thought she was going to die, we FedExed photographs and a draft obituary to *The Times*. She was ninety-three and had a fever of 108. Our actions did not feel hasty. When she finally did die, just when it seemed she would dwindle indefinitely in her bed upstairs, she died in her sleep. I hope she didn't call out for someone who wasn't there.

The writer staffing the arts desk that morning normally wrote about antiques. Her name was Elita, and she asked about the cause of death. 'She was ninety-four, she died in her sleep,' I said. 'She had been failing for a long time.'

'*The Times* always specifies the cause of death. What does the police report say?'

'Police report?' I said.

'You didn't call the police? In New York we have to call the police. Do you have a death certificate?'

I could tell I was making a bad impression on Elita, reluctant writer of art obituaries.

'The death certificate says natural causes, old age.'

Elita asked if she could speak to my boss. 'Of course,' I said. 'But what about her photograph? You will run that picture of her, won't you?'

'No. Look, we didn't print a picture of her husband when he died, and he was a lot more famous. We like to be consistent.'

I put her on hold. I began to feel sorry for any other somewhat-famous widows whose deaths were being reported on Elita's shift.

Charcot-Marie-Tooth disease is a hereditary disorder of the peripheral nervous system characterized by weakness and atrophy, but she did not die of it. She had lymphoma and lost all her hair when she was seventy-seven, but she didn't die of that either. Last year she had a record-breaking fever, and she did not die of that.

She lived through the fever. No one knows why.

I know I went into her room to look at her while waiting for the funeral director to arrive, but I can't remember if I kissed her. I always imagined that I'd want to. I remember the fifty-four white drip-dry blouses in the closet. And two long rows of specially made suede oxfords, the kind with the fringed flap covering the laces. The shoes weighted her withered feet as they dragged the ground. They kept her from floating up.

VIII

The days begin early at the hotel because I can't stop thinking about Mrs Albrecht. It is a problem that cannot be solved awake or asleep. What was the story of her life, why should I try to recollect it, what was she to me?

What do you want to know about her? That she was famous

or disciplined, that she did or did not walk with a limp? She was famous, famous enough to have her picture taken but not famous enough always to have it published. And she was disciplined, she hated stopping for lunch. She did walk with a limp (people thought she had rickets) and missed out on all the dances at the Bauhaus. She could not climb a flight of stairs without making a sound so she never became a sneaky person. She preferred the warming up of the orchestra to the actual performance. She loved that in America glasses of water always came with ice and pillowcases without buttons. She did not believe in voting or sunsets. She preferred counting volcanoes and assassinations. She knew that she could not have every single thing worth having in life, so she did not try to.

I cannot remember what I said to her, I cannot remember if I said goodbye the last time I saw her alive. She told me about the crossing once. I remember later on someone told me she often lied about it. I have forgotten most of what she said, except that she threw up almost continuously, the seas were stormy and the trip took longer than usual. When they arrived she was a slim and somewhat minor celebrity in a fur coat. After gathering around her husband for several minutes the reporters suddenly exclaimed, 'Hey, let's get one with the wife!' – as if it were a new idea to photograph a man and a woman together on the deck of a ship.

IX

I can hear the guests next door shower and listen to television in the mornings and at night. The voices sound wobbly, twisting through sheetrock and the thin fiberglass shower unit.

Water thunders through the hollow bathroom. It is familiar, but surprising. I would like to wash my hair, but I just washed it a few hours ago in a small campaign to divide the day into segments of less and less to do.

I walk through the woods in a thin kind of daylight and feel transparent, or insubstantial, except for the occasional bare branch slapping my coat sleeve. I picture myself in the landscape, in a panorama of inaction.

This is supposed to be about a woman and a hotel, why she went, what she did there. How did she get there? Was there a journey involved? Her gray raincoat, her straight black hair, her eyes, slightly hooded, what will become of her?

Every day something empties out: air, light, the possibility of telling a story, having a story, or recording the boredom. Why do we say we're 'bored to tears'? What are we mourning?

I project the dreamed movie of my life, somewhere in the future of enframement, nothing broken, everything continuous, at the center of a spinning landscape, or sinking in a cool green pool after lunch.

X

Mrs Albrecht liked me as much as she could bear to like anyone young, female, and ambulatory. She said I was noisy, that my real name was 'Boom-boom.' Mornings she sat in her wheelchair, shrouded in an enormous white terrycloth robe, staring at a boiled egg. A plastic sip cup of coffee mixed with Ensure trembled in her hand. With excruciating deliberateness, the cup moved toward her mouth. She drank. She swallowed some. She coughed in a serious way several times, but I was used to this and knew not to be alarmed. I'd stand behind her, to her right, looking at my shoes, hoping she wouldn't comment on them. I'd say 'Good morning! How are you?' and wait for a response.

Even when the windows were open, the faint smell of urine was everywhere. Her ears and hands and nose seemed to get larger all the time, or was it that the rest of her was shrinking?

'What do you hate?' I'd ask her.

'That skirt you're wearing.'

'Sorry you don't like it.' On this particular day it was leopard-printed denim, short, and had been on sale for nine dollars.

'Hello, pussycat,' she said.

XI

I have been told that when you die you cannot breathe, not even through a straw. There are things I'll never be able to do again, things I used to be able to do without concentrating. Time isn't endless and shadowy anymore. From now on, time will be an insanely narrow and ill-conceived corridor connecting nothing. And instead of those romantic shadows, I'll see only a headache-inducing glare.

The present is very close and often makes me feel faint. I see those bright spots dancing. Everywhere I look the spots want to look, too. I am learning to tolerate it. This is what it is like to look for the future.

XII

Dear Mrs Albrecht:

Hotel stationery is romantic. The idea of it is romantic. You would approve of the bony, lowercase lettering across the bottom:

h o t e l   l o n g a c r e .

Last night I dreamed that I could not sleep because you were lying in the other bed, propped against an enormous pile of mittens, wearing the white terrycloth robe you were buried in. I was afraid to close my eyes. I was afraid to go near you. I woke myself up, certain that everything was my fault.

I remember one night when I was five telling my mother that I was afraid to fall asleep because the world could end during the night and I might not wake up. She told me not to worry, that I'd be in heaven before I knew what happened. A while later when I was still awake in her bed, unable to be comforted by thoughts of a place as scary as heaven, she said, 'You know, dear, rest is eighty percent of sleep.'

It's not that I think of you as being asleep, because I know death is not really like sleep. It's just that when the doctor announced that you died 'in your sleep,' I wondered how we'd ever know if that was true. You might have awakened because you were feeling bad, and then died. You might have been lying there, looking at that painting that hung opposite your bed, the one Joseph made in the 40s that was supposed to be an abstract allegory of your marriage. (I always wished it had been painted in something more than black, white, and gray.) Maybe the TV was on in the nurse's room and no one heard you calling.

Monday is a popular day to die. The promise of the weekend is past, the dread of another week before. When you were learning English you walked through a field in North Carolina explaining to Joseph that 'pasture' was the opposite of 'future.' I think of that all the time.

I don't go to your house anymore. I try not to drive anywhere near it, in fact. I still have the key to the front door, and I know where everything is inside. The beaver coat, the one you wore in the newspaper photo taken on the SS *Europa*, still hangs in the hall closet. And even though your bedroom is now an office, that little statue of Isis remains on the bookshelf.

I do drive to the cemetery from time to time. I sit there with the windows rolled down looking at the mail, or balancing my checkbook. I don't get out of the car, though, and I know you wouldn't mind.

Who says goodbye to paintings, I wonder. No one driving by its shoebox exterior could tell that 818 Larchwood Drive contained a great collection of modern art. Before leaving I tried to memorize your husband's paintings, as alike as Easter eggs, nested squares of color. Did you tell me they reminded you of hearts beating? Your own work is a kind of ancient writing, loosely woven glyphs painstakingly plotted on a loom. Solemn and hardly ever ethereal, always weighted by the labor of weaving, and impossible to memorize.

The day I left the Foundation I told myself I would go back sometime, that part of me would always be at my desk, looking up out of the basement window. Or I'm in your studio, sitting at the aluminum work table where we sat when I helped steady your hand while you signed your name a few hundred times. Sometimes I picture you in your wheelchair at the top of the stair, waiting in a Chanel knock-off and smelling of L'Origan a full hour before a visitor was due to arrive. It was from that post above the railing that you used to call down to us. That's where you ordered us to cut off a branch of a tree in the front yard because it blocked your view of the mailbox.

On my last day at the Foundation I sorted some of your old letters at the table in your soothing white kitchen. Four small paintings, yellow and orange squares within squares, hung opposite me. I loved them as if they were related to me, but they were the blankest faces I have ever seen.

I have always loved airmail, a ghostly form of travel. Some of the envelopes were pale blue with navy and red striped edges. Aerogrammes from Brazil bore exotic yellow and green slash marks. In them you wrote about painting the kitchen, about the days seeming long, about the unpleasantness of working with wool in August. You wondered whether Joseph remembered to wear his hat on cool days, or took his vitamin pill. Your English was peculiar, cadenced, careful. The complete text of one letter was simply 'Without news –.'

I touched the linen-patterned Formica, the vinyl dinette chairs, and what you always referred to as the 'first Chemex coffee pot in North America,' grateful that if people don't go on indefinitely, at least objects do.

XIII

If I have lunch early at the hotel the day is ruined, but sometimes this can't be helped. If the day is going to be bad, it's better just to get it over with. Have lunch early, have dinner early, go to sleep early.

Hotel rooms are easier to be in than rooms in houses or

offices. You're supposed to be inert in hotels, supposed to watch *Cujo* dubbed into Dutch on TV, or stare at the view if there is one, one that you either can or cannot afford. You are not supposed to make your bed or clean up after yourself. You're supposed to pick up the phone and ask the people who wait on the other end to bring you mineral water and baskets of fruit. Complain if the peaches are too hard and the rolls are stale. And where is the bathrobe you asked for yesterday?

I used to go more places, I have been in other hotels, much livelier than this one. I have been in many hotels trying to forget what I am doing there. In Spain or Italy I drank too much and said things that made a lot of well-dressed people laugh. The next day I couldn't remember what the joke was.

I would like to tell you that I have danced in circles of lamplight outside the Congress Hall in Nuremberg, that I have crawled the pilgrim's route to the church of Hagia Sophia in Istanbul, that I have run cold water over my wrists to keep from fainting in Algeria, but I have not done these things. I have stayed in my hotel room in Cologne, afraid to venture out to a restaurant in the evening, eating an entire cake bought from a bakery for my supper.

I slide through cities and buildings and plazas and mountain ranges, talking to no one. It is cheaper this way, but sadder. There is no comfort. This is how it starts.

Haole Go Home!: Small Gestures from the Hawaiian Secessionist Movement

ZEV BOROW

I

Honolulu is 2,560 miles west of the coast of California. It takes about eight days to get there by boat. If you fly it's an eleven-hour plane ride from anywhere on the East Coast. (It's only nine from Tokyo.) Once you've arrived, you'll find the locals say 'mahalo' when they mean 'thank you,' and really do wear flower-print short-sleeve shirts. Look up, and maybe you'll notice that the thin fingers of gauzy, pink clouds responsible for the city's biblical sunsets roll in from the east instead of the west, opposite of nearly everywhere else in the Western Hemisphere. (This because of the Pacific trade winds.) Turn on the television in your hotel room or condo, and you can watch a local anchorperson delivering the news in front of a giant relief of a world map. On it, the Hawaiian Islands are disproportionately large. Japan, the Philippines, and China fill up the left-hand corner of the screen, and the blue expanse of the Pacific extends all the way to the right. The mainland United States never makes it into the frame, even when it's time for the guy who does the sports.

II

On November 23, 1993, President Clinton signed US Public Law 103-50. Co-sponsored by Hawaiian Sens. Daniel Akaka (D) and Dan Inouye (D) and passed by both houses of Congress, the resolution formally 'apologizes on behalf of the people and government of the United States to native Hawaiians' for 'the illegal overthrow of the Kingdom of Hawaii on January 17, 1893, with the participation of agents and citizens of the United States, and the deprivation of the rights of Native Hawaiians to self determination' and 'expresses its [the United States'] commitment to acknowledge the ramifications of the overthrow of the Kingdom of Hawaii, in order to provide the proper foundation for reconciliation between the United States and the Native Hawaiian people.'

III

Hawaii's vast physical and cultural distance from the rest of the United States is, of course, part of its attraction. You don't need a passport, the convenience stores have all your favorite haircare products in stock, and there's native culture to ogle. You can even visit a royal residence; smack in the heart of downtown Honolulu lies the recently restored Iolani Palace – the only royal palace on US soil, once home to King Kalakaua and Queen Lili'uokalani, the last rulers of the independent nation of Hawaii.

It is easy to forget that the eight oases of cooled lava grown lush in the middle of the Pacific are in fact the 50th state of the union, and not, as they once were, a foreign country. Mililani Trask, however, never forgets. And if you stand with her on the steps of Iolani Palace, she won't let you forget either.

Trask is serving her second term as the elected Kia 'Aina, or Prime Minister, of Ka Lahui Hawaii, a native Hawaiian sovereignty organization founded in 1987 that now boasts over 20,000 members – members who prefer to call themselves citizens not of the United States or the state of Hawaii, but of Ka Lahui. In English, Ka Lahui translates, roughly, to 'the nation,' as in the Sovereign Nation of Hawaii. Trask, along with her sister, Dr Haunani-Kay, Director of the Center for Hawaiian Studies at the University of Hawaii and the chief public voice of Ka Lahui, have succeeded in pushing the concept of native Hawaiian sovereignty to the forefront of Hawaii's cultural and political landscape.

IV The Sisters

'When I was six or seven, my father brought me and my sister here. It was in shambles.' Mililani Trask gestures over her shoulder toward the looming presence of Iolani Palace, a square, two-story white mansion in a style best described as Polynesian-plantation. 'He said, "This is where our Queen lived." He took us to the archives next door and showed us real pictures of her.' Her eyes soften for a moment. Then Trask, 46, takes a final deep drag from her fourth cigarette of the morning, exhales, and hardens her focus once again. 'He told us, "We were a great nation, we always were committed to peace, and this is what they did to us. But some day we will live to see this place restored, and with it the dignity of our people." He died, but in 1993 he looked down from where he was and he saw his daughters leading the march.'

A former practicing attorney, Mililani is, at her core, both an advocate and a negotiator, and now as head of Ka Lahui, a politician with constituents. Her sister, Haunani-Kay, on the other hand, is a fire-breathing academic, most often delicately described as the 'more difficult' of the two. On the islands, and especially among the native Hawaiian community, Mililani is the more prominent. (A 1995 *Honolulu-Advertiser* poll of native Hawaiians found her the third-most-respected public figure in the state.) But on the continental US and abroad, it is Haunani-Kay, one year older, who is the face and voice of not only Ka Lahui, but often the entire sovereignty movement. She does interviews on NPR and lectures on the topic at hundreds of colleges and seminars each year, where, she says, for many who attend, 'It's something to do. "Let's drive to UC Berkeley and hear Trask talk about Hawaiian Sovereignty."'

Both Trasks are outspoken, intense, and aggressive, but while Mililani seems perpetually harried, the force of her convictions barely keeping total exhaustion at bay, Haunani-Kay has a controlled, almost regal bearing, tinged with razor-sharp, if calculated, menace. Her office on the University of Hawaii's Manoa campus is lorded over by a large framed poster hanging behind her desk: a blown-up grainy black-and-white photograph of Malcolm X staring out a window, clutching a submachine gun. Bold black letters across the bottom read: By Any Means Necessary. It is draped on three sides by a lei of fresh flowers.

'Mililani and I have pretty much the same political opinions,' says Haunani-Kay. 'I handle a lot of the press, because the press is afraid of me. It's harder to be head of Ka Lahui than to be head of Hawaiian Studies. I get a paycheck. The general public, especially whites, say, "Haunani is hard, Mililani is kind." Hawaiians don't do that. They'll say, "Haunani says outrageous things, but politically they're on the same side." It's kind of like the Kennedys: You had Jack, and you had Bobby . . .'

V

Polynesians from various islands in the South Pacific first settled what are now the Hawaiian Islands nearly 1,800 years before the first white Westerner, Capt. James Cook, waded ashore Kauai, in 1778. When Cook arrived, as when he left (in a coffin, after being killed in an attack by natives in 1789), the islands were governed by several rival warrior chiefs. It wasn't until 1810, when one chief, Kamehameha (after being suitably outfitted with Western artillery), embarked on an inter-island cannon campaign that a unified and sovereign Hawaiian monarchy was established. Throughout the middle of the century, American settlers, mostly missionaries and planters, arrived in droves, cultivating much of Hawaii's land for sugar and pineapple crops, and a good portion of its people for Christianity. Still, during this time King Kamehameha I's descendants solidified their power, adopted a constitution, and entered the Kingdom of Hawaii into diplomatic and trade treaties and conventions with 22 countries around the world, including most of Europe and the United States.

In 1893, an American-led group of foreign planters and missionaries, giddy with plantation profits (that would balloon further without the hindrance of US import tariffs), and backed by 162 marines from the USS *Boston* (moored conveniently in Pearl Harbor), staged a bloodless coup. On January 17, a 13-member self-proclaimed Committee of Safety, led by Sanford B. Dole (of Dole pineapple fame), declared the Hawaiian monarchy ended, martial law enforced, and a new provisional government in power 'until terms of union with the United States' could be negotiated. The United States foreign minister in Hawaii immediately recognized the new government, and at dusk on that day Hawaii's Queen Lili'uokalani, a devout Christian, schooled in English, and long-mesmerized by the relatively new experiment in democracy 2,500 miles to her east, yielded her throne and her country, with these words:

I do, under protest, and impelled by said forces, yield my authority until such time as the government of the United States shall, upon facts being presented to it, undo the action of its representative and reinstate me in the authority which I claim as the constitutional sovereign of the Hawaiian Islands.

Lili'uokalani urged Hawaiians not to take up arms and to await the result of her appeal to the US government. The US foreign minister also appealed to the US government, writing the State Department: 'The Hawaiian pear is now fully ripe, and this is the golden hour to pluck it.' An annexation resolution was hastily drafted and submitted to the Senate by President William Harrison, but was withdrawn a month later by the newly inaugurated president, Grover Cleveland.

Less covetous of far-off beachfront property than Harrison, Cleveland sent an envoy to Honolulu to investigate the American role in the overthrow. Later that year, in a speech to

Congress, he called the coup: 'a substantial wrong' and 'a lawless occupation under false pretexts.' 'The United States,' he told Congress, 'cannot fail to vindicate its honor and its sense of justice by an earnest effort to make all possible reparation.' Four years later, in 1898, a new US president, William McKinley, signed a redrafted annexation resolution, and Hawaii officially became a US Territory. Sanford Dole was appointed governor. Cleveland later wrote: 'I am ashamed of the whole affair.'

VI

In 1978, the Hawaiian state legislature created the Office of Hawaiian Affairs (with funds from both the state and federal governments) to further the causes of native Hawaiians and, in part, to work to redress some of the historical injustices they had suffered.

Native Hawaiians are at the bottom of almost every social indicator. As a group they have the lowest median income in the state, the lowest literacy rate, the highest rates of incarceration and substance abuse, and some of the worst health statistics in the entire nation. At the time of Capt. Cook's landing in 1778 there were close to 300,000 full-blooded native Hawaiians living on the islands. Today, native and part-native Hawaiians account for about 13 percent of the state's nearly 1.2 million population. The 1990 census listed 138,742 native Hawaiians in the state.

VII

In August of 1993, three months before President Clinton signed the formal apology, 15,000 pro-sovereignty demonstrators watched Hawaii's former governor, John Waihee, raise the flag of the Kingdom of Hawaii over Iolani Palace. Waihee, along with the state's entire congressional delegation, came out in general support of the movement. (Current Hawaiian governor, Benjamin Caeyatano (D), and both Senators Akaka and Inouye have all come out in 'general' favor of the movement. All three declined to be interviewed for this article. Instead, each faxed copies of his written position: eerily similar, vaguely worded politicalese.)

In 1994, a bill was submitted to the Hawaiian state legislature requesting a plebiscite be put to the Hawaiian people, posing the question: 'Shall the Hawaiian People elect delegates to propose a Native Hawaiian government?' A 20-member election council was formed, funded in equal parts by the state and OHA. By that time, the agency was flush with funds after suing the state in 1995 and winning the right to a 20 percent revenue interest on the 1.7 million acres (nearly one-fourth of the land in the state) of ceded public and Crown lands that had belonged to the Kingdom of Hawaii. (Upon annexation, those lands had been transferred to the control of the federal government, and then, upon admission to the Union, to the state of Hawaii.) OHA's 20 percent revenue interest translated to more than $300 million.

The Trasks and Ka Lahui opposed the vote because they felt it was an attempt by the state, primarily through OHA, to co-opt, even subvert, the sovereignty movement. As

Haunani-Kay Trask puts it: 'It's absolutely ridiculous to think that a native vote on sovereignty can be funded by the state. OHA is a state-funded and controlled agency.' She cites several international legal scholars (whose written opinions were solicited by Ka Lahui, and are now featured prominently in the organization's literature) who opine that any sovereignty vote in any way connected with the state jeopardizes the integrity of the movement as a whole, because its results could be construed as a native-determined mandate to follow a state-directed course. 'It's absolutely ridiculous,' she says. 'We're talking about forming another country.'

VIII

'Well, let me just say this, it's nonsense!' John Goemans has just ordered dinner at Sam Choy's, a seafood restaurant ten minutes from Waikiki Beach that is, nevertheless, packed with locals. 'It has existed for so long, and nobody has wanted to say anything against it. And now you've got a whole generation who has been fed a bunch of hogwash, and they believe it, and they're going to be angry when it doesn't come to pass. It doesn't take a rocket scientist to know there's not going to be a sovereign nation carved out of the United States of America.'

Goemans, a former state attorney, first came to Hawaii immediately after it was granted statehood. One of his former roommates at the University of Virginia Law School, Ted Kennedy, had asked him to help run John F. Kennedy's presidential campaign on the islands. With his ruddy complexion and sharp New England inflection, Goemans himself could pass for a distant Kennedy cousin. In 1995, he agreed to take on the case of Freddie Rice, a white Hawaiian rancher whose family had been living on Hawaii since before the time of the overthrow. Rice wanted to sue the Office of Hawaiian Affairs (OHA) for barring him, and anyone else not of over 50 percent native blood, from voting in the elections for the nine OHA trustees.

'In Hawaii, we've created a special group entitled to privileges out of all proportion, and unavailable to most citizens of the state of Hawaii,' says Goemans. (Native Hawaiians, thanks in a large part to the work of OHA, enjoy a number of government-sanctioned privileges, ranging from shopping discounts and low-interest loans to unimpeded land and grazing rights.) 'And that's contrary to the US Constitution. But there are a couple of basic fallacies. First of all, the "illegal overthrow," that's a redundancy. All overthrows are illegal. Until you win, then they're legal. Another is that Hawaiians lost sovereignty in 1898. Hawaiians had no sovereignty in 1898. All sovereignty was with the monarchy. Hawaiians were royal subjects. They had nothing to lose because they had nothing. Serfs aren't sovereign. We're talking democracy here.'

IX

Goemans and the Trasks became unlikely allies. Both supported the Coalition Against the Native Hawaiian Vote, a band of sovereignty groups anchored by Ka Lahui that worked to wage a bitter campaign against the vote. In fact, the Trasks often agreed more with Goemans than they did with other native members of the coalition.

Ka Lahui differs from most other native sovereignty groups in that it espouses not total independence from the United States, but a nation-within-a-nation approach. It seeks to place native Hawaiians within the existing US federal policy, which affords all Native Americans the right to be self-governing. Given the right to self-rule, Ka Lahui would then negotiate a land and economic base and form a government. (Though not championing a complete return to monarchy, Ka Lahui would likely support a Windsor-like entity within a democratic, constitutional government.) Compared to the visions of those activists who support total independence, theirs is a realistic scenario – the principal reason why they are taken seriously, or at least more seriously, by Goemans.

'It's logical,' says Goemans, 'to say we want a sovereign nation, and we're not a sovereign nation if we have to depend on the state of Hawaii to do anything for us. If they posit the overthrow was illegal and they want to try and set up a sovereign nation with a king, or a parliament or whatever – that's logical. It ain't gonna happen, but it's logical. It's not logical to say we want to have a sovereign nation and you, the Hawaiian taxpayers of the United States of America, are going to fund the process of the establishment of that nation.'

X

More than 80,000 eligible native Hawaiian voters had until August 15, 1996, to mail in their ballots. On September 6, a federal district court handed down its ruling that the vote was constitutional, but could only be considered 'a barometer to gauge momentum and popular support'; that neither the state legislature nor the Hawaiian people were legally bound by its results. (The court also suggested the plaintiffs sue again if OHA moves to hold a constitutional convention to form a binding mandate on sovereignty.) Only 33,000 voters, 39 percent of those that were eligible, returned ballots. (Eight percent of the total Hawaiian population.) Of that 39 percent, 73 percent voted yes on the question of electing delegates to propose a native Hawaiian government.

XI

John Goemans is appealing the federal court's decision because it did not rule the vote's eligibility requirements unconstitutional, and the role of race with regard to the sovereignty movement remains hotly contested. Hawaii is one of the most racially and ethnically diverse states in the Union. (As of the 1990 census: 33 percent white; 22 percent Japanese; 15 percent Filipino; 13 percent Hawaiian; 7.5 percent Hispanic; 6 percent Chinese; 3 percent black; and percentages of Hispanics and blacks have grown substantially since.) Many sovereignty activists are of mixed ethnic heritage, and Ka Lahui, while opening up 'citizenship' to all races, only allows full-blooded native Hawaiians to vote in its elections.

'One of the reasons I came here was that I thought Hawaii really had something to offer the nation, as an example of how a multi-racial community could live in relative harmony,' he says, finishing up dinner at Sam Choy's. 'That was the beauty of the place.'

Then, looking around the restaurant, he adds: 'Hawaiians are fully assimilated here. You don't look around and say, oh, look at the poor Hawaiians. They're everywhere – in the boardrooms, the courts, everywhere! The day after I filed the suit I got hundreds of phone calls, from Hawaiians and non-Hawaiians, thanking me for what I was doing.' (A *Honolulu-Advertiser* poll taken before the referendum vote found only 53 percent of native Hawaiians favored 'some type of sovereignty.' Support is substantially lower among non-natives.)

'All this sovereignty stuff has made people angry,' Goemans says. 'There's a new racial defensiveness.'

At that, a waitress, who isn't white, asks if he'd like any dessert, prompting Goemans to turn toward her, smile, and bellow: 'Of course I would, I'm an American!'

XII

The group of nearly 50 sovereignty supporters gathered at the Quaker Friends Meeting House on a quiet street near the University of Hawaii-Manoa campus believe in positive vibes. It's a Thursday evening, and they have come together to share breadfruit (with coconut milk for dipping), guava juice, cookies and iced tea, and to talk sovereignty. Specifically, they are here to forge a consensus on a white paper on Hawaiian sovereignty that could be sent to various international bodies, including the United Nations.

It is something of a rare occasion, this gathering of representatives from most of the major sovereignty organizations. Mililani Trask is there, as are Dennis 'Bumpy' Kanahale, 'Head of State' of the Nation of Hawaii; Dr Kekuni Blaisdell, leader of Ka Pakaukau, a coalition of smaller sovereignty groups, and Poka Laenui, formerly known as Hayden Burgess, a former

OHA trustee. Leaders from sovereignty groups on neighboring islands are also present.

Kanahale and Blaisdell had been together that afternoon at a rally on the lawn of Iolani Palace to mark the 99th anniversary of annexation. Blaisdell, a slight, light-skinned 72-year-old man who greets people with a hug and the traditional rubbing of noses, is the head of the University of Hawaii Medical Center. At the Palace that afternoon, he led a small protest highlighted by several speeches and a Marxist red banner that, in obligatory ragged white bubble letters, screamed: 'End Colonialist Aggression!'

Kanahale is wearing an electronic monitoring device around his ankle, as he is required to do while he awaits his impending second trial (the first was declared a mistrial) on charges of harboring a fugitive. The trial has become something of a minor *cause célèbre* in Hawaii, since Kanahale leads what he considers to be an independent nation and has been involved in several militant pro-sovereignty actions. Taking a page from the Black Panthers' handbook, Kanahale and a small gang of his supporters confronted several state and federal judges and 'served them papers' for crimes committed against the native Hawaiian people. In the late 1980s he even made statements about stockpiling weapons. He has, by all accounts, mellowed, but is one of the only activists that seems to have any potential for violence, or anything approaching cliché, El Jefe-like, revolutionary charisma.

Both Kanahale and Blaisdell support total independence from the United States. Blaisdell calls Ka Lahui's proposed nation-within-a-nation model a 'sell-out,' while Kanahale says simply: 'We're not looking to be American Indians. We don't want to live on a reservation.' Even Poka Laenui parts with

Ka Lahui on the idea of nation-within-a-nation status. That's why in her opening comments to the assembled group, Mililani Trask makes it clear she's there only to try to work out a consensus on a possible white paper, not to debate independence versus nation-within-a-nation.

This meeting, like the rally at the Palace that afternoon and most other sovereignty events, large and small, begins with the group standing in bare feet – no shoes are allowed – holding hands, and chanting a native Hawaiian verse, followed by a moment of silence in deference to 'the Creator,' and a call to be 'one with the world and the spirit.'

Despite Mililani's best efforts, the next two hours are filled by nearly every person in the room giving his or her general opinion about sovereignty, not about the proposed white paper. Clearly agitated, Mililani goes through almost a full pack of cigarettes. Another woman in her mid-20s tells the group she thinks the movement needs to make itself more attractive to non-natives, that 'we can't deny who we are now, that we all wear blue jeans and Western clothes . . .' Mililani just lowers her head.

Little concrete is accomplished, there are repeated calls for increased cooperation and vows never to forget the struggle. Perhaps the most unifying and telling sentiment is expressed by one activist from Maui, who stands up and says to the group: 'It still gets to me, how the hell did this happen to us? We were a nation. This land was ours, is still ours. How could it ever not be?'

Few beside Mililani seem bothered by such unfocused soliloquies. In fact, many seem to find a simple comfort in being around fellow sovereignty supporters. Watching it all, it's hard not to wonder if the meeting is anything like those Hawaii's rival chiefs had upon first dealing with the West 200 years ago.

XIII The Odds

An independent Hawaiian nation: 10,000:1

A sovereign native nation-within-a-nation, with powers greater than any American-Indian entity: 100:1

A state-sponsored model with less autonomy, likely to draw the ire of the Trasks and other activists: 6:1

Fleets of planes stuffed with tourists continuing to descend from the skies: 1:1

XIV

'It was a frustrating night,' Mililani would later reflect. 'At this point in the game, I'm trying to work with people, considering the needs of our people: homelessness, medical, housing. But as far as independence, until there are free elections and the people say that is what they want, Ka Lahui isn't going to champion it. We took a vote of Ka Lahui citizens, and only 19 percent voted for independence. When I first came back to Hawaii, I wanted only independence. But when I started talking to people in the community, they weren't saying independence, they were saying: "My kids are sick. We don't have a job." Nation-within-a-nation is a realistic way to address those things, and our political sovereignty. We're not talking about reservations.'

Haunani-Kay, as always, is more direct: 'Ask Kekuni and

Bumpy what they're going to do about the seven military bases in Hawaii. The 7th Fleet goes out of Pearl Harbor. The US is suddenly going to say, "Oh yes, here's sovereignty, we're taking all our ships out?" It's not that I don't want to see a totally independent Hawaii, but you need to give me an on-the-ground analysis of how we're going to get there. Kekuni thinks we can shame the US away! Has the United States ever been shamed out of anything?'

But concerning the movement's spirituality, both are in agreement. 'Without that feeling in the room,' says Mililani 'we'd be nowhere.' Haunani-Kay agrees. 'It's at the core,' she says, 'of the movement, of being Hawaiian . . . it's at the core of what most Americans don't, can't, understand.'

XV

a) 1998 is the 100th anniversary of annexation, and nearly all the sovereignty factions see it as an ideal time for a final, victorious push.

b) 'Hawaii – an independent country? But we've got condos there!'

c) There are currently 88 Native-American nations seeking secession from the United States, but none of them is armed with a public apology, which reads more like a confession, signed by the President of the United States.

XVI

Just before last August's Annexation Day rally in front of Iolani Palace was about to break up, a small group of sovereignty activists formed a circle underneath one of the huge, dripping banyan trees that shade the Palace lawn. They joined hands and began a native Hawaiian chant. Moments later, a gusty trade wind caught hold of their voices and seemed to carry their voices up and into a surprising crescendo. It was loud enough to startle some of the office workers nibbling on their lunch in the nearby gazebo. A family of tourists with University of Missouri sweatshirts caught the sound while walking up the steps of the Palace, stopped, listened, and kept walking.

XVII *Epilogue*

This piece was originally assigned by *Civilization* magazine, which is based in Washington, DC, affiliated with the Library of Congress, and the winner of something known as the 'National Magazine Award.' Halfway through the editing of this piece, *Civilization* hired a new editor, a man named Nelson Aldridge Rockefeller. Previously the head person at *American Benefactor* magazine, Mr Rockefeller decided that *Civilization* would have a new 'celebrity guest editor' for each issue. Oprah was mentioned. This piece was dropped, not fitting the new 'feel' of the periodical. Last February, *Civilization* re-launched. Martin Scorsese was the celebrity guest editor. His picture was on the cover. At the time of this writing, Bill Blass, the clothing designer, was busy editing the newest issue.

Solicitation

REBECCA CURTIS

I was waiting for my lover – I would say boyfriend, but my
boyfriend reminds me to say lover, not boyfriend, because we
are in school and boyfriend sounds silly for a person in school
– and it was late. When my bell rang I thought – here's my
lover! – so I opened my top-door, and at the bottom of the
stair I saw the face of the crack-lady, although of course I
didn't know yet who she was.

I'm your neighbor, the crack-lady called up through the
glass, I live next door.

Now I had a neighbor who lived next door and he was
black and his name was Tim, and I liked Tim very much, so
when the crack-lady said she lived next door I believed her. I
did not want to be rude to a friend of Tim's.

You know Tim? I said.

I'm your neighbor, the crack-lady said. I live next door.

So I walked down the stairs and I opened the bottom door,
the one that goes outside, and then we were body to body.

I need your help, the crack-lady said. I need your help real
bad.

Yes, I said.

She explained that she needed diapers for her baby, who
was out of diapers, and that she needed my help to get the
diapers. She said, Sister, I need your help.

I knew we were not sisters. But it was nice of her to say

245

so, and if what she really wanted was crack, I thought, I would force her to have diapers instead by going with her to the store, which was only one block away, and which stays open until long after midnight.

The street was crispy and our feet made a fine noise stepping together.

So you know Tim? I said.

Who's Tim? she said.

Tim is my neighbor next door, I said. Don't you live next door?

I'm new, she said.

At the store we went together, my neighbor and I, to the diaper aisle. Everyone saw us together in the diaper aisle, looking at the diapers. I felt that in some sense this made me her mother. I'm gonna get some diapers to last a while, my neighbor said, touching a pack of mega-bonus-diapers.

Please don't, I said. I don't have much money. Please get the cheap diapers.

All right, she said. She chose some diapers. These are the cheap diapers, she said.

They were not the cheap diapers but we took them to the register.

At the counter the counter-boy looked at us funny. I did not think anything was so funny. I did not like his funny look.

I need a receipt, my neighbor said.

Do you need a receipt? the counter-boy said to me.

That made me angry. He had heard us ask for a receipt.

Yes, I said, we need a receipt. I thought it was something to do with welfare, that if you were on welfare, you had to have receipts.

My neighbor left me outside the store. She took a cigarette butt from the butt-can. I need a cigarette, she said.

Good night, I said. I went to my house. I sat on my couch and felt alone. By the time my lover rang my doorbell, I knew I had been fooled.

What's with the diapers? my lover said.

Nothing, I said.

She already brought them back, he said.

Well, I said. It's a very crispy night.

I don't like you living on this street, he said. I'll be happy when you live with me, on my street.

The next night I was sitting with my lover. We were watching a movie about basketball. When the bell rang I thought – here she is! But when I looked down from the top-door I saw a man at the bottom that I had not seen before.

I went downstairs. Hi, I said.

Is your boyfriend home? he said.

My lover? I said.

Yes, he said. Is he home?

Yes, I said. I went upstairs. He wants to speak with you, I said.

While my lover went down, I sat on the couch and waited. I heard their voices – like trucks on a highway – I could not hear their words.

My lover came back. What did he say? I said.

He wanted two dollars, my lover said.

Did he want the two dollars for crack? I said.

For milk, my lover corrected. He wanted two dollars for milk.

Oh, I said. Milk-man, I said. Then, Do you know him? I did not understand.

No, my lover said. I do not know him. My lover laid back on the couch. He started the movie about basketball which he had stopped before. They know this house, my lover said, and they know you live in it, and I do not like you living on this street. I'll be happy when you live with me, on my street.

Okay, I said.

Now I do live with my lover on my lover's street. It is a very pretty street, much prettier than my old street, and the snow has begun to collect itself so that we may have a white holiday.

This morning, well noon, that is when we wake up, since we are awake late at night, our doorbell rang. Can you get that? said my lover (who generally likes to answer the door but was naked), I'm naked.

At the door was a man. He was a shaggy man wearing a red wool hat. He looked a lot like the father in *A Time to Kill* – he had eyebrows of wrath and an ivory smile. Got any bottles today? he said.

Sorry, I said. I shut the door.

Who was that? said my lover, pulling on pants.

Bottle-man, I said.

Oh, he said. Bottle-man.

I stood there.

I opened the door. The bottle-man was down the street, wheeling a shopping cart toward the house of our neighbor. Hey! I said.

He turned. Got bottles? He rolled toward me.

I carried two cases of bottles from the kitchen and I put them on the porch. Wait, I told the bottle-man, who stood on the porch with his cart, there's more.

What are you doing? my lover said.

It's Christmas, I said. It's the holiday. I picked up two more cases and carried them out. The bottle-man was waiting on the porch. I was glad to give him so many boxes of bottles.

Happy crack! I said.

He shrugged. Happy crack to you too, he said.

Inside, I was happy, but my lover, no longer naked, was not happy.

You are weird, my lover said.

Was he a crack-man? I said.

No, he said. He's a bottle-man.

Oh, I said.

Now I am often confused. Crack-man, bottle-man, father, neighbor, crack-lady, sister, mother, boyfriend, lover, pretty-street, crack-street, all these distinctions are slick and leave their colors on one another, but I have the idea that one white day soon my God will speak, and then my headphones may save my life.

Fat Ladies Floated in the Sky Like Balloons

AMANDA DAVIS

Fat ladies floated in the sky like balloons.

That was the year we forgot our dreams and woke, bewildered, muttering. It was spring when I noticed them turning in the sky, this way and that, drifting gently on a breeze. They looked lovely from a distance but somehow I knew it was a bad sign. It could mean only one thing: my ex-boyfriend was back in town.

Sure enough, I ran into Fred Luck later that day. I was walking home from grooming the dogs when there he was on a bench by the town square watching the fat women twist against the cloudless sky. You! he yelled and leaped up. He was a man of surprises.

It's been a long time, I replied. I couldn't quite look him in the eyes. I kept thinking don't do it don't do it but somehow I sensed it was only a matter of time. He had eyes like licorice: shining and bitter.

Eloise! Fred called again, though he was only inches away. I've been waiting for you to walk by!

You can't just march back into someone's life, I tried to say, but it came out: Oh, Yes, Well.

We stood for a moment studying each other, each with our motives hidden in our sleeves. Actually mine weren't very well hidden. Fred, when he could take the time to focus on me, had been an incredible lover and I was feeling a little bit lonely.

Fred, I started.

It's Jack now, he said, I changed my name.

Jack Luck? I asked. I was thinking with noodles. I was thinking with duck sauce and white rice.

He nodded. I think I look more like a Jack than a Fred, he told me, and shoved his hands deep into his pockets.

It was true. He did the name Jack justice.

You were bringing up the property value of Fred though, I blushed. Redeeming it, kind of.

Thanks, he said and smiled.

That part was simple. I brought him home when I knew my house would be empty and made dinner. On the way there he told me how wrong he'd been to leave, how much he'd missed me. I knew his words were empty, the empty husks of beetles long wandered off, the shell game I always lost. Still I let him touch me. Gentle now, I said.

He had his problems. Disappearance wasn't the worst of it, nor was the plight of the innocent fat ladies. Fred couldn't control himself. He was what Florence, my godmother, called bad news.

He's a natural disaster and you're trailer city, Florence rasped, then took another drag of her cigarette. He's an itchy rash, a pimple under the skin. He's a toothache and you're just numbing the gum, girlie. You need to pull his mean self out and toss it away.

But I love him, I said in the smallest voice those words could afford.

Oh, girlie, Florence said. That's the worst of it.

When we first met I was more trusting. I had just begun to groom dogs and I thought it sweet when Fred showed up at the shop to meet me. I was so swept along by his sexy ways that I didn't complain when he launched the Apesons' poodle into the highest branches of the sycamore in front of the library or somehow elevated the Hendersons' Affenpinscher and left it running circles in the air above the kennel roof. I thought to myself, he's an unusual guy, soul of an artist, I'll have to smooth some edges is all. Then he impaled the Lorsinskis' cat on a lamppost and dropped a city bus on the Lawsons' Dalmatian.

How the hell did he learn those tricks? Florence had asked me, sucking on a cigarette, curled in smoke.

I don't know, I told her, twirling my hair.

Well, why can't he stop it?

I don't think he knows what he's doing until it's too late, I answered. I was looking out the window of her house at the Meyersons' puppy, romping around in their yard. I don't think he means to, I said, but I wasn't entirely sure about that.

I'm leaving something out. See, the other thing was my laugh. I have a terrible laugh, all my life a wretched, horrible laugh. When I laugh, sounds come out of my throat that violate the rest of the world. My laugh causes injury: it makes people nauseous or crazy. Stop that awful sound, they scream, running from my vicinity with their hands clamped over their ears. It's so bad that the movie theater wouldn't allow me in to see films. That's a violation of my rights, I told them, until they set up private screenings. The projectionist would leave the building and sit on the sidewalk. I went and got him when each reel ran out.

So you can imagine what it meant to meet a man who didn't mind. The first time I laughed around him – we were sitting on my porch when a nervous frantic giggle escaped and I tried to snatch it back with my hand, to stuff it back down my throat – he just tucked a curl behind my ear and whispered, You are so beautiful.

And like that I was putty. It didn't even bother me that the potted plants that had been resting so quietly beside us on the porch were floating near our heads. It didn't even bother me when they smashed to bits during our first kiss. All that mattered was Fred and the way he held me. All that mattered was the idea of watching a movie with someone else.

Now by the time Fred became Jack, I had married a guy named Steve. So of course I brought Jack home to meet him. Steve wasn't his real name – his real name sounded like a kind of sausage – but he'd paid me a lot of money to become his wife and felt Steve made him sound like a naturalized citizen. Though he didn't like my laugh, he'd hired me to be his wife so he wouldn't be deported to the gray, depressive country that spawned him. When Steve learned of Jack it seemed to upset him, though his inner life wasn't always clear to me. We had trouble communicating.

You and me are bloodletting, he said while Jack was in the bathroom.

You and me are bouillabaisse, he tried again. Bakers.

No, I said, flipping the pages of a shiny magazine. I didn't even look up.

Borrowing, he said. Burrowing.

Blowing? I offered. I enjoyed frustrating him.

No! You are not understanding. You and me like tree, he tried.

Bush? I flipped a page.

No!

(Flip, flip.) Brain!

Jack is borrowing wife, he began again, his desperate hands flailing about. Husband forgets husband is forgotten.

I threw down the magazine and rose from the armchair as Jack reentered.

Back later, I said.

See, love was not part of the bargain. I know love never is, etc., etc., but I expected more respect. I'll be your wife, I had told him. Professionally. Like a job, I'd said. You hire me and that's my job: wife. Nothing else.

Right, he'd said, beaming. Wife.

It wasn't until later that I realized how little he understood.

So he didn't like Fred. But everyone liked Fred. It was part of the way of the universe: people met and liked Fred. That was how the world was formed. But not Sausage Steve. The first thing he said when he met Fred was: He is not the good man. He is not the husband for you.

Right, I told him, you hired me. He disappeared. He's just my obscenely perfect ex-boyfriend who has a strange effect on people.

Steve didn't get it. He is the no good, he muttered and glared at Fred.

Jack né Fred was many things, I must agree, but not really a bad person, exactly. I mean he acted irresponsibly, sure, but generally because of a helpful impulse, I thought, not a malicious sensibility.

Still, I felt things in the back of my head, forgotten dreams maybe, fleeting thoughts, the sense that I had a running list of things I was losing, things left behind. When we walked out of the house, I looked at Fred but he had his hands in his pockets staring at the night sky, the fat ladies blocking the stars like black holes, like gasps of breath, like forgotten clouds. I shook my head at the way that I felt, yearning for his touch, the anger I'd been storing hidden somewhere distant. He waited for me to catch up, then he put his arm around my shoulders, kissed my forehead and I followed him home.

In the morning we had breakfast at a diner near the park. I sipped coffee and Fred gnawed a banana muffin. The staff watched us, frightened – they had seen the damage Fred could do. This probably isn't such a great idea, I began in my head, but what I said was, Nice day.

On the radio there was much debate over how to get the fat ladies down from the sky. They waved happily in the daylight but I imagined they must be hungry by now.

But I thought maybe this was the evolution of things, the way the world spun. Maybe this was true for the fat ladies too – that one minute something was an orange and the next it was a peach. And maybe they would drop quietly as they lost weight until they landed here like the rest of us, drawn, haggard, and dreamless, all their glorious roundness gone.

In the Kingdom of the Unabomber

GARY GREENBERG

In 1998, the author, a psychotherapist and occasional college professor, began a correspondence with Theodore J. Kaczynski. Herewith, the results so far.

I

Please Forgive My Intrusion into Your Life

The first time I got a letter from the Unabomber, I had my wife open it.

I was at work, the letter had come to my house, and neither of us wanted to wait to see what Ted Kaczynski, whose out-going mail was by then inspected by the United States Bureau of Prisons, had to say. Sealed in a #10 envelope, the letter was addressed in the careful block capitals that the post office says will guarantee maximum efficiency. He even put his return address, in the same frank print, in just the right spot. No fool, Kaczynski knows that the mails will only work for you if you work with them.

The first letter, which arrived in mid-June of last year, had not come unbidden. Six months earlier, just after he'd pleaded guilty to the Unabomb crimes, I'd written Kaczynski a letter. Although I had paid close attention to his case for nearly three years, from his emergence as a composite sketch demanding space for his manuscript in a national publication to his arrest, incarceration, and abortive trial, my letter wasn't fan mail. Instead, it was a pitch.

Here's how it went:

> *January 24, 1998*
> *Dear Mr Kaczynski:*
>
> *Please forgive my intrusion into your life. I am not sure if this letter will gain a sympathetic reading, or any reading for that matter. But after thinking long and hard about writing it, I'm taking the chance.*
>
> *I would like you to consider allowing me to write a biography of you. I am sure you have had many requests from other people to do this, and for all I know you are already working with someone. Or, for that matter, you may be opposed in principle to the very idea. In the event, however, that neither of these are the case, I hope you'll read on and think about my request.*
>
> *I know nothing of you, of course, except what the news media have decided to tell me, so what I am about to say is no doubt presumptuous — it's just my reading between the lines. It seems to me that you are one of the notable antimodernists of our age. At least since saboteurs hurled their sandals into machines and Luddites rioted in factories, people have deeply (and sometimes violently) objected to the fundamental tenets of the modern world. This protest is not against one or the other work of technology — against, say, nuclear weapons or automobiles — but rather against the worldview that underlies and makes possible the creation of any particular machine or device. And, as many antimodernists have discovered, this worldview does not tolerate radical protest. It must either co-opt it or eradicate its opposition, the latter through*

outright killing or mere discrediting. I believe this is one of the reasons that there has been so much interest in finding a psychiatric diagnosis for you: not, as the various lawyers have claimed, to ensure that you are competent or sane to stand trial, but rather to dismiss your protest as the ravings of a lunatic.

I should acknowledge here that I have firsthand knowledge of this misuse of the mental health profession, as I am a psychologist. My research and writing, however, have always been deeply critical of many of the practices of my profession, particularly insofar as it tends to pathologize what it does not understand or cannot tolerate. I have no wish to understand you as 'schizophrenic' or 'paranoid' or any of the other labels that have been thrown at you. To the contrary, I wish to tell your story partly in order to show how limiting and harmful those labels can be, both for the person who is labeled and for the society which might otherwise benefit from listening to him or her.

I should also mention that I know something of what it is like to try to live by antitechnological principles. Like many of our generation, I spent a number of years in a cabin in the woods with no plumbing or electricity, trying to live off the land. Circumstances forced me out of my refuge, but I will always remember both the difficulty and the joy of life off the grid. I will always remember the suspicion and outright dislike I aroused in people who could not understand what I was doing, and how precious the few who did understand were to me. Without wishing to seem presumptuous, I think I recognize in your story some of my own, and I think I see in your decision to live as you have an integrity that I deeply respect.

I believe your story deserves to be told with a sympathetic voice in a manner that does justice to the deep truth of your principles. I feel certain that I can tell it this way. I am an experienced writer and interviewer, and I would greatly appreciate the chance to use my skills and talents on your behalf.

If you are interested in pursuing this any further, you are welcome to use the enclosed envelope to write me or to call collect if you can arrange for that. Or, if you like, I can come to see you. Whatever you decide, I wish you well, and I hope to hear from you soon.

Regards,

Gary Greenberg

My prospective subject was interested enough in the project to ask, through his lawyer, for more information about me. So, during the spring, I wrote Kaczynski a short autobiography. I told him about my therapy practice and my teaching, even a little about my personal life, and I sent him some of my academic writings – two articles and a book. I heard nothing directly, and in mid-May, 1998, after he'd been sent to the Supermax prison in Florence, Colorado, I sent him a gentle reminder of my existence. His first letter came in response.

Kaczynski couldn't know that he had written this letter on my 41st birthday, but despite myself, I allowed the coincidence to take on some meaning. Midlife had left me wondering about my professional craft, hard-pressed to fulfill therapy's promised miracle – not the offer of quick cures for psychic suffering, but the extension of a hope as American as Plymouth Rock: that with honest hard work, some weeping here and some soul-searching there, anyone can pursue and find happiness. The miracle embedded in this promise is that it keeps alive the possibility of a good life amid the execrable social order that Ted Kaczynski wanted to destroy.

The first letter itself wasn't much: a four-page, single-spaced document, handwritten with pencil. There were no signs of erasures or corrections. The prose didn't so much flow as march steadily from the beginning of an idea to its end, with nary a false logical step in the parade. Above all else, the letter conveyed a calm rationality, a sharp intellect, and a distinct courtliness. Kaczynski had detected my impatience to hear from him and explained, without complaint or self-pity, the restrictions under which he labored, the difficulty in getting money for stamps, the necessity of submitting letters to prison officials, the fact that he did not get my book because, according to some inscrutable prison regulations, he was not allowed hardcover editions. He informed me, out of fairness he said, that he was probably going to write an autobiography, but he allowed that a book by someone else would still be a worthwhile addition to the knowledge about him. He seemed accustomed to thinking of himself as a historic figure.

And then he asked me a question, based on the articles I had sent him: Did I really believe, he wondered, that there was no such thing as objective truth? After all, he said, a nuclear bomb's effects are predictable and deadly regardless of the culture in whose midst it explodes. He wanted to know how my relativism, which he'd detected in my critique of psychiatric practice, could encompass this fact.

I wanted to know why he chose that particular example.

Even more, I wanted to know how the person who had fashioned this note, with its politeness and sensitivity, its levelheaded clarity, its measured expression of frustration – how this person had spent 17 years of his life perfecting a technique for building bombs and delivering them to people he didn't know.

But most of all, I was taken with the queer quiddity of it,

the fact that I was holding in my hands a letter from the Unabomber. I don't have much sense of the allure of the artifact. I've stood in Monticello's preserved rooms, passed in front of the Liberty Bell, trod the ground at Gettysburg, paid due respect to the cause or the person or the event without hearing history speak or feeling the moment. But holding this letter, I glimpsed the engine that drives the history buff, the collector of autographs, the high bidder at auctions of John F. Kennedy's clothing. I wasn't finding my place in the flow of history, in the great unfolding of human events. None of that matters anymore anyway. All that's left is spectacle, and I had something spectacular in my hands: a letter from a man whose name everyone knew. Ted Kaczynski had written me a letter – by hand, no less. He wanted to know what I thought about heady philosophical matters. I felt hooked up, plugged in, reached out and touched. I went out and rented a safe-deposit box.

II

A Letter with Five Footnotes

The second letter I got from Kaczynski came in early July; it was 20 pages long. It was addressed, 'Dear Gary,' and signed, 'Best regards, Ted Kaczynski.' From then on, we were on a first-name basis.

Some of the letter was personal: Kaczynski agreed with me that living in the woods was alienating, but that hadn't bothered him as it had me. Some of it was revealing: he told me that he had long had a recurring nightmare in which he and his cabin were transplanted to an island in the midst of a huge shopping mall. He paid me a compliment, telling me that he thought I was someone with whom it was possible to have a rational conversation. He insulted me, using one of my papers as an example of the way that philosophical writing buried its insights in 'bullshit.' Most of the letter was as dry as a math textbook. It had five footnotes, which ranged from simple amplifications of what he was saying to quibbles with me about my interpretation of early Christian martyrdom. The Unabomber had written me a treatise.

I should explain the occasion for this outpouring. The paper he criticized had nonetheless hit close to home for Kaczynski; it had an indirect but significant bearing on his case. The article was about a curious development in my profession. On a day in 1973, the psychiatric industry had eradicated a disease that had theretofore resisted all attempts at treatment and ruined many lives. After two years of contentious meetings, disrupted conventions, and what one psychiatrist called 'fevered polemical discussion,' the American Psychiatric Association officially deleted homosexuality from its *Diagnostic and Statistical Manual*. The love that dared not speak its name was now safe to discuss with the doctor. Not only was homosexuality no longer an illness, it had never been. It was all just a misunderstanding, and the doctors were very, very sorry.

This change was both good and bad news for the industry. The good news was that it explained why those millions of couch hours had failed to make desire flow in its proper channels. The psychiatrists hadn't lacked skill; they had just tried to use it to fix something that wasn't really broken.

This good news led to better: a new disease called 'ego-dystonic homosexuality.' To the relief of therapists everywhere, gay people still needed professional help – no longer to try to reorient their sexual compass, but now to combat the effects of living in an intolerant society. Homosexuals were suffering not from homosexuality but from internalized oppression. The very doctors who had legitimized the stigma now stood at the ready to help its victims reclaim their dignity and accept what they once sought to eliminate. Of course, no one was going to get their money back, or even credit toward treatment of the new disease. This wasn't penance or community service, but capitalism at its most exuberantly irrational.

The bad news, though, was grim. As one psychiatrist said, 'If groups of people march and raise enough hell, they can change anything in time . . . Will schizophrenia be next?' You can see the problem: all the hellraising in the world won't stop cancer from eating up your insides, but enough marching might relieve psychiatrists of the power to make pathology out of deviant behavior. This would be a disaster for the industry. And even if it didn't materialize, its very possibility was troublesome. The unmistakable hustle of therapists to keep up with the times, to avoid eating the dust of the sexual revolution, revealed psychiatry's darkest secret: that most diagnoses are moral judgments wrapped in medicine's cloak, and that therapists are really clerics disguised as scientists.

My paper was about the industry's response to this bad news, how it had been caught with its pants down but still managed to maintain its professional dignity and protect its franchise on the scientific understanding and treatment of human behavior. It's one of the great public relations coups of the 20th century, and it was of vital interest to Kaczynski because, in his view, if psychiatry had lost its franchise, he might not be in his current position: left to rot in Supermax, where his bed and table are made out of molded concrete and exercise takes place in a kennel.

Instead, he'd be dead, or at least under a death sentence.

To understand why my paper got a 20-page rise out of Kaczynski, you have to know a little Unabomber history.

Kaczynski's lawyers knew a hopeless case when they saw one. There was a warehouse of evidence against him: bomb-related hardware, journal entries lamenting his failures and applauding his triumphs, various eyewitnesses to his whereabouts. Even Hamilton Burger couldn't have booted this one. Worse, the federal government had a new death penalty, and the Unabomber seemed a fitting early target: he'd committed heinous crimes, embarrassed the FBI by eluding them for almost two decades, and seemed entirely unrepentant. To his lawyers, this meant that there was only one possible plan: to find a defense that would minimize their client's chances of getting executed. But to Kaczynski, this was an end that served the lawyers more than their client. And this wasn't fair, as he wrote to attorneys whose support he sought after he had been convicted:

The principle that risk of the death penalty is to be minimized by any means possible . . . is very convenient for attorneys because it relieves them of the obligation to make difficult decisions about values or to think seriously about the situation and the character of the particular client.

The problem, in Kaczynski's view, was that the single course that would save his life was to turn to the psychiatrists and make him out to be a crazed killer. After all, if you're going to kill in cold blood, which is what a juror is asked to order, your victim had better be a villain and not someone to whom you can, as we therapists say, relate. Fortunately for defendants with good lawyers, there is no end to my profession's ability to commonly denominate the most heinous act or the most loathsome personality: Charles Manson had a mother too. Thus is revulsion turned to empathy, and all transgression's horror reduced to the banal recitation of trauma everyone might share.

So the defense rounded up its investigators and psychiatrists to prove that this hermit, with his poor hygiene and inscrutable mailing list, was a nut. They even arranged, in a strange fulfillment of Kaczynski's bad dream, to bring his cabin to Sacramento for the jury to examine.

'You've got to see this cabin to understand the way this man lived,' said Quin Denvir, his lead defense lawyer. What you would see, Denvir explained to the press, is the external manifestation of a demented mind. 'The cabin,' he said, 'symbolizes what had happened to this PhD Berkeley professor and how he came to live. When people think about this case, they think about the cabin.'

Back in the early 80s, when I lived in my little cabin, I knew people who thought I was nuts simply by virtue of my chosen lifestyle. If I had had legal trouble, I don't think I would have wanted my lawyer to be among these doubters. But that was Kaczynski's situation. His lawyers wanted to save him from execution, and to do so they were willing to turn the better part of his adult life into a case study. Kaczynski didn't want his life saved that badly.

He did manage to make the psychiatrists and psychologists they sent his way aware of his opposition. The doctors went in under various covers: to help him with his sleeplessness in the noisy jail, a condition that one doctor called Kaczynski's 'oversensitivity to sound'; to give him tests that might prove that he was neurologically intact; to assist in the preparation of his defense. And they all came back empty-handed: no raving lunacy or other florid symptom to report. Kaczynski refused to talk about his feelings, terminated interviews when clinicians started to talk about his mental illness, and told his lawyers repeatedly that he would not cooperate with their defense.

Kaczynski had opted out of American culture in the late 60s, at just the time that everyone was learning to speak the language of therapy, but it wasn't ignorance that kept him from a crying confession of psychic pain. He knew just what the shrinks were up to – not only in terms of his trial, but in the larger sense: they were trying to tell his story in their language, which was unacceptable to him.

Many clients refuse to accept the therapist's authority, but most are reduced to the squirming prevarication we call 'resistance': missing appointments, changing the subject, disavowals of feeling. But Kaczynski just up and said it. Dr David Foster, who met with him five times in 1997, wrote, 'Early on in our sessions, he looked me in the face and said, "You are the enemy."' For an academic paper I wrote about his psychiatric diagnoses, Kaczynski elaborated on this comment:

[What I was doing at the time] was simply laying on the table in a civil, or even friendly way, as a matter that needed to be taken into account in our discussions, the fact that Foster and I were on opposite sides of the ideological fence, that he as a psychiatrist was an important part of the system I abhorred, and that he was in that sense an enemy.

Now, there's only one thing to do with a person who won't behave like a client: throw the book at him. In Foster's version, Kaczynski's candor reflected 'his paranoia about psychiatrists,' itself part of his 'symptom-based failure to cooperate fully with psychiatric evaluation.' Thus, there are no principles in this world, only symptoms; no politics, only pathology. Of course, Foster, like all the others, knew what everyone else knew: that this man was the Unabomber, so he must be crazy. The fix was in from the beginning. Even his defense lawyers were in on the game, ultimately arguing that Kaczynski's disagreement with them about the mental-defect defense was more evidence of his mental defect. No wonder they all thought he was paranoid – they were out to get him.

Finally, after months of trying to resolve this conflict, after endless motions and countermotions and chambers conferences, even after some highly unusual letters from Kaczynski to Judge Garland Burrell – virtually begging him to relieve him of his lawyers – on January 5, 1998, the day his trial was to begin, Kaczynski stood up and said, 'Your honor, before these proceedings begin, I would like to revisit the issue of my relations with my attorneys. It's very important.' Kaczynski and the lawyers filed back into the judge's chambers, where he once again explained that he could not endure the daily injustice of a portrayal that could not be refuted. And now, he said, he was done with these lawyers. He wanted a new one: Tony Serra, a San Francisco lawyer who had lurked on the margins of the case for 21 months, and who had promised to not use a mental-defect defense.

Serra proved to be unavailable. On January 7, Burrell ruled that Kaczynski's lawyers could introduce mental-status evidence, even against their client's wishes. Later that day, Serra finally surfaced, offering to take over the case, but not for nine more months, a delay that Burrell was unwilling to grant. Here is Kaczynski's account of what happened next, taken from his appeal. It's in the third person; Kaczynski the lawyer referring to Kaczynski the client:

During the night of January 7–8, Kaczynski attempted suicide by strangulation. When he applied the arrangement he had devised for strangling himself, he felt that his sight was growing dark and that he was losing consciousness; but too slowly, so that he feared he might become unconscious yet not die, and might perhaps be left with disabling brain damage. Hence he released the strangulation device, intending to try again with a better arrangement . . . On the morning of January 8, before court opened, Denvir and Clarke [his lawyers] came to see Kaczynski at the holding cell outside the courtroom. Kaczynski said to them in agitated tones, 'Look, I can't take this . . . Isn't there any chance that the judge might still let me represent myself?'

Denvir and Clarke were shaken by Kaczynski's obvious desperation, and they agreed to help him secure his right to self-representation.

But Kaczynski was crazy, or so the psychiatrists said, and a crazy man cannot represent himself. Now, at long last, the Unabomber was going to have to submit to the mental health experts: Judge Burrell refused to rule on the request for self-representation until Kaczynski cooperated with a psychiatric evaluation. Sally Johnson, a psychiatrist who had come to prominence when she determined that John Hinckley was insane, was flown in.

Johnson worked at amphetamine speed. In five days, by her

own report, she read the full Unabomber archive, which by now took a single-spaced page simply to list and included 'the complete set of writings obtained from Mr Kaczynski's cabin in Montana,' reportedly some 20,000 pages long. She interviewed all the lawyers on both sides, his mother, his brother, all but one of the seven experts who had weighed in on his mental status, and the town librarian in Lincoln, Montana. She made a pilgrimage to Kaczynski's cabin in its new home in an airplane-hangar-turned-warehouse in Sacramento. And she met with the defendant himself for 22 hours. Then she wrote a 47-page, single-spaced report that concluded, provisionally, that Kaczynski was a paranoid schizophrenic.

This in itself was nothing new; it had been the conclusion of all the other doctors, but they had had to coax the diagnosis either out of Kaczynski's known history or his current orneriness. They had, for instance, taken the fact that he used his own composted shit to fertilize his garden (a practice not quite so unusual as it sounds; there's even a name for it: humanure) as evidence that he suffered from 'coprophilia,' an unhealthy interest in feces. His hardscrabble, third-world life showed a lack of self-care. And his failure to accept that he was truly deranged was 'anosognosia,' the condition of being too sick to agree with the psychiatrist, a hallmark feature of schizophrenia, and a word to bear in mind the next time you disagree with a psychiatrist. But Johnson needed to do no diagnostic conjuring. In 22 hours, she had taken the measure of the man, gotten a full frontal view of the Unabomber, and she'd concluded that he was really and truly crazy, at least provisionally.

The Diagnostic and Statistical Manual of the American Psychiatric Association, which is a sort of *Audubon Field Guide* to human foibles, is very clear that paranoid schizophrenia is not just one of those diagnoses you send in to the insurance company to ensure reimbursement. It's really not enough simply to think psychiatrists are the enemy, at least not in the current edition. You also have to have delusions, and Johnson thought she had found them, as she wrote toward the end of her report:

In Mr Kaczynski's case, the symptom presentation involves preoccupation with two principle [*sic*] delusional beliefs. A delusion is defined as a false belief based on incorrect inference about external reality that is firmly sustained despite what all most [*sic*] everyone else believes, and despite what constitutes incontrovertible evidence to the contrary . . . [I]t appears that in the middle to late 1960s he experienced the onset of delusional thinking involving being controlled by modern technology. He subsequently developed another strong belief that his dysfunction in life, particularly his inability to establish a relationship with a female, was directly the result of extreme psychological verbal abuse by his parents. These ideas were embraced and embellished, and day-to-day behaviors and observations became incorporated into these ideas, which served to further strengthen Mr Kaczynski's investment in these beliefs.

So here was the final proof that Kaczynski was crazy: he thought technology controlled his life, and he believed that his parents had made mistakes that had made his life miserable.

As delusions go, these are problematic. Technology surely mediates our lives, even if it does not control them outright. And the question of parental abuse is an epistemological black hole. Rarely, if ever, does a therapist get corroboration (or incontrovertible contradiction) of a client's claim that he or she was subjected to bad parenting. Indeed, it is often the case that therapists 'help' their skeptical clients to see that they were abused.

Dr Johnson would have had a partial answer to these objections: it wasn't what Kaczynski believed so much as the tenacity of his belief that was troublesome. Try as she might, she couldn't persuade him of the folly of either of his 'delusions.' 'When challenged on the initial premise [of either belief],' she wrote, 'he appeared perplexed and it was evident that he did not challenge the belief system on his own regardless of existing evidence.' Even worse, 'he does not challenge [his beliefs] in response to new information.'

Johnson promised to give Kaczynski her notes from their interviews but never did. That's too bad, because it would be interesting to see just how this conversation between two people who disagreed on basic premises went. One thing is clear, though: there was no way for Kaczynski to respond (other than agreeing with Dr Johnson that technology wasn't such a bad thing and that his family was functional) that would not reinforce his diagnosis. What the psychiatrist overlooked, however, was that by her logic – in which their disagreement was about not politics, but reality itself – one of them had to be crazy. But it might not have been Kaczynski.

So Kaczynski was found guilty of schizophrenia, but still competent to stand trial, which meant that he was competent to defend himself. But Judge Burrell, whose knickers had been twisted by this mathematician's unassailable logic and dogged insistence on obtaining the protections of the system he hated, played his last card. When he denied Kaczynski's motion to represent himself, Burrell made no use of Johnson's report; he simply ruled that the motion had come too late, even if Kaczynski had repeatedly indicated that he was ready to proceed immediately. He had to go through with his lawyers' defense.

Kaczynski had been bamboozled. Now he had the worst of both worlds: the psychiatric exam he had never wanted, and the certain prospect of hearing its findings reiterated in open court. He felt he had no choice but to plead guilty. Again, from his appeal:

After Judge Burrell's ruling, Kaczynski had to choose one of two alternatives. He had to either accept the plea bargain, or allow Denvir and Clarke to begin immediately their portrayal of him as a grotesque and repellent lunatic. With extreme reluctance, Kaczynski chose the plea bargain.

Five months after he made this choice, when Kaczynski got my paper on the bankruptcy of psychiatric diagnosis, he must have thought that even if I didn't already know all that had happened to him, I would probably understand and believe him when he said he'd been bushwhacked. That might be why he wrote me a 20-page letter in response. There was someone inside the industry who wouldn't think he was crazy simply because he didn't like psychiatry. He must have figured he could use such a person, and he turned out to be right.

III

The Franchiser

So what's a nice guy like me doing with the Unabomber for a pen pal? If, as Kaczynski himself once asked me, I objected to his diagnosis, why not just write a paper for some professional journal and be done with it? Why cultivate a relationship with him? These questions should come up with any journalistic foray into another person's life, but because Kaczynski is a killer, they require answers.

One answer is that we had some common interests: we'd both lived in cabins without modern conveniences, shaken our fists at airplanes, and read Jacques Ellul. That's what I explained in my first letter to Kaczynski. But there was something else we had in common, something I'd left unsaid: both of us wanted to get published.

Is this too glib? Perhaps, but surely there's no author or aspiring author who doesn't recognize Kaczynski's wish to be heard and resonate with its desperation. No over-the-transom prayers or letters to agents or walls plastered with terse rejections. He got what hardly anyone gets, let alone someone who lives in the woods: a virtual power lunch with Katharine Graham and Arthur Sulzberger. It's a comment on many things other than Ted Kaczynski's character that a person goes to such great lengths to achieve such ends.

But more was at work here than a grudging respect, something more personal: he'd run some serious interference for me, clearing an opening at exactly the time I was figuring out how the game was played. Just before his trial began, and before I sent my first letter to Kaczynski, my own book proposal, submitted in the normal way, had been rejected. The book was going to be called either *Is Your Bathroom Breeding Drug Users?* or *Oxygen was My Gateway Drug.* My plan was to report on the cultural side of the drug war; all those 'Just Say No' posters, D.A.R.E. classrooms, and drug-free workplace initiatives deployed in the battle to convince the citizenry that it's in their best interests to stay off drugs other than nicotine, caffeine, alcohol, and Prozac. I was going to go behind enemy lines, as it were, talk about how this war machine looked to one of its targets. A major publishing house agreed to consider it.

My agent delivered the news. 'They think it's a really good idea. But the first thing someone is going to do in a bookstore is look at the cover and say, "Who is this guy? Why should I listen to him?" Gary, You just don't have a name.'

'But that's the point,' I said. 'The book is about what happens when a guy no one knows starts to poke around in big things. It's an Everyman thing. Think,' I said, imagining how a real writer would pitch it, 'Michael Moore on drugs.' I winced at the inadvertent (and unappealing) double entendre, and decided to tack.

'Well, what do I do to get a name?'

'Just get an article published in *Rolling Stone* or somewhere like that. The *Wall Street Journal*, *Playboy* – anywhere really. Except *High Times*. Don't get published in *High Times*.'

The funny thing is that she was serious. I hung up. And I swear this really happened: the words came to my mouth. 'You want a name?' I said to the phone. 'How about Ted Kaczynski?'

Stanley Elkin, who never quite got himself a name, wrote a novel called *The Franchiser* about a man who gains a strange inheritance from his wealthy godfather. He is given the right to borrow money at the prime rate in perpetuity. This lucky legatee, Ben Flesh by name, uses the leverage to buy franchises: Burger Kings, Travel Inns, Texaco service stations, all the roadside's hideous familiarity. He spends his days driving from one franchise to another, a man with nothing but names, none of which is his own and all of which he owns. It's a Great American Novel.

Elkin recognized the peculiar genius of franchising: you don't buy anything but a name, and then you are simultaneously made someone and freed from the burdens of actually being anyone. So when Michael Jordan, announcing his retirement, referred to himself as 'Michael Jordan,' or when Bob Dole, running for President, referred to himself as 'Bob Dole,' it wasn't some kind of identity problem or rhetorical affectation; it was the exercise of the franchisee's greatest privilege: to trumpet a name that means so much to so many.

So I was going to try to get a name like Elkin's franchiser did: by going out into the marketplace and procuring one, which in this case meant convincing the owner to sell it.

As names go, Ted Kaczynski was not without its burdens. This man had, after all, killed people in a most terrifying way, people who were doing nothing more than sitting down to open their mail. Surely I could find a name with less opprobrium attached.

But I recognized something familiar in Kaczynski's antimodern, antitechnology politics. In his pamphleteer style, he had written about things I'd studied and written about in my academic career: notably, that technology wasn't simply an assemblage of tools that awaited our use, wise or foolish. Rather, technology was a way of being in the world, one with some very peculiar psychological characteristics and social consequences. For, as various philosophers and novelists had been pointing out for some 200 years, it seemed to leave us fully aware of, but unable to do anything about, the way our devices alienated us from each other and the natural world, and, more to the point, threatened great peril.

The problem, in Kaczynski's view, was that technology had a life of its own, because technical progress had trumped all other possible ends to which humanity might be put. He made the point this way in 'Industrial Society and Its Future,' better known as the Unabomber Manifesto.

The system does not and cannot exist to satisfy human needs. Instead, it is human behaviour that has to be modified to fit the needs of the system. This has nothing to do with the political or social ideology that may pretend to guide the technological system. It is the fault of technology, because the system is guided not by ideology but by technical necessity. Of course the system does satisfy many human needs, but generally speaking it does this only to the extent that it is to the advantage of the system to do it. It is the needs of the system that are paramount, not those of the human being.

The worst of it, according to the Manifesto, was that technology didn't take away our freedom forcibly, in a manner that would have us up in arms like the villagers in *Frankenstein*. Rather, enchanted by its near-magic powers, we had become collaborators in our own enslavement:

When skilled workers are put out of a job by technical advances and have to undergo 'retraining,' no one asks whether it is humiliating for them to be pushed around in this way. It is simply taken for granted that everyone must bow to technical necessity and for good reason: if human needs were put before technical necessity there would be economic problems, unemployment, shortages or worse. The concept of 'mental health' in our society is defined largely by the extent to which an individual behaves in accord with the needs of the system and does so without showing signs of stress.

None of this was original to Kaczynski, although it had probably never appeared in the *Washington Post* before. The

Industrial Revolution has always had its naysayers, artists and philosophers and social theorists who question what it is doing to us. Crucial among these questions, at least for a psychologist, is how we manage to be shaped by technology without either knowing it or being able to do anything about it. William Blake, an early antimodernist, captured this process with his image of 'mind-forg'd manacles,' shackles that are so compelling and comfortable that they become undetectable, and show up only obliquely, as symptom. That's the job of the therapist: to come along and reveal to a person the way they are, without knowing it, imprisoned by their own unacknowledged history. But some cases of self-imprisonment are harder to understand and point out than others. And the one that Kaczynski noted is perhaps the hardest of all. Technology not only helps us to accomplish things, with the occasional failure or accident or frustration; it also constructs us as the kind of people who are hard-pressed to be sufficiently critical of technology.

Perhaps the mental health industry, as Kaczynski implied, is inescapably another of the sorcerer's apprentices. That's one way to explain the difficulty of understanding, at least in psychological terms, this central mystery of technology, the way it seems to keep us blind to itself. But the fact is that no one really understands how we can listen to another report about the greenhouse effect even as we drive our cars, festooned with 'Save The Earth' bumper stickers, to fetch a loaf of bread. No one really knows how we sustain this level of what psychologists call cognitive dissonance or why we barely perceive it. Neither can anyone explain why we are not wracked by guilt and anxiety or at least repelled by our own bad faith. And because we (psychologists, that is) don't really understand these things, we can't do anything about them, even if we want to. Such has always been the problem with thoroughgoing indictments of modernity: they're long on critique and short on solution.

The Manifesto's proposed therapy parted ways with this aspect of antimodernism:

The only way out is to dispense with the industrial-technological system altogether. This implies revolution, not necessarily an armed uprising, but certainly a radical and fundamental change in the nature of society.

And it offered a very loose treatment plan:

'It would be better to dump the whole stinking system and take the consequences.'

My philosophical kinship with Kaczynski – in which I don't think I was by any means alone; as Robert Wright wrote in *Time*, 'There's a little bit of the Unabomber in most of us' – stopped short of this let-the-chips-fall confidence. I like the fact that I don't have to worry about getting smallpox, and I'm not quite willing to say that the whole system ought to be jettisoned, or the citizenry rallied to arms by random violence, as Kaczynski evidently wanted.

But the fact that he was a killer perhaps only increased my interest. Was it possible that Kaczynski's moral depravity was understandable as the snapping of a weak link in a chain pulled too tight? Was it possible that his terrorism was only the leading edge of a series of even more desperate acts to come as that cognitive dissonance came to be less and less tolerable? That his very character seemed to bear the imprint of large social and historical forces, that he seemed to know what those forces were, and that he was very, very famous –

all this made the franchise irresistible, despite my squeam-ishness.

But there was a problem even beyond the obvious ethical one: in the public eye, Kaczynski had only been a political figure for a blink. Quickly, as William Glaberson of *The New York Times* reported, he'd been transformed into a pathetic lunatic.

It seems hard to believe now, but it wasn't very long ago that the Unabomber seemed like a serious person. To read about him in many newspaper and magazine accounts was to hear of a mysterious philosopher: dangerous yet compelling, brilliant, intriguing. Yes, he was troubled, even evil – but he was a man of ideas.

Now he's just a nut. Or, perhaps worse, a fraud.

Glaberson reviewed 'scores' of articles and TV news accounts to chronicle this shift, singling out the *Washington Post* and the *Los Angeles Times* (and leaving out his own paper, which had undoubtedly known all along that the guy was a sandwich short of the whole picnic) for their about-faces. He got pro-fessional counterculturist Todd Gitlin to explain the Kaczynski jokes: In many of the jokes, the Unabomber seems 'pathetic more than evil,' said Professor Gitlin.

It may be that the humor comes from a deep fear of the harm that a disturbed criminal can do. 'There is something that is very difficult for society to confront, and that is that crazy people have the means to do damage,' Professor Gitlin said. 'If you think of him as a joke, then you don't have to confront that: he has become shtick.'

Environmental terrorist to madman-bomber to punchline: the metamorphosis is so complete that Gitlin forgot that

Kaczynski started out as something even more scary than a disturbed criminal.

Celebrity culture doesn't just hand out names for free. Kaczynski, having gotten famous (and published) by unsanctioned means, had to pay the price. He couldn't be forgotten, and he certainly couldn't be bought out of his beliefs. So he had to be turned into kitsch. And, to make things worse, his fashioning as a pop-culture trinket was largely brought about by his own lawyers, at least according to Glaberson:

The shift in public image which began with Mr Kaczynski's arrest for carrying out an 18-year campaign of bombings that killed 3 and injured 28, accelerated after his lawyers said he was a delusional paranoid schizophrenic who believes people have electrodes implanted in their brains.

To keep Kaczynski safe for democracy, his license to seriousness had to be revoked. If he's crazy, after all, then he can be famous without being meaningful, his unsettling denunciation of modern technology reduced to the entertainment of a lunatic's raving.

And who, besides the lawyers, was responsible for this outcome, this down-the-rabbit-hole reversal of logic whereby a rational, if contentious, belief — that there's something wrong with the way technology has colonized our landscapes, both interior and exterior — becomes the mark of insanity? Therapists, of course; the people trusted, for no particularly good reason, with the authority to decide who is a genuine apostate and who is just plain nuts, whom we should listen to and whom we can dismiss. The first person who might have predicted this outcome was Kaczynski himself, who worried a lot more about therapists' inability to distinguish pathology from dissent than about their implanting electrodes in his brain. The culture indulged his anxiety, and its agents were my own colleagues.

In the end, I'd just as soon forgo franchising and stick with my own name. But Ted Kaczynski – the antimodernist, cabin-dwelling, diagnostically labeled, famous murderer/writer with a cause – that name was the next best thing, a name I could use without too much misgiving at the fact that I was a user.

Does this mean that I am guilty of exploitation with intent? In trying to explain how his identity was constructed by the mass media, Kaczynski and I corresponded about Janet Malcolm's famous passage in *The Journalist and the Murderer*: 'Every journalist who is not too stupid or too full of himself to notice what is going on knows that what he does is morally indefensible.' Malcolm, who has turned self-reflection into a writing style that defies Zeno's paradox, is getting at the way that all journalists must be franchise-seekers and thus must use others for their own gain. Some writers, like Malcolm, manage to franchise themselves; others get their name recognition from the journals they write for; but the rest of us don't have these luxuries. The writer must be determined in his attempt to get the other to give him a name, particularly when his subject is not for sale.

I never hid my ambition from Kaczynski, never claimed that I was in it solely for the intellectual stimulation or to make the world a better place. As our correspondence unfolded in August and September, he often asked me why I was so interested in him and his case. So I wrote to him about my ambition and my misgivings about my ambition:

My wanting to write about you . . . is, after all, an act of appropriation; I am seeking to take something from you and weave it into something of mine . . . Much as I might not want to, I must admit to being among those who want to get in on the ground floor with you. I have certain aspirations as a writer and a commentator on modern mental health practice, and getting to know you serves them. I don't know how this makes you feel (although I'd be glad to hear), but it would be disingenuous of me to claim this was not the case. All I can do is try very hard to make sure that my aspirations do not lead me to exploit or otherwise hurt you . . .

I don't know if I would have been so honest had I not figured Kaczynski for someone exquisitely sensitive to being manipulated. Here is the truth of what Malcolm says. It is impossible even for me – the agent of these words and acts – to say if my honesty was in service of the Right and the Good, or if it was just another sales pitch. In fact, it's hard to say if this kind of confession without absolution is cheap or noble or just superstitious: if I'm only frank enough about my sins, then I can continue to get away with them.

That's why later on, when another of Kaczynski's associates called me a fibber, I didn't object. Somehow, I thought he had a point.

But I'm not sure that honesty, even for the best reasons, is a good moral defense. I mean, there I was worrying about how it made the Unabomber feel that I might be exploiting him, confessing my wish to appropriate his story to a man who had appropriated the very lives of other people. Either I'm casting scruples before swine or turning the truth into a shill.

In the end, it's hard to know if the wish to be heard is about the message more than being the famous messenger.

We know ourselves too well to parse motive. Honesty just isn't up to the job.

IV

A Brief History of the US Postal Service

Or maybe motive is simple to understand; as simple as an explosion.

Terrorism, after all, is about finding the fulcrum. The terrorist takes a little powder and salt and places it in the best possible proximity to the place where things pivot, thus turning his marginality to Archimedean advantage. Leverage is a form of laziness, really.

The postal service was Kaczynski's ultimate and best fulcrum. It wasn't enough to leave bombs in parking lots and university labs, as he had in the early stages of his terror campaign. Even when a Sacramento businessman, apparently clearing away a bomb disguised as a road hazard to spare someone else a flat tire, was killed, it didn't, perhaps, attract a concerted enough focus. This may be because altruism is not a critical pivot point of our society. That someone got killed when he stopped minding his own business might inspire as much contempt for him as fear for ourselves.

But the postal service, that's something else entirely. It's the most primitive and venerable of the ligatures that hold us together. The engineers of our Republic were so convinced of the importance of a trustworthy post to a functioning and cohesive society that they made its establishment an early order of business. The Continental Congress, in a symbolic shot across Britain's bow, appointed Benjamin Franklin to wrest the delivery of mail from the Redcoats in 1775. The Articles of Confederation put aside their fear of central government long enough to establish a national post office as a power superseding state control. And the Marshall Court's famous implied powers doctrine determined that a post office was essential to Congress's ability to execute its Constitutional duties. Some people even think the post office was what made it possible to keep such far-flung territories as California on board with the rest of the Republic.

No doubt this history, like most history, is far from the minds of millions of Americans opening their day's mail. And that's the point. No one wants to wonder if the next package is a bomb. All the protection implied in those ominous signs about tampering with the mail, in the inviolability of the envelope's seal, is evidence that Kaczynski indeed had found a pivot close to the heart of things.

The postal service was, in any event, a fitting way to communicate with a man who eschewed and hated modern technology, and who wrote very good letters to boot. I could communicate with all the other important people in my life face to face, or with the quick ease of email or telephone. But it took us 18 days, at a minimum, to accomplish one exchange of letters. An express mail letter could take as many as seven days to get from my post office to his cell. Much of the delay was easy to account for: letters had to be read going in and out, presumably to be certain that he and I weren't conspiring to commit mayhem. (Indeed, I often wondered what the readers made of our letters, which discussed everything; I think of them as the silent witnesses to our relationship.) But I always thought it was possible that the deliberate pace of our exchanges was the post office's means of revenge.

If that's true, then it's just more evidence that Kaczynski found the right fulcrum. This discovery, of course, is the terrorist's best hope. But, you may rightly wonder, what did he want to do with his leverage? David Gelernter, whom the Unabomber maimed, has written of his belief that Kaczynski was just trying to find a way to get his name in lights the easy way. I think Gelernter's at least half right. I don't believe that Kaczynski really wanted to get famous or rich. But I do think he wanted badly to be heard, not only because he wanted to point out the disaster of what he called industrial society but because he knew that it was in the nature of that society to drown out a voice like his own. He knew he had no chance of having a voice through the conventional means, so he set out to cheat.

So there's your motive. Kaczynski had found a fulcrum. And he was going to be my lever.

V

The Mark of Zorro

But what about the rest of the letters? a reader must be asking at this point. My answer is, I'm getting there.

I'm not trying to be coy. It's just that the letters tell a story, but without their context, they are only pure commodity. I never said it straight out, but I'm sure I implied to Kaczynski that I wouldn't be so baldly exploitative, just as I'm sure I implied that I wouldn't quote from them without his permission. That's why, even though lawyers tell me I could make a case to do so, I've refrained; not only because, as one magazine editor put it to me, 'He doesn't have much better to do than file lawsuits from prison,' but because I have to live with myself.

Fairness, though, demands and allows at least some description. There are 27 letters, a stack one inch thick. They date from June 9, 1998, to June 1, 1999. Twenty of them came between August 11 and December 11 of 1998. They're on lined, usually white but occasionally yellow paper, mostly written in pen. Kaczynski's evenly spaced block letters are neat and unadorned. His left margin is ruler-straight, his right taken to the edge of the page unless that would disrupt the orderly rhythm of his print. Perhaps Kaczynski's penmanship is his attempt to mimic his impounded typewriter, the one on which he wrote the Manifesto. Maybe he misses it.

Kaczynski's grammar and syntax are as precise as his handwriting. His carefully unbroken infinitives and faithfully maintained parallel structures read like examples from Strunk and White. I imagine sometimes a schoolboy's pride in following the rules, his relish of a job well done, lurking in all this compliance; Kaczynski's rebelliousness, his love of the wild, stops here.

In his letters, Kaczynski is sometimes pedantic and other times argumentative. But leavening them throughout, in addition to his unfailing politeness and moderation of tone, is a sense of humor that stops just short of wise-ass. In this, he reminds me of a very smart adolescent boy whose sharp intellect and way with words can, if only momentarily, put his insecurity out of mind. In a word, Kaczynski's letters are jaunty, a quality that I don't have to quote in order to show.

I just have to tell you that when he signs his name, he often underlines it with a scrawled 'Z' that looks, for all the world, like the mark of Zorro.

VI

'He Probably Never Felt a Thing'

One last word on motive. The problem that grabbed my attention went way beyond Kaczynski's image. The real opportunity here, the one that made the franchise seem valuable to me, was to write about the way all things Unabomber had been fashioned. Kaczynski hadn't thrown a wrench into the machinery of mass culture so much as he had kicked it into high gear.

Take, for instance, the story of Hugh Scrutton, the man killed by a bomb Kaczynski left in a parking lot in Sacramento in December 1985. Here's how the Government Sentencing Memorandum describes the victim:

Friends recall Hugh as a man who embraced life, a gentle man with a sense of humor who had traveled around the world, climbed mountains, and studied languages. He cared about politics, was 'fair and kind' in business, and was remembered as 'straightforward, honest, and sincere.' He left behind his mother, sister, family members, a girlfriend who loved him dearly, and a circle of friends and colleagues who respected and cared for him.

And here's Kaczynski's account of the killing, decoded by the Government and presented in the same memorandum:

Experiment 97. Dec. 11, 1985. I planted a bomb disguised to look like a scrap of lumber behind Rentech Computer Store in Sacramento. According to the San Francisco Examiner, Dec. 20, the 'operator' (owner? manager?) of the store was killed, 'blown to bits,' on Dec. 12. Excellent. Humane way to eliminate somebody. He probably never felt a thing. 25,000 reward offered. Rather flattering.

The contrast couldn't be clearer. One man – chortling to himself in his ramshackle cabin – exults over having obliterated another – an honest, hardworking man who was performing what the Sentencing Memorandum called a 'simple act of courtesy, trying to remove what looked like a potential hazard to others.' It's effective rhetoric: no one can read this account and not be moved or think that the killer deserves to lose the same rights he stole from the victim.

But here's an interesting thing, one that tells us that more is at stake here than simple justice: The 'act of courtesy' by which the Government said Scrutton was killed seems to be a fiction, one of those tales that gains its truth by some combination of plausibility and repetition, that takes hold because the cultural climate is just right for it. It's a little piece of mythic filigree that was added to the story slowly and imperceptibly over the 13 years between the murder and Kaczynski's sentencing.

Scrutton's violent and untimely end is awful enough, so awful, one might say, that it doesn't matter if the Good Samaritan story isn't precisely true. But, by the same token, one might also reasonably wonder why and how the embellishment came about in the first place.

At first, the simple horror of the death could be conveyed in a workmanlike account like the *Sacramento Bee*'s:

A Sacramento businessman was killed Wednesday when a bomb that had been left behind his store blew up in his face, authorities said.

The blast shortly after noon mortally wounded Hugh Campbell Scrutton, 38, owner of RenTech Computer Rentals in the Century Plaza shopping center . . .

The device exploded just moments after Scrutton left his store through the back door and headed for the parking lot, according to reports. The blast blew Scrutton about 10 feet.

The first person to arrive at the scene said Scrutton cried out, 'Oh my God! Help me!'

Scrutton, of Carmichael, was pronounced dead at 12:34 p.m. at University Medical Center. He reportedly took the full force of the blast in his chest. There were no known witnesses.

Investigators placed the time of the blast at 12:04 p.m. They said Scrutton was on his way to the parking lot when, they believe, he spotted an object, which may not have been identifiable as a bomb.

[Sgt. Roger] Dickson said it appeared that Scrutton, who had only keys in one hand and a book in the other, may have leaned over to examine or move the object when it exploded. 'The injuries were consistent with that kind of movement.'

Eight days later, the *Bee* put a little more face on Scrutton.

'Mr Scrutton was an exemplary citizen with an unblemished character. I am certain that he was not a specific victim of the bomber,' said Lt. Ray Biondi, head of the Sacramento County Sheriff's Department homicide bureau. 'Anyone who happened by the business could well have been the victim.'

Three months later, Scrutton was still on Sacramento's mind – now as the victim of an unsolved crime. And, the *Bee* reported, he was still an exemplar.

'Hugh was the best boss I ever had,' said a RenTech employee, who asked that his name not be printed. 'He was an honest, kind person. And that really makes it harder, because it's such a shame when someone that nice is taken from you.'

So far, the mythmaking is gentle and slow and almost invisible: a good and law-abiding man had gotten blown to pieces in a parking lot. Even unadorned, it shows us that the terrorist had found his pivot: the dead man could have been you or me.

By 1994, however, it began to seem that Scrutton's death was one in a series of bombings carried out by someone *Playboy* called 'The Scariest Criminal in America.' And suddenly, Scrutton had a motive:

It is five minutes before noon on December 11, 1985. Hugh Scrutton, 38 years old and single, opens the back door of his computer rental store in Sacramento and steps out into a bright day, where his death waits just a few feet away in a crumpled paper bag. Sunlight glints off the chrome of cars and pickups parked in the big asphalt lot that opens to the west. A 15-mile-per-hour wind blows south off the eastern hip of California's Coastal Range and rattles the bag. Scrutton steps past it, then turns.

There are two Dumpsters right by the door, he thinks. Why do people do this? Jesus, just drop the damn thing in.

Scrutton bends down and reaches for the bag with his right hand. There is no time to consider what happens next.

It's hard to understand how a *Playboy* fact-checker could fail to question a reporter's claim to know Scrutton's thoughts at the moment of his death. But the flourish of altruism, first spotted here, fits in, certainly better than if *Playboy* had had Scrutton seized by a need to keep his parking lot clean or a hope that the bag contained cash. Scrutton isn't quite yet the Good Samaritan, but he is good enough to hate litter. He may be better than you or me.

The embellishment was soon an integral part of Scrutton's story. The month after the *Playboy* article appeared, Thomas Mosser, a New Jersey advertising executive, was killed by a bomb in his home. Mosser's death was almost immediately identified as another in the series, and *Newsday* reviewed the earlier victims, including Scrutton.

Hugh Campbell Scrutton walked out the back door of his RenTech computer rental store. He bent down to clear what looked like clutter, about two feet from the door.

Sgt. Dickson's 1985 speculation has now become a fact, even for the paper that initially reported it as a theory: 'Scrutton . . . bent to pick up what appeared to be a pile of litter,' the *Bee* reported in November, 1997. He didn't just trip on or idly kick the bomb. He had a motive, one that, six months later, became part of the United States Government's official story about Hugh Scrutton.

Robert Graysmith's true-crime book, *Unabomber: A Desire to Kill*, gives us this version of the Good Samaritan story:

On December 11, 1985, only two weeks before Christmas, Scrutton got up from his desk and made ready for a lunchtime appointment

. . . He opened the rear door of his store and looked out upon a windswept parking lot in the strip mall and pulled up his collar. Near a Dumpster he saw a block of wood about four inches high and a foot long. There were sharp nails protruding from the block, a road hazard or, even worse, a real danger to the trash men or the transient who occasionally came by to pick through the Dumpsters. He bent over to move it. It was heavy. Lead weights had been inserted in the lower two inches of the block.

Graysmith's rhetorical economy here is remarkable, each image used for all it is worth and then some. Bums and trash men in need of the protection of a hardworking businessman, an inhospitable parking lot, a lead-heavy road hazard (not just trash, but dangerous and inconvenient trash), the now-famous wind, and, serendipity for the storyteller, Christmas. Graysmith hardly needs to take up residence in Scrutton's blasted life to venture this explanation. He just needs to know his audience.

Decorated as a Good Samaritan, the innocent but hapless bystander takes on the glow of decent people's highest aspirations. It's not enough to vilify the bomber simply for murdering someone or to appeal to the usual explanations – passion or dementia, revenge or hatred – to account for Scrutton's death. Because these are political crimes. The Unabomber was a subversive, in the most elemental sense of the word. He wanted to turn things upside down. What kept Industrial Society going, in his view, was a belief in technology that amounted to a dangerous delusion. And he wanted to disabuse the rest of us of our illusion by blowing up whichever you or me kicked or tripped on or tried to steal or safely discard the parking-lot bomb. Not because he was crazy or randomly depraved, but because he believed something that was at least coherent.

And that's why Scrutton's story had to be adorned, why he couldn't be left as the victim of random cruelty. At stake, after all, is this central problem of modern life: that we pursue and sometimes achieve happiness with such blithe disregard for consequence. The filigree tells us just what terrible kind of monster Kaczynski is: the kind that would kill an altruist.

VII

The Plea Bargain

But if Kaczynski was so bad, then why was his plea bargain – which, after all, ensured that he would not be put to death – met with such relief? Why was George Will left to weigh in virtually alone with his thin-lipped outrage at a society too namby-pamby to strap a convicted murderer to a gurney and shoot him up with lethal drugs?

The editorial pages, which from coast to coast declared justice the victor, had their own explanation, perhaps best summed up by the *Los Angeles Times*.

With Kaczynski's guilty plea, the victims, the nation and federal prosecutors should gain some satisfaction. His admission that he committed these horrific crimes should bring a measure of solace to the Unabomber's surviving victims and the families of victims. His incarceration . . . will keep him safely locked away for life. Moreover, federal prosecutors and taxpayers save the millions of dollars a Sacramento trial and, later, a federal trial . . . would have cost.

In management-consultant parlance, it was a win-win deal. The defense lawyers had saved their client's life, despite over-whelming evidence that he had murdered with malicious intent. The prosecution had avoided uncomfortable questions about the FBI crime lab's work in the case and the legality of the search of Kaczynski's cabin. David Kaczynski, the Unabomber's brother, who had turned him in only after the Government assured him they would not seek the death penalty, had been spared the mark of Cain.

But, as with Scrutton's altruism, there's more to this story, something first made clear by William Finnegan, reporter for the *New Yorker* and author of the most perspicuous account of the trial's abrupt end. Behind the Kaczynski trial, he said, lurked the O.J. trial. In his view, the most relieved party was the presiding judge, Garland Burrell, who had sidestepped the shit that his colleague Lance Ito was still scraping off his shoes. The ill-fitting glove, the lying detective with an interest in screenplays, the race card, the strange coincidence of a dog and a houseboy both named Kato – these icons of humiliated justice would be denied their Unabomber equivalents.

The *Sacramento Bee*, the hometown paper, recognized this motive. The *Bee*, presumably read by people close to the victims (not to mention the disappointed restaurateurs and hoteliers, the street vendors and cab drivers who had watched the O.J. trials and anticipated the arrival of the medicine show to their Main Street), had to explain the whimpering ending with something less abstract than justice. After reciting all the winners and remarking that closure had been achieved, the *Bee* drew a bead on another thought:

In addition, this result avoids the spectacle of having the government prosecute an obviously deranged defendant or – worse yet – watching him meander through reality attempting to defend himself.

Although judged competent to stand trial, it has become increasingly evident that Kaczynski is greatly disturbed. His behavior, the contentions of his lawyers and the diagnosis of a respected government psychiatrist have made that clear. No good would be served by the circus that his trial could so easily have become, that could only have brought disrepute on the process.

The New York Times also noted that 'Mr Kaczynski's mental illness threatened to disrupt the progress of any trial,' turning it into what the *New York Post* worried could only be a 'distasteful spectacle.' Even Butch Gehring, described by the *San Francisco Chronicle* as 'the closest thing Kaczynski had to a friend in Lincoln, Montana,' had '"worried that [Kaczynski] was going to turn this into a weird sideshow, and that wouldn't have been good for anyone."' The Unabomber trial had packed its tents and gone, and the citizenry was safe from its freaks and barkers, and, most of all, its deranged ringmaster.

Listening to these protests over the degradation of public discourse and of the otherwise reputable justice system, you have to wonder whose satellite dishes those were outside Ito's courtroom, who wrote all those front-page headlines, who dispatched an army of America's reporters to broadcast each evening's lead live from Los Angeles in the first place. Did the unanimous consent to the Kaczynski verdict signal the newsies' own shame at what had just unfolded? Or were they simply relieved that temptation too great to pass up – a cold-blooded murderer meandering his way through reality just can't be bad for ratings – had been removed from their reach?

Of course, it's also possible that the production values of this spectacle were all wrong. The O.J. trial had so many things going for it: a well-dressed celebrity defendant, colorful lawyers, a media-friendly judge, the Hollywood backdrop. All the players seemed to know their parts. And the 'deep cultural issues' reiterated as the excuse for carpet-bombing America with O.J. news – domestic violence, the cost of a good legal defense, racism – were perfect for a viewership desperately in need of reassurance that all these hours of watching and talking and reading about it were something more than shallow self-indulgence. These themes could be endlessly indulged without anything important ever getting said or anyone important ever changing anything.

But Kaczynski took control of his own spectacle, made life impossible for the scriptwriters. Even after he was put in jail, he eluded capture by headline and soundbite. Every time the posse caught up with him, he beat it cross-country and left a cold trail. Was he the pedantic pamphleteer? The Last Honest Man, holding out for a world safe for spotted owls and self-reliance? The supremely confident terrorist? The brilliant but troubled recluse? The paranoid schizophrenic who had judges and lawyers (and reporters) chasing their own tails? One and a half years after his arrest, they still didn't have him figured out.

Kaczynski's ability to keep everyone guessing should not have come as a surprise. He was, after all, an expert at finding the fulcrum, measuring the exact length of the lever necessary to get the job done. He'd gotten America's newspapers of record – papers that are generally very clear about what and whom they publish – to print, at their own expense, a 35,000-word manuscript that systematically denounced everything they stood for. And if the events leading up to the plea bargain were any indication, this prank was small potatoes compared with the havoc this man could wreak if he got the whole apparatus of spectacle under his control. No wonder they were relieved.

VIII

In Which the Author Discovers That the Unabomber Is a Complicated Man

July and early August brought more letters. They took a surprising and unsettling turn toward the personal, at least insofar as we seemed to be searching for common ground.

This wasn't all that hard to find. Partly that was because certain subjects were off-limits, notably anything to do with the Unabomber crimes. Kaczynski had made it clear from the beginning that he wasn't going to put anything in writing that affirmed his guilt, as all he had really done at his plea bargain was to concede that the Government was probably going to win its case. He needed to keep his options open for a possible appeal.

So we discussed our mutual interests – back-to-the-land living, the politics of psychiatry, books. Kaczynski asked me to send him a book, *Ecoterror*, by Ron Arnold, free marketeer. The book linked the Unabomber and Earth First! terrorism to Al Gore's wonky environmentalism, arguing that all this concern with spotted owls and old-growth redwoods was just cover for people too faithless to place their fate (and that of the earth) in the care of the 'invisible hand.' I thought the book might make Kaczynski angry, and I told him so (wondering what an angry Kaczynski would be like in writing), but he surprised me by saying that he liked it quite a bit, because it polarized issues, and without polarization, revolutionary change just can't happen. This had been one of the Unabomber Manifesto's first points: that liberal politics were bound to fail to reform anything because Leftists were too busy being nice. Kaczynski liked the trenchant tone of Arnold's argument: he recognized him as a fellow polemicist.

Kaczynski's letters were dense, carefully argued, and full of promise. He stopped short of saying he'd cooperate with me in writing his biography, but he was clearly willing to discuss the matter. Even more promising, he had told me I could come to visit him, although, as I found out in early August, he was currently unable to get his visitor's list approved by the prison.

I spent a good part of the summer getting to know the Unabomber. I was trying to convince him that I was a worthy writer and interlocutor, someone he'd be wise to trust his life story to. But I was also interested in a way I had not anticipated: Kaczynski's thinking was careful and calm and deep, and his material ranged from Russian history to Hobbes's *Leviathan* to Desmond Morris. He pulled out obscure facts from his mental archive – telling me once, for instance, that he didn't bathe very often when he lived in Montana, but that bathing wasn't all it was cracked up to be, and in fact there was a law on the books in Indiana (he thought) that made it a crime to bathe in the winter, which Kaczynski thought meant that pneumonia was more of a problem than body odor. (He often apologized if he couldn't cite sources, but I never thought he was making this stuff up.)

Although I resisted treating Kaczynski as a case study, I couldn't help but make some clinical observations about him. I was discovering that he was just as complicated and full of self-contradiction as the rest of us. While he tried to live a life of complete consistency between his beliefs and his actions, in some ways he embodied the biggest opposition of all. He was at once a mathematician, a man of science, entirely convinced of reason's superordinance as a means of negotiating the world, and at the same time a savage critic of rationality's greatest achievement: technology. It's impossible to divorce Descartes's ego cogitating its way to certainty from Henry Ford's Model T slipping down the conveyor belt – both grow from the desire to hold the world firmly in our grasp, to make it yield to us. Most of us see the resulting, nest-fouling problem. Kaczynski saw it too, but he seemed unable to turn this infinite loop of alienation into the wry irony the rest of us are so good at. It just pissed him off.

A differently constituted man might find the tension of being stretched across this great rift of modernity unbearable. Perhaps this is why the psychiatrists who evaluated him found him to be schizophrenic even though, at least in their presence, he never behaved like a schizophrenic. Maybe they divined the desperate, irreconcilable conflict in his politics, and concluded that a man unable to gloss over this problem like the rest of us ought to be crazy.

That's as far as my clinical speculation went. And though I'd known going in that I wasn't courting Kaczynski as fodder for some pet theory of mine, I wasn't prepared when I discovered that, instead, I was beginning to like him.

That didn't mean, however, that he couldn't be difficult.

I wasn't the only person who wanted to get to know the Unabomber. Kaczynski complained throughout the summer about all his correspondents and the inefficiencies they caused him. So in August, he decided to do something about it: he introduced us to one another. His idea was that we would cooperate, stop asking him the same questions separately and help him to cut down on his workload. We were to share his letters among ourselves, garnering more information than we would individually. He wanted to hold a slow-motion press conference.

I did wonder what else a man kept in a prison cell 23 hours a day had to do. But the letters were clearly labor-intensive – long, interesting, and handwritten with no sign of revision. Either thoughts sprang fully formed from his head to the page or he was drafting multiple attempts. I wouldn't have minded a scratch-out here, a logical slip there, but this would have been intolerable for him. He was, after all, the man who complained to his journal about all the time and trouble he had to go to in order to perfect his bomb-building techniques. Human frailty, at least the variety revealed in failed bomb experiments or poorly turned phrases, was an abomination to him. Better to wrangle us than his own perfectionism.

His method for winnowing his workload was, well, methodical. He divided his correspondents into groups and wrote a letter to each group introducing its members to one another and urging them to work together. (He cc'd the letters and was perhaps the last man in the industrialized world who used actual carbon paper to do so.) Kaczynski divided us into three phyla. First, the authors: Vermont Law School professor Michael Mello, and Montana-based writer Alston Chase, and me. Next, the social theorists, the people who wanted to talk about the Unabomber's ideas: Russell Errett, Derrick Jensen, and me. And finally, the shrinks who wanted to explain the Unabomber to the world: a forensic psychiatrist and me. I didn't know exactly what to make of my inclusion in three groups, but I took it as a good sign.

What I did know was that, like much of what Kaczynski did, this act was at once strange and reasonable, obnoxious and considerate, obtuse and clever, naïve and subversive. It was, at one level, all pure and equal exchange: we would get more bang for our 32 cents and he would get relief from his writer's cramp and crowded calendar. Didn't that make sense? At another level, it was revolutionary, detesting competition itself and maybe building anti-industrial cadres in the bargain.

But what kind of self-respecting writer lets others ask his questions? What kind of entrepreneur cooperates with others? We all wanted to tap the Unabomber's well, and he wanted us to share. More to the point, he thought one of us was just as good as the next. His was a kingdom of equals in which no one had a unique claim on his attention. It's a stunning appraisal: that a group of people full enough of themselves to think they could consort with this icon of monstrosity could cooperate in this fashion simply because Kaczynski had determined that it made sense to do so. Even more stunning, though, was that no one appeared to object to the terms.

Because what are you going to do when you want something badly from someone? There's only one Unabomber, and he knew it. His move may have reflected his own commitment to reason above all else and his tone deafness to the subtle music of human interaction. But it also was born of the sheer imperiousness enabled by his emergence into the public eye. He seemed to have an innate knowledge of how to handle his new situation: he responded to our clamor by telling us to work it out among ourselves and get back to him with the results. Maybe he couldn't send out bombs anymore, but he could still use the mails to treat people as pure abstraction. I imagined him reveling in his new-found popularity, this man who had been described over and over as the consummate nerd. Terrorism in the age of celebrity had suddenly given him friends and influence.

IX

The Six Stages of Moral Development

Kaczynski's taxonomy of correspondents provided more than insight into his character. It was also a passport to other parts of the Unabomber kingdom. It's a great conversational entrée: 'Hi, this is Gary Greenberg calling. I got a letter today from Ted Kaczynski suggesting I get in touch with you.' So all the Unabomber's men were willing to interrupt their breakfasts, to talk about Kaczynski with an understated delight.

Some of this was merely checking out the competition. But perhaps the others felt what I did: the relief of finding someone else who spoke the secret language, for whom Kaczynski had become a household fixture – not as notorious criminal but as a point of obsession, not to mention a source of vexation. Perhaps he occupied an empty seat at the dinner table in their homes too.

I had already been in contact with one of the men on the list: Michael Mello, who had written an article for a legal journal comparing Kaczynski's trial to that of the abolitionist John Brown. At the time I discovered Mello's article, I was reading *Cloudsplitter*, Russell Banks's historical novel about John Brown. It was hard to miss the parallels between these two terrorists: both were quixotic figures who insisted that the stench of corruption washed over all and left no one (except themselves) to see, let alone to decry, the original sin. Both hovered around the margins both of society and of the groups that were ostensibly on their sides, honing their solitary anger to a fine point, finally unleashing it upon victims who seemed largely innocent. But when it came time for their day in court, guaranteed by the Constitution, Brown got a real trial that discussed real issues; Kaczynski only got a psychiatric evaluation and the judge's dry recitation of his crimes. Mello's article (and a book he was writing) dealt with what he saw as the injustice to Kaczynski of this outcome.

I called Mello because I wanted a copy of his article, which I had then only read about. I wanted to talk to someone else who might be thinking that Kaczynski had gotten a raw deal, legally speaking. We discussed Kaczynski's diagnosis. Mello had come to conclusions similar to mine about the politics of his 'schizophrenia,' and was pleased to hear them confirmed by someone with a PhD in psychology. Perhaps he recognized in my willingness to take on my profession his own apostasy: he had left capital-defense practice because he believed that he and his cohorts had been turned into collaborators with the executioner; due process had been turned into window dressing. In Mello's view, to continue to play a fixed game was to give it a legitimacy that it didn't deserve. By helping to maintain a pretense of fairness, his colleagues were also helping to keep the real horror of state-sponsored murder at bay. Neither was Mello content to retreat quietly to the clapboarded law school on the White River's banks. He published *Dead Wrong*, an urgent indictment of the capital-defense bar that alienated many of his former colleagues.

But the first thing Mello told me about himself was that he'd been a law clerk for Judge Robert S. Vance, a federal judge killed by a letter bomb (not one of Kaczynski's) in 1989, that he'd loved Vance as a father and harbored a special hatred for mail bombers. I think Mello told me this not only to reassure me that he was no tree-hugging Unabomber groupie, but also to make his interests clear. Michael Mello is dedicated, above all else, to the rule of law; he may hate what you do, but he believes in your inalienable right to be fairly tried for it.

Mello wasn't just writing about Kaczynski's case. In the interests of justice, he was helping Kaczynski prepare an appeal of his guilty plea, on the grounds that he should have been allowed to represent himself. A new trial's primary effect would be to expose Kaczynski to the death penalty before a jury disabused of the notion that he was a pathetic madman. Lawyer-assisted suicide, Mello called it.

Lawrence Kohlberg was a psychologist who got famous by claiming the moral-development franchise. He theorized that our sense of the good develops like other faculties and functions: some combination of time and experience leads us through predictable stages on the journey toward moral maturity. Some people, he said, stopped their moral development earlier than others; indeed, he found six stages along this path and even devised a quick way to assess the pilgrims' progress: he wrote a series of short short stories whose characters found themselves in moral dilemmas and solved them in various ways. Kohlberg's subjects simply said what they thought of the solution and why, and scorers then assigned them a place along the moral continuum. It was a vast improvement over religion.

One of Kohlberg's vignettes is the story of Heinz, a man whose wife will die without a medication that is too expensive. Having exhausted all other avenues, Heinz burglarizes the pharmacy. Should he have done this? Subjects who think he should have and who reason that principle trumps law every time earn Kohlberg's highest honor: they have achieved Stage 6 and become moral paragons, because they use their autonomy to stick to universal moral axioms rather than submit to a law. They're pioneers clearing the ethical frontier with reason's scythe. No wonder that Kohlberg cornered this market: his hero stepped out of a Western.

It's also no wonder that Mello found both Kaczynski and John Brown so compelling, and that Kaczynski trusted him. All three were Kohlbergian exemplars. Each had his own trump suit – abolition, the preservation of wild nature, equal protection under the law. Each was ready to cover the same ace – the proscription of murder – and damn the consequences. By the time our conversation had ended, Mello had invited me into the game. He wanted me to write a foreword to his book on the subject of Kaczynski's psychiatric diagnoses. I was no longer a spectator; I was to be a participant in weighty events.

X

'Let's Roll'

August brought one more thing. I started to think about how to develop my franchise.

In some ways, this was a purely practical consideration. I was by now in hip-deep. I was getting a crash course from Michael Mello in laws relevant to Kaczynski's case, capital-defense strategy, and the technicalities of appeal, not to mention a library of material to read: Mello's book, transcripts of Kaczynski's pretrial hearings, all the motions and counter-motions that told the story in starched legal language. I was renewing my acquaintance with those antimodernists I'd told Kaczynski he reminded me of, dusting off Thoreau and Jacques Ellul and opening Kirkpatrick Sale for the first time. I was preparing to write about Kaczynski's diagnosis for Mello's book, which meant digging into the long and dismal history of psychiatry's attempts to come to terms with its inescapably political nature. Although my practice was already only part-time, and I had but one course to teach in the fall, I found myself looking for ways to minimize these commitments as well without placing undue economic burdens on my family. My new obsession wanted as much time as it could get.

So I decided to see if I could interest someone in paying me to write about the Unabomber. I thought that if I dropped his name into a query letter, I might actually get a response. I pitched an article to *Harper's*, the *Atlantic Monthly*, *Rolling Stone*, and another national magazine that I'll call *Glossy*. I told them that I was a psychologist in contact with Ted Kaczynski and that I had certain provocative things to say about him: that his diagnosis was founded on fallacy; that he was best understood as another antimodernist; that in both his reign of terror and his treatment by the courts, the media, and the psychiatrists we could see some of the deep fissures of American society and culture. I added that he had indicated that I might come see him, reminded them that he had heretofore avoided all media contact, and suggested that my visit might make a good peg for the article, which I described as a 'long and thoughtful memoir.' And, I told them, I looked forward to their quick response.

The *Atlantic* asked me to send the article when I'd written it. *Harper's* sent me their rejection form six weeks later. *Rolling Stone* didn't reply at all. But *Glossy* bit hard, just two days after I mailed them the letter. A senior editor there was very interested in the interview, and I reminded him that a visit was still tentative, that many things remained to be worked out. But, I told him, 'no matter what happens, this is going to be a very interesting story.'

Without an interview, however, it seemed that I was just another guy floating his fantasies over a barely open transom. 'Maybe the thing you should do,' he said, 'is let us know when you've got the interview. And we'll go from there.'

'Do you want to see some of my writing in the meantime?'

'Yeah. Sure. Send it along.'

So it wasn't going to be as easy as I had hoped. Knowing the Unabomber, getting 20-page letters from him, being on a first-name basis with him wasn't going to make up entirely for my lack of a name. It also seemed that it might not even matter what Kaczynski said in the prospective interview – whether we talked about books or cabin design or his hit list or what he watched on television – or how thoughtfully I wrote about it. All that counted was bringing the public a sensation they hadn't yet experienced: face time with Kaczynski. But before I could even begin to get discouraged, the phone rang.

'Let's roll,' said the editor, his circumspection gone, along with any memory of the phone call we'd ended five minutes before.

I said, 'Okay, where to?'

He told me that he had just spoken with the editor-in-chief, who had said that no matter what happens, this was going to be a very interesting story. So he wanted to fax me a contract, get it signed and returned today. Up to 5,000 words at $1.50 a word, plus travel expenses. With foreign rights, which the editor said were a near certainty in this case, it came to around $10,000. That would buy me a lot of time to work on this project.

I signed the contract.

But I didn't tell Kaczynski about any of this, at least not quite yet. I'd never promised to tell him exactly what I was up to, or to refrain from this kind of thing. He knew I was a writer and he was accordingly cautious. Still, I caught the whiff of my own dishonesty. But, I assured myself, I'd find a way to tell him. When the time came.

The time came the next week.

Kaczynski had also been thinking about how to make use of our contact. A letter that Mello gave me, in which he'd written to Kaczynski about me, made it clear that he and Kaczynski were already talking about ways that a writer who would put his PhD in psychology behind a claim that the Unabomber's diagnosis was a travesty could give them aid and comfort. And Kaczynski had a very specific idea about how I should do this. He wanted me to read the book he'd just finished writing, comment on it to him, and then consider the possibility of interviewing him and his family to come up with a fairer assessment of the Kaczynskis.

Truth Versus Lies arrived in early September, a 548-page typescript. It was Kaczynski's point-by-point, fully documented refutation of all the unflattering things the media had said about him. (I signed an agreement not to divulge the contents of this book until they had otherwise been made public. At press time, it had not been released by its publisher, Context Books. So my discussion will refer only to what has already been reported about *Truth Versus Lies*.) His thesis was that his brother, David, and his mother, Wanda, rather than acknowledging the Kaczynski family dysfunction, had portrayed Kaczynski to the national press as mentally ill. A willing and gullible media had then amplified this account until Theodore Kaczynski had become, in the public eye, just another lunatic.

Kaczynski's reaction is understandable. Surely there isn't a public figure alive who hasn't at one time or another imagined taking on the media as Kaczynski does in *Truth Versus Lies*. It must be hard to watch your image get conjured out of whatever little tropes are in demand at the moment. This loss of control over personal identity – which is just about all any of us has left – must temper some of the delights of fame. It might even unleash a desire for revenge beyond a lawsuit.

Still, most people would simply settle for bad publicity and tough it out. And even the most headstrong person would pale at the prospect of countering a tale with as much resonance as the one that emerged about Kaczynski in the months after his arrest. The loving but helpless mother and brother choking up as they describe Kaczynski's descent into madness to a public that has little patience for political diatribe but infinite hunger for therapeutic confession – most people would hold their breath as this tsunami washed over them, hope it left them something in its wake, and turn their attention to important matters, like their upcoming capital murder trial. But most people aren't the Unabomber.

Another thing most people would do, if they had the chance, is burnish their image. Who could resist, in the telling of one's own story, the autobiographer's license to vanity? Well, aside from quibbling over details like whether or not he really panicked when he was spotted while leaving off a bomb (as was once reported), Ted Kaczynski could. He is unrepentant in the book, addressing the Unabomber crimes only obliquely and often providing details that can only make people like him less – as, for instance, his dispute of a news account about a dirty limerick regarding a co-worker that he'd scrawled on the workplace wall: Kaczynski's rebuttal was that he'd scrawled the limerick on a machine.

I suppose the all-trees-and-no-forest approach of *Truth Versus Lies* could be read as evidence that Kaczynski is mentally ill. But surely it is not evidence of neurochemical explosions of schizophrenia and the resulting disorganization of mind. Quite the contrary. The book is remarkable for its controlled tone, the steady focus it brings to bear on a sprawling archive of personal and public history. And underlying it is a method that is both coherent and quaint. It conjures a world, part nostalgia, part desperate hope, in which great issues are discussed in measured tones and brought to incontrovertible resolution by reasonable men in dark-paneled rooms. In that imagined world, people will look at the facts and soberly reconsider their conclusion that a man who lives in the woods and sends bombs through the mail to people he doesn't know, who renounces the bounty of industrial civilization and fertilizes his garden with his own shit must be crazy.

So it's not entirely true that *Truth Versus Lies* is devoid of self-flattery. It's just that one of the qualities most worth having, in Kaczynski's view, is rationality, which he has by the bucket. I think the only hero he ever wanted to be was Rudyard Kipling's hero of 'If', the one who kept his head while all about him were doing otherwise.

He wasn't even blaming others for what he had done. Even if he was claiming that he was just another abused child, he offered no excuses. An author who would tell the truth must withstand its reflection upon him and settle for the cerebral satisfaction of possessing the facts.

After reading the manuscript, I told Kaczynski that his approach to the problem wasn't likely to change any minds, that his chosen method was like using Euclidean geometry to argue with a hurricane. I added that I thought the manuscript could backfire and give new currency to the image he was trying to discredit. And then I seized my opportunity: I told Kaczynski that if he really wanted to redeem his public image, he might consider allowing me to interview him for a national magazine, and that I happened to know of a magazine that was interested.

XI

Dr A. Tumbles Down the Oubliette

Glossy may have given me a contract on the basis that something interesting would likely happen, but my editor continued to make it clear that they weren't going to let me fill up space between cologne ads with mere ideas. The interview was still essential, the contract merely a no-cost option they had taken out on my relationship with Kaczynski in the event that it blossomed into an on-the-record meeting. And, despite the serendipitous timing of Kaczynski's request for my comments on his book and his family, I still wasn't sure a meeting would ever take place.

And there was another problem. A version of the letter in which Kaczynski suggested an interview as part of an evaluation of him and his family had gone to the forensic psychiatrist he had listed in his taxonomy of Unabomber correspondents. Michael Mello had given me a copy of this psychiatrist's pitch to Kaczynski, and it was clear that Dr A. knew his business. The letter, originally sent to Kaczynski's lawyers, enumerated the eight reasons Kaczynski ought to allow him to become 'the vehicle through which your thoughts and feelings are communicated.' Among these were his skill at 'putting my own thoughts and feelings aside and honing in on the communication of others,' his license 'as a psychiatrist [to] attest to your views as real and well thought out, rather than being dismissed as simply based on factors such as revenge or paranoia,' and his 'access to a wide spectrum of media contacts. However, I am not the media!' Indeed, Dr A. was not many things: 'I am not a celebrity, nor do I seek notoriety . . . I carry no agenda of selling newspapers or advertising space. I do not operate in sound bites and do not need to editorialize.' He was even willing to give Kaczynski editorial control. And Dr A. worked to a rousing conclusion:

In summary, Mr Kaczynski, I believe that I would be the perfect instrument to achieve the goal of telling your story to the world. You have a message and I have the means and expertise to assure that message is heard in a credible, unbiased, and complete manner. I will defer to your judgment as to the medium used for our interview, audio, video, film, or whatever.

In his letter to us, Kaczynski said that he wanted Dr A. and me to work out how we would split up our duties. If we couldn't do that, then he might have to choose between us. Dr A. had started where I had: with Kaczynski's caricatured lunacy, his thwarted wish to be taken seriously. He'd also started with similar ambitions, but he'd given a very different chase. He'd sent his pitch, with its shameless recitation of credential, on proper bond through proper channels. He'd offered Kaczynski editorial control, denied self-interest, promised a happy ending. All of this was the opposite of my ragtag approach and my clear insistence on bringing my own ideas to bear on Kaczynski's story. I worried that Dr A. – who, after all, had great references and good media contacts – knew something that I didn't: that Kaczynski would respond well to naked ambition, so long as it seemed like good bedside manner.

I called Dr A. and we sized each other up. We spoke vaguely of getting together. Then I searched the Internet and found out that Dr A. had been on a national news show, for about ten seconds; he'd had a bit part in the O.J. trial. I wrote to Kaczynski:

[Dr A.] is a prominent forensic psychiatrist. He participated in the O.J. Simpson [trial] and appeared on [a national news show] as a result. I think he and I are sufficiently different that our work would be complementary rather than redundant; and I think we are similar enough that we can work together.

I knew that this one-two punch – the mass media and O.J. – would very likely knock Dr A. out of the ring, and that I had delivered it perfectly: from a neutral corner, a sharp jab disguised as a pat on the back. That I had told nothing but the truth was bad enough, but the real chill in my spine was the simplicity of this assassination. I just wrote it.

By mid-September, Kaczynski had decided that Dr A. was not a promising candidate, due in part to his role in the O.J. circus. Maybe Dr A. deserved his fate, for his bad faith and worse writing. Maybe Kaczynski needed to be protected. That's not why I did it, though. I did it because he was in the way.

XII

The Unabomber Plays Shrink

Kaczynski did say interview. But even with Dr A. out of contention, difficulties remained. Kaczynski had something far more clinical in mind than I did, not to mention something far more useful to him than to me. I wasn't ready to take on the Kaczynskis, to get down in the epistemological tar pit of a family squabble and emerge with the authoritative version of who dragged whom into the muck. I didn't want the franchise that badly.

It's not that it wouldn't have been interesting to talk with Wanda and David about their notorious kin. Especially David. The story of these brothers – with all its love and betrayal, the intimacy that allowed David to recognize the Manifesto as Ted's work, the bitter disappointment of two men too close to forgive each other's differences – seemed of biblical proportion. No doubt that I'd come back from an expedition into this primordial ooze with a story to tell.

But Kaczynski didn't want a travelogue. He wanted an evaluation. He wanted to use my expertise to debunk theirs. And even if he expressed his commitment to the truth rather than a particular outcome, I didn't want to be his house shrink.

I just wanted to give *Glossy* what it wanted so it would give me a name so that I could write a book about the thing that interested me so much that I'd almost forgotten about my drug book: the deep historical and cultural resonances of the Unabomber story and the complex, disturbing, and (so far) obscure character at its center.

Market forces made me do it – made me spend the next couple of months in hot pursuit of an audience with the Unabomber. An alternating current of come-hithers and get-losts ran from his cell to my mailbox, sometimes twice a week. The man of perfect logic was clearly confused about what to do. In one letter, he gave me an unequivocal no, followed by a request for more information about me and a suggestion that I write an article about him, at which point he would reconsider. Kaczynski knitted and unraveled promises like Penelope.

Milan Kundera has said that love is constant interrogation, which may help to explain why my colloquy with this serial killer kindled intimacy: we were questioning each other. For his part, Kaczynski asked all about me: my household income, my practice, my pet psychological theories, the cars I drove, my wife, how I planned to raise my son, my hobbies. At the end of that long litany, he asked how often I masturbated – then quickly explained that he was joking. It was his chance to play shrink, he said, to let me know what it felt like. I didn't answer the question, but I did tell him about a time that I found myself on the wrong end of a therapist's questions, when she tried to interpret my critical view of psychotherapy as so much adolescent acting-out.

Kaczynski's questioning was unfailingly polite, and he often apologized for his ambivalence. It wasn't anything about me personally; in fact, he said, he liked me and thought I wrote well. He pointed out, however, that I'd already gotten some things wrong: in my response to his book, I'd written, 'You . . . seem (and I'm not certain if you mean this, or if I have read your book accurately) to have been unhappy for much of your life,' but Kaczynski responded that since his decision to leave academia for the woods, that had not been the case. He also said that I'd misunderstood his motivation for challenging his conviction: he didn't so much want to clear his name as to avoid a long time in prison.

But beyond mistakes that could be corrected, there was a perhaps insurmountable problem. He was afraid that even if I got all the facts right, I would still get him wrong. He understood that I wanted to be more than the Unabomber's amanuensis, that I had ideas of my own. And he was concerned those ideas might make me misrepresent him. Of course, he allowed, it was possible that I might see things about him that he himself could not, that the error might be his and not mine. But it was also possible that I would be mistaken, see things that weren't there and turn him into someone he was not. And this, he told me repeatedly, would horrify him.

For Kaczynski, it was impossible that more than one story could be true. Like any good empiricist, he was sure that the world and the people in it could be divided into the really there and the not. My credentials only deepened his worry that I would get his story wrong and then accuse him of bad faith for his disagreement. But the real issue was deeper: it was the inevitability that my values would seep into my account of him. His personality would then be no more than a platform for my own ideas, and he would be stuck with yet another story about him that wasn't true, only this time with his own consent.

Kaczynski hadn't gone into that cabin just to avoid an electric bill. He'd gone there to keep himself intact, away from the institutions – corporations, universities, psychology – that would make him into their own versions of him. He thought that he had the best command of the facts of his life.

It was impossible to argue with any of this. Of course I wanted to use Kaczynski's stories to tell my own. So I agreed with him:

While I am disappointed with your turning me down, I am neither surprised nor mystified . . . I know I am a pig in a poke from your perspective, and I am pleased to have gotten so far with you as to even be talking about these things. While I remain hopeful that you might change your mind (and grateful that you hold that possibility open), I respect your decision and the reasoning on which it is based. As I have said many times, I don't know how I would act, were I in your situation.

I reassured him about my scholarly intentions:

I think that the best reassurance I can give you is to remind you that I have no interest in offering you a 'better' evaluation and/or diagnosis than the other shrinks have. I'm not interested in diagnosing you; I would be hard-pressed to think of a less interesting way to write about you than trying to fit you into one of the categories in the DSM. Even if I could find one, then what would I have said? The way that my expertise as a psychologist enters into this picture (besides giving me a credential that will make it possible that people will actually listen to me; I know that's cynical, but it's true) is that I know from the inside the inadequacies of diagnosis, and in general the problems related to power embedded in the mental health industry. In my last letter to you, I tried to outline how I can use my credentials and knowledge to this end.

And my personal intentions:

I don't think you are doing me an injustice, nor is there any reason (from my end) that your decision should strain our relations. I only hope that I have not strained our relations by asking in the first place. I think I have already told you that there is no quid pro quo in my request for a meeting. We can continue, I hope, to correspond, and as circumstances change perhaps your decision will change as well. In the meantime, this process (wherever it leads) can only help us to get to know one another better.

I pushed:

Here is an idea. If what I have written here inclines you to further contact with me, then consider my proposal [for an interview] to you in the last letter. Think of it as a trial run, an audition . . . You can let me interview and write about you and then see if you like what I do in a relatively low-risk setting. This will give you a crucial piece of information about me: whether or not I can be trusted with your words, and whether or not I am true to my own. It will also give you the chance to meet me face to face and fill in your picture of me. Again, I think the bird-to-stone ratio is favorably high.

I backed off:

I know it remains possible that all my reassurances and attempts to address your concerns might not be enough. Thus far, that is the case, and so I have no choice but to give up on [the interview] for now and seek other ways to enlist your aid.

And it almost worked.

XIII

A Successful Audition

By October, Kaczynski's doubts began to give way to concerns about the technical difficulties of the interview: who else would be present, what documents I'd have access to, how I could get press credentials. He proposed a topic for the interview — a discussion of the exact ways in which his defense team had deceived him about the mental-defect defense. He put me on the list of people he'd be allowed to call on the telephone (in the event we had to make arrangements quickly) and suggested I call his defense lawyers about the possibility of their monitoring the interview. He never mentioned the interview without hedging, but at least his flat objection had given way to if-only logistics.

Then I had my audition. I sent Kaczynski my foreword to Mello's book. It was the 13,000-word version of my argument that his diagnoses were more political than psychiatric. The doctors said that Kaczynski's insistence on living his low-tech life, his hatred of the incursions of the modern world into the Montana woods, not to mention his aversion to psychiatrists, were the evidence of his illness, but, I argued, these things could only be symptoms if one already assumed he was delusional, which was, of course, what the evaluators were supposed to be proving. Without this assumption, his attitudes and actions, which were undoubtedly deviant, were no more inherently pathological than, say, the claims of certain women that they are married to God and that they must wear strange clothing and live in convents to uphold their marriage vows. The psychiatric reports reasoned in a circle; their authors had all committed the basic logical fallacy of assuming their conclusions. None of which was to say, I hastened to add, that Ted Kaczynski was not mentally ill; one can't, after all, prove a negation. But it was clear that the diagnosis was ill founded and thus deeply suspect.

Kaczynski liked my paper so much that, he said, he would be willing to have me come to interview him as soon as I wanted. But there was a catch: he'd recently been in touch with a lawyer who was considering taking his case. In lawyerly fashion, this man had advised Kaczynski to curtail all contact with the outside world. So the final decision would have to await a discussion between the two of them.

What Kaczynski didn't know was that, courtesy of Michael Mello, I knew this lawyer, Richard Bonnie. Bonnie had read the foreword and liked it. It had figured into his willingness to consider taking on the case, helping to convince him that, at least insofar as the psychiatric evaluations were concerned, it was indeed possible that Kaczynski had been unfairly pressured into his plea bargain. Bonnie, through Mello, knew of my contract with *Glossy* and my negotiations with Kaczynski about an interview. He saw the value of such an interview, under properly controlled circumstances, to an appeal based in part on the injustice of Kaczynski's diagnosis. So, he told me, he would tell Kaczynski that he ought to go ahead with it, and that we would be coming out to see him in January.

It looked like I'd gotten my name.

XIV

Pimping for Kaczynski

If there was a moment when I understood just what that meant, it was when I spoke with Serena.

Serena wasn't the first agent I'd had truck with. A young agent from a large New York agency had called me in September, having caught wind, through a mutual friend, of my bid for the Unabomber franchise. We'd gone to lunch at a swank Midtown place. He was a smart man who was interested in Kaczynski as a cultural phenomenon as well as a business opportunity. He didn't glaze over when I talked about antimodernism and the Luddites and Thoreau, even countered with some thoughts of his own about the relationship between art and violence. Business only came up as the hovering waiter removed our empty plates. A book would be great. And, having heard the story of Kaczynski's planned appeal, he suggested that an article for an outlet like *The New York Times* Magazine, about the problems of the plea bargain, with a focus on Mello's guerrilla lawyering, would be an easy sell around the time the appeal was filed. He had only two caveats: this story had legs, but they wouldn't run forever; and without face time, I didn't really have anything an agent could sell.

He paid for lunch, 75 bucks or so. So far, that is the entire remuneration my Unabomber franchise has yielded. The food was delicious.

It turned out he couldn't be my agent. His agency had a conflict. It represented a real reporter with an interest in the Unabomber story. Since it seemed that I had no need of an agent until I had secured an audience with Kaczynski, I decided to search no further. But just after I got my invitation, *Glossy* started to play its hand in a way that made me rethink this decision. My editor emailed me, using our shorthand for Kaczynski's name.

As I've continued to think about this piece, I think I've hit upon a strategy that may work best for all parties involved: a straight, lengthy Q&A, bracketed by an intro and conclusion by you. I like this because it gives the reader what he/she really wants, which is to hear TK himself speak, and also because it will allow you to focus more of your attention on the conversation itself, drawing him out, letting him speak, and less on trying to come up with a narrative strategy. Of course, quite a bit depends on what

TK says in the interview. But as we get closer to the event, let's discuss this.

He may well have thought this strategy would truly serve all of us, or at least that his touch was deft. He may have thought I would be relieved not to have to trouble my pretty little head with narrative strategies, or at least that I wouldn't detect the condescension of his email. But his meaning could not have been more clear: I was useful to *Glossy* only to the extent that I could get to see Ted Kaczynski on their nickel, and once I'd done that, my job was to stay out of the way.

I was in high dudgeon, not yet smart enough to realize that I had merely discovered gambling in Casablanca. Hadn't I told them what I wanted to do? What about my long and thoughtful memoir? A Q&A indeed! They wanted me to pimp for the Unabomber!

Of course, this wasn't entirely a surprise. From the beginning, my editor had made his concerns clear. 'I think we ought to start talking about the article,' he had said to me a month or so before he hit upon his strategy. 'You know, get some sense of where you're going to take this thing.'

So I gave him that day's riff on the Unabomber, which was all the strange symmetry in his life. Kaczynski's worst nightmare wasn't getting caught; it was getting caught and then being called a nutcase, which is exactly what happened. And then the fact that he'd predicted it, through some fairly sophisticated analysis of the psychiatric profession, became more evidence that he was crazy. He hated technology, and the prison he ended up in is the most technologically advanced prison ever built, not to mention that his cell is about the same size as his shack in the woods. There's something vicious

about all this self-fulfilling prophecy, I told the editor, vicious
like Blake's Tyger.

He was silent for a moment. But he wasn't mulling over
Blake. 'You know, I've been thinking about this piece, too.
And I keep remembering Tom Snyder's interview of Charles
Manson. All I really wanted to see was Manson, you know,
what was he like and all that. And this asshole with a good
haircut kept getting in the way. It was like he thought he
was more important than Manson. We really want to avoid
that kind of a situation.'

So I guess I should have known they weren't terribly interested in what I had to say. More to the point, and speaking
of fearful symmetries, I suppose I shouldn't have expected to
reap anything other than what I sowed. They hadn't, after all,
responded to my query because it was well written.

But still.

I took out my contract. What really worried me was the
part about how they had 'the right to adapt, crop, enhance,
change, and edit the Work.' Did this mean they could re-
assemble my words as they saw fit, to make sure the article
gave the readers what they really wanted?

I called a lawyer, a New York lawyer. 'You signed a contract?' he said, graciously leaving off his suffix: 'You fucking
moron.' I read him the clause in question. He told me he'd
have to see the whole thing to be sure, but that they probably
had more latitude than I wanted them to have. His advice
was either to give *Glossy* what they wanted or something they
couldn't use at all, and then go on to write the article I was
interested in for someone else.

That seemed like good counsel, but it also worried me.
What if *Glossy* did such a hatchet job that they destroyed

my connection with Kaczynski? What would happen to my franchise then? $10,000 was a lot of money to me, but it was chump change to anyone else. And it would be a shame if all the fruit of my labor were a Q&A with my byline squeezed into the corner of Kaczynski's beard.

Enter Serena. She was the agent of a friend of mine. She spared me the lawyer's tact. 'Look,' she said. 'If you let *Glossy* publish this, it's just going to hurt you. They're not even a top-tier magazine, and they're trying to squeeze you out. Anyone can see that. Fuck *Glossy*.'

'But the contract.'

'Fuck the contract, too. You've got something here. So this is what you do. Put together a book proposal. Doesn't matter who writes the thing – you can, or I can find someone else to. Then a month before the book comes out you put an excerpt in *Vanity Fair*. Twenty thousand dollars. Then when the book comes out, you've got a bestseller. You can't let some second- or third-tier magazine – and they're not even at the top of their tier – blow this for you.'

Oh, Serena! Sweet co-conspirator, blowing bestseller kisses into my ears and spanking me at the very same time. Fucking *Glossy* with me, a ménage à trois. Concupiscence made me weak in the knees. I mean that literally – the part about my knees going weak. When Serena unveiled her plans for me, I swooned for a moment. This was my big chance. Serena was going to show me how it was done, New-York style.

In the movie version of this story, I say to Serena, 'But, darling, how do we know this is a bestseller when it isn't even written yet? And what happens when I decide I don't like my contract with you?' and ride off into the sunset with principle between my knees. Real life being what it is, however, I told

Serena I'd have to think about all this. 'Well, if you like,' she said, obviously exasperated with my dithering at such a critical time.

It wasn't so much the prospect of dishonoring my contract with *Glossy* that worried me. I could probably have justified that. The more disturbing thing was the prospect of becoming the person Serena thought I should be: the kind who lets someone else write his book proposals, who types his book with one eye on his bank account and the other on *The New York Times* bestseller list, who writes in disregard of all the assurances he's given his subject (and himself) about exploitation and pandering.

Which doesn't mean I wouldn't have liked to see my name on the Bestseller List. There were just things I couldn't do to get there, or so I thought. But I'll never know how much of a scoundrel I really am. Because not long after I decided that I really couldn't be the kind of person Serena wanted me to be, and before I could reconsider that decision, matters were taken out of my hands.

XV

'If I Were a Tattletale . . .' (The Greenberg Embargo)

Through no fault of his own, Beau Friedlander's entry into the picture marked the beginning of my end.

Friedlander, a 29-year-old publishing entrepreneur, had an idea for Context Books, his new company. It would produce books that might otherwise go unpublished – not for their lack of literary merit, but for their failure to fit into the bottom-line calculus of mainstream publishing. His planned debut nonfiction book fit the bill perfectly: Theodore John Kaczynski's *Truth Versus Lies*. (Friedlander might have had a little of the franchiser in him: he was also publishing Michael Mello's book about Kaczynski – the one with my foreword in it.)

I first called Friedlander at the end of November. Up to that time, Michael Mello was the only person I was in regular contact with about Kaczynski. Our frequent conversations were long and rambling and remarkably free of competitive undertone; we seemed to have an understanding from the beginning that there was plenty of room for both of us in the Unabomber world. When I read him Kaczynski's letter approving the interview and he said, 'Well, I guess you're going to be the first of us to get in there,' he seemed far more pleased for me than envious. Mello was generous with time and documents and connections. In return, he asked for very little: mostly, I thought, just the company, the opportunity to talk with someone who could understand his sympathy and loyalty toward Kaczynski, and appreciate the difficulties they brought him.

So when I called Friedlander, partly to check him out, partly to tell him that I wanted to retain copyright to my foreword, I was expecting to find more of this camaraderie. At first, it seemed that I was right. Friedlander praised my foreword, told me he was glad I was going to see Kaczynski (Mello had told him), and then asked if I had thought about publishing more articles. I told him I had my hands full with this one, recounting my recent dust-up with *Glossy* over their wish for a Q&A.

'Oh, fuck *Glossy*,' said Friedlander. '*Playboy* or *Penthouse* is the place for a Q&A. I think I can give you a name at *Playboy*.

And the place for your article is *Vanity Fair* or the *New Yorker*. We really ought to try to get something placed there.' We were a 'we.' Friedlander was going to help us. He was particularly concerned that we were only getting published in *Glossy* and asked me to send him my query letters so he could figure out what I had done wrong.

But then I asked Friedlander a question that Mello and I had been discussing since we'd heard he was going to be Kaczynski's publisher. Had he considered, I wondered, that publishing *Truth Versus Lies* might make things worse for Kaczynski? I wasn't only worried about Kaczynski's wellbeing. I also wanted to know what made Friedlander tick. If he was in some way sympathetic to Kaczynski or his politics, then why would he publish a compendium of complaint about Unabomber family dysfunction that was likely to further discredit him even as it sensationalized the story? And if he was only in it for the name brand, all cynicism and no heart, then did I want to be part of his 'us'?

Friedlander answered by defending the book on both literary and historical grounds, and added, 'If I were a tattletale, which I'm not, I'd have to tell Ted what you're saying here.'

The threat itself wasn't a problem: I'd already told Kaczynski what I thought. But the fact of the threat, its redolence of schoolyard brutality, unnerved me. Mello and I had the freedom with each other to grouse about Kaczynski behind his back, each safe in the knowledge that the other's complaints weren't going to hurt our mutual friend. But here Friedlander was telling me that his loyalty ran deeper: he would report to Kaczynski anything he heard related to him. It was the first time I thought I might go the way of Dr A.

One of Freud's best ideas was repetition compulsion, the

notion that our secret histories – trauma and loss and plain disappointment – set the course and direction of desire before we even know it. Following the trail of my pursuit of Kaczynski, I could find the wish not only to be heard saying something worth saying, but to be part of something, a member of a club I'd want to join. From there, it's a short couch trip to boyhood disappointment, regret at playground ineptitude. I'd fancied myself, with Mello and (I'd hoped) Friedlander, one of the boys at last. We would all be pals. We would do swell things together. But Friedlander's threat made it clear that I was living in the wrong neurosis: it was a father thing, and we were vying for favorite-son status. As Freud pointed out, that struggle was bloody and relentless.

But it wasn't Friedlander who got me in trouble with Kaczynski. It was Mello. In early December, I got a letter from Kaczynski. A glance at the salutation would have revealed that there was a problem: no 'Best regards' or jaunty 'Z', just a cold 'Sincerely yours' and a formal 'Ted J. Kaczynski.' In a measured but sharp tone, he told me that he had received information that raised questions about my motives and honesty. The list of charges, compiled mostly from what Mello had told him about me, was long, comprehensive, and fully documented, even containing a footnote. It was also damning enough to make Kaczynski reconsider his contact with me.

I stood accused by the Unabomber of any number of transgressions, all of which pointed to my being a double-dealing, self-serving person no better, in his view, than your average journalist. Mello, according to Kaczynski, had written that I'd obtained a big-time literary agent who had arranged for me to publish a story about Kaczynski's appeal (and Mello's role in it) in *The New York Times* Magazine, and that the article was due to appear the week of April 19, the week after the *Glossy* article would hit the newsstands. Mello had also made it clear that I thought the interview was more of a certainty than Kaczynski did, and he implied that I had been trying to pry information out of him, so much so that he had had to remind me of our information-sharing agreement.

Kaczynski's distress was understandable. From his obscured view, solid information was hard to come by. All he'd had to go on about me was what I had told him, and the fact that Mello was telling him a story about me that was at odds with my own meant that his worst fear might be true: the Unabomber was worried that I was a loose cannon. And he wanted an explanation.

Here was a difficulty. Almost everything Kaczynski was concerned with was not true. But there was no way to prove that without casting doubt on Mello, whom I thought of as a friend and who was probably Kaczynski's most trusted ally. Mello, along with Friedlander and Richard Bonnie, had been cc'd on Kaczynski's letter. In fact, the day before I got my copy, he'd left a baleful message on my answering machine: 'We're in a terrible mess here,' he'd said. At the time, I thought he was worried for both of us.

I called him after I got the letter, told him I hoped he could help me out. Mostly, I wanted to avoid conducting a suit of claims and counterclaims through the mail and with the Unabomber as the arbiter, so I asked Mello to tell Kaczynski that he had been inaccurate.

'I have trouble with the word "inaccurate,"' he said.

I was on my own.

So I wrote a long letter, explaining myself. I had had lunch with an agent, but had not signed on with him. I had discussed with the agent and Mello the possibility of a '*New York Times* Magazine article,' had drafted a query for the article but never sent it out. I hadn't intended to deceive Kaczynski by not telling him of these things. Indeed, I wrote, some proof of this had no doubt already arrived at his cell: a letter I'd mailed a week ago asking what he thought of the prospective article. I had discussed publication dates with Mello in order to understand how the dates of Kaczynski's appeal would best dovetail with *Glossy*'s schedule, but I had no dates, and no other contract. I had not intended to pry information out of Mello, I said; to the contrary, we frequently had long and rambling conversations in which information freely flowed. I added that I knew Kaczynski had not given final approval for the interview, but my conversation with Bonnie had seemed quite decisive to me. I also allowed that I was angry with Mello, that I didn't understand how this had happened.

What I didn't say was that Mello had gone out of his way to get around what he and I were calling 'the Greenberg embargo,' Kaczynski's request that Mello not give me any documents or information without prior approval. Or that Mello had asked me to put in a good word for him with the big-time literary agent. Or that I thought Mello had had no business in writing Kaczynski about the interview before either Bonnie or I had had a chance to do so. Whining self-justification was bad enough; whining denunciation seemed even worse.

Besides, Kaczynski had me dead to rights about one thing: I was ambitious. Of course, he'd known that all along, but he had perhaps been lulled by my apparent honesty. So I wrote a second letter. This time, I just took the bullet. It didn't matter, I said, whether or not Mello had reported accurately on me. The fact was that I had talked with him about things that I hadn't told Kaczynski, half-baked ideas and possibilities of plans. And that wasn't fair to any of us. I couldn't stop thinking or talking about this business, but I would hereafter refrain from doing so with anyone in touch with Kaczynski unless and until I was ready to discuss the matter with Kaczynski himself. And, I concluded, I would try to keep my ambition in better check from here on out.

I sent the letters express mail and waited. It's hard to imagine that important affairs of both the heart and state used to be carried out through the mail: the indirectness, the delay – these seemed almost unbearable under the circumstances.

And I'd overestimated the loyalty of my new pals.

I faxed a copy of my letters to Friedlander and called him a little later. In our conversation the day the letter came, he had made it clear which side of the triangle he was on: 'Well, I guess you really stepped in it,' he had said. My response, he now said, seemed effective, if a bit long-winded. Except for one thing: 'You're still fibbing.' I hadn't, he said, told the whole story about the agent. And I hadn't sent Kaczynski the early query letters, the ones I'd sent Friedlander just the last week. It would be unfortunate, he continued, if he had to send them to Kaczynski, but he'd do it if I didn't. In the meantime, Kaczynski had told him not to talk to me, so our further contact depended on Kaczynski's response.

At least Friedlander told me that much. Mello didn't call me when I faxed him my letters. When we finally spoke, he only growled, 'I'll talk to you tomorrow.' Which he never did. Two days later, I got a faxed copy of his letter to Kaczynski. Whatever inaccuracies he'd conveyed, he wrote, were only my distortions and exaggerations accurately reported. Thus, he was forced to conclude that I was untrustworthy. So he was removing my foreword from his book. (This fax, as it turned out, was his way of informing me that I'd been fired.) Mello never said it straight out, but the advice implicit in his vitriol was that Kaczynski follow his lead and put as much distance between me and him as possible.

So when, the following week, I got a letter from Kaczynski apologizing for jumping to conclusions about me, expressing relief that my explanation was so satisfactory (as I had come to be one of his favorite correspondents), and wishing me season's greetings, I wasn't exactly packing my bags for the interview. As I explained to Friedlander when he called to welcome me back to the fold, I just figured my letters had gotten to Kaczynski before Mello's.

XVI

Therapists Call It Closure

Kaczynski soon retracted his apology. Letters from Mello and Friedlander, he wrote, had made it clear that I had been underhanded. I was still useful to him, at least to the extent that I was willing to say that my industry had done him wrong, so he would proceed with me, but only with the protection of a cooperation agreement that would give him substantial control over me. I'd be hearing from his lawyers.

I told him that I'd be willing to give up some of my autonomy, but not without something substantial from him – like exclusive biography rights or access to his legal team during his appeal. I never got his counterproposal.

Kaczynski wrote me two letters during the winter, apologizing for being too busy preparing his appeal to stay in close touch. He asked me to keep writing him, as he enjoyed hearing from me. But the feel of a slack line in my hand was dispiriting, and, after a few notes, I let my end drop.

Until the end of April, when Kaczynski finally filed his appeal, Richard Bonnie had decided not to take the case, leaving Kaczynski to handwrite a 124-page brief for himself. He appended a draft of my ex-foreword as an appendix, in support of his claim that he wasn't crazy and thus should never have been forced to choose between a mental-defect defense and a guilty plea. You could look it up. It's Exhibit 9 of Theodore John Kaczynski's Pro Se Motion Under 28 U.S.C. §2255 to Vacate Guilty Pleas and Sentences and Set Aside Convictions. This is how Kaczynski introduces me to the world:

In respect to the ideological bias of the experts' reports on Kaczynski, see the essay by psychologist Dr Gary Greenberg, attached as Exhibit 9.

Kaczynski . . . emphasizes that Dr Greenberg's essay contains certain errors of fact and erroneous conclusions. In attaching this essay to his petition, Kaczynski does not mean to express agreement with everything that the essay states or implies.

I guess he was still mad at me.

Kaczynski didn't ask for permission, or even inform me of his plans to use the ex-foreword: I found out from Richard Bonnie. Neither was his disclaimer enough to temper his perfectionism. He corrected one of my errors of fact: I had written, 'his portrayal as a paranoid schizophrenic was, in his view, the result of lies told to the reporters, attorneys, and investigators by his family.' Kaczynski inserted 'partly' between 'view' and 'the,' perhaps feeling the license to do so because I was talking about his view. And so he got what he wanted: he made sure any public comment of mine about him would be to his maximum advantage, and that either I would get him just exactly right or he would get to point out my errors.

So the Unabomber used me before I could use him. But that doesn't mean I came up empty-handed. Even if I didn't get the franchise that Mello and Friedlander did, the one that had Mello interviewed on 'Good Morning, America,' talking about his correspondence with Kaczynski, and Friedlander holding forth in *Time* about Kaczynski's TV-viewing habits, I still got to take a trip to the pulsing, bloody heart of things, where raw human desire is transformed into power and money and sent coursing through the veins of the body politic. I came back without my $10,000 or even a souvenir T-shirt, but I got something better: I'm writing this article, after all. You don't know me from Adam, but you got this far, and you might not even have started if it weren't for his name in the title. I do hope I won't be taking undue advantage of my celebrity connection if I tell you what I think some of the morals of this story are.

I'll start with a confession: the reach of my ambition exceeds my grasp. The reason I gave up so easily when Mello and Friedlander brought me down, that I didn't retaliate or plead my case against theirs and let the Unabomber judge the merits, is that I didn't have the heart to do what had to be done to close the deal I had sought in the first place. It was one thing to set Dr A. up for a fall, quite another to do in someone I actually knew. But let me be clear: I restrained myself for no one's sake but my own; faced with a glimpse of my naked ambition and its rapacity, I faltered. I reached the limits of irony, its ability to distance me from my own actions, and at the moment when ruthlessness, pure and single-minded, was required, I turned tail.

Because I am a fibber. Oh, I'm telling you the truth, and I told Kaczynski most of the truth. But I told myself that what I was doing was morally defensible, that good intentions would somehow outweigh or make up for the way ambition transforms people into commodities in a marketplace. And I was wrong. Moral purity of the kind that would redeem a franchiser is impossible. The system, as Kaczynski referred to it, knows where you live. Even if you move to a cabin in the woods.

It isn't just would-be writers who have to worry about their scruples. Therapists, too, must turn other people, or at least their suffering, into business opportunities. The moral defense for this is that it's really nothing personal; we're scientists, after all, treating medical conditions, not people selling love by the hour. And to maintain this defense, we must speak the language of pathology, the same language that gives us a name for the sickness that we are certain Ted Kaczynski must have.

But this intuition – that a person who perpetrates horrific crimes must be ill – needs some examination. My experience of Kaczynski, in which he was reasonable, polite, coherent, fair, and respectful, even when he was being difficult, only comes as a surprise against the backdrop of his violence. Certainly, a killer may be insane. But a person who is sane, sober, and rational, may do terrible things. As in the case, I think, of the Unabomber.

This statement is only vexing if we have already decided

337

that behaving immorally is a criterion of mental illness. I believe this decision has already been made. It's implicit in the psychiatric case against Kaczynski: such specious reasoning can only bear scrutiny if it's what we already expect to hear. But a case like the Unabomber's forces us to look at this decision, and particularly at the way it puts my profession in charge of public morality.

Take my word for it; this is not a good idea. Not because my colleagues and I are scoundrels, although some of us may be, but because the mental health industry will reduce the political to the personal every time. It is our business to do so. Then we are stuck talking about health and illness instead of about right and wrong. Right and wrong, with their reach toward central questions of what it is to be human, are words worth discussing when it comes to serial killers, not to mention other important concerns, like what technology is doing to us and our world. Health and illness, aspiring only to scientific certainty, are, in comparison, hopelessly impoverished.

A society unaccustomed to understanding individuals' behavior as anything other than the result of their psychological states – their childhood traumas and neurochemical imbalances, say – cannot account for the political dimensions of everyday life. It cannot, for instance, raise the question of exactly what is wrong with what Kaczynski did. We perhaps could stand to be reminded of the public agreements that stipulate why we aren't supposed to kill, no matter the cause, and then perhaps we could decide what other people and practices are falling short of the standard that he violated. But the Unabomber case can't force this much-needed conversation if Kaczynski is merely a madman. Then it's enough to know that he is not one of us.

338

But he is. Indeed, *Time*'s assertion that 'There's a little bit of the Unabomber in most of us' may not be all hyperbole. And it's not just the resentment inspired by the maddening little daily encounters – the questions that go unanswered because the computer is down or the thought interrupted by the cell phone or the privacy lost to the demographically precise database – that links us with Kaczynski. It's the knowledge of what lies behind these petty outrages. That's why, when we tell these stories to our friends, we cast ourselves as the heroes battling a wickedly impersonal world, struggling on the side of humanity against the machines and their feckless operators.

Because we know that something is not quite right out there. And it may be too much to assert, as the Unabomber did, that we are the trusties of modernity's prisons; it is certainly too much to kill random people for being collaborators. But it is not too much to say that the problems posed by technology are vast and complex and crucial, far outpacing the engineer's ability to repair a glitch or rethink a poor design. For it's not just the dangers and difficulties – the greenhouse effect and the nuclear waste and the extinction of various species – that ought to give us pause. Technology is etched deeply on our characters, perhaps as deep as our souls. In many ways, it gives us who we are: the kind of people who can flick a switch, hear the furnace rumble faintly in the basement, and take reassurance from its promised warmth without a moment's hesitation over where the oil came from or how it got here or what will become of its smoke. The kind of people who know the answers to all these questions, but what are you going to do, freeze? Move to a cabin in the woods?

We must wink at ourselves to get by. The little bit of the

Unabomber in all of us may be an animosity toward an identity so thoroughly in the debt of bad faith.

The manufacture of the Unabomber as a crazed killer is highly efficient. It applies the balm of explanation to terrible events. It maintains a comfortable distance between him and us. It erases the nagging but crucial public questions raised by the story of a man unable to withstand the dissonance with which all of us must live. And in their place it gives another nugget to be consumed on the way to the next, a story in a glossy or not-so-glossy magazine, written by someone who knows an opportunity when he sees one.

Mollusks

ARTHUR BRADFORD

My friend Kenneth and I were looking through some old automobiles we had found out in a field. We thought maybe there was something valuable in them. One time Kenneth found an old radar gun in a similar situation, the kind cops use to check a car's speed. It didn't work, but he kept it for parts.

These cars out in the field seemed like they had once been on fire. The paint was all bubbly and peeled. There were plants and other vegetation growing up practically through the floorboards. Under the seat of an old Ford I found myself a silver cup. Solid silver, imagine that.

Kenneth crawled inside a green Pontiac which was set apart from the rest of them. He'd been in there not even a minute when I heard him yelling for me to come over. I took my time and he kept yelling, 'Hurry up! Hurry up, you gotta see this . . .'

So I made my way around to the passenger side-door where I could see Kenneth gazing at something he'd found in the glove compartment. I peered inside too and what a sight it was. Right there in that glove box sat a quivering yellow slug about the size of a large loaf of bread.

Kenneth and I watched it for a while, just to see it move. Its skin was all glistening, covered with slime.

'Jesus Christ,' said Kenneth.

So we decided to take the giant slug home with us. Actually, it was Kenneth's idea. He said, 'I know what we're gonna do. We're taking this puppy home.'

Now I wouldn't necessarily have thought of it that way but then it's Kenneth who has the business sense. He is several years older than me and used to make his living doing this sort of thing. We found ourselves a big plastic bag, the kind they give you at the supermarket, and I held it open while Kenneth rolled the slug over. It just fell in there, plop. That slug was heavy, like a big ham, a little softer maybe.

Here's what we had scavenged in just about fifteen minutes at that place: a silver cup (solid silver, mine), an old Zippo lighter (broken, Kenneth's), and a giant slug (maybe ten pounds, Kenneth's, mostly).

I held the slug on my lap on the drive back. Kenneth wanted me to be very careful with it. 'Don't break its skin,' he kept saying. 'Don't let any salt get on it.' Right, where was I going to find salt?

We went straight to Kenneth's house. He lives in a nice place but it's all trashed since he and his crazy wife Teresa never throw anything away. I heard Kenneth say this once, he said, 'It costs ten dollars a month to have them fuckers come over here and haul away the garbage. Why should I pay that? Give me one good reason?'

Kenneth was particularly excited at the prospect of showing the slug to his wife Teresa. He was so excited that he screeched into the driveway and knocked over some plastic milk crates full of trash. 'Whoops,' he said, and then he hopped out of the car.

'Teresa baby, you got to COME QUICK! You got to come out here and see this! You got to see what we found today!' he yelled.

Out comes Teresa and her eyes are all wide like she can't wait to see what we have in store for her. Teresa is very small, childsize almost. She and Kenneth make a funny couple, what with him being so uncommonly stout. I don't know what Teresa thought we had in that plastic bag, but it sure wasn't a big yellow slug.

She screamed and then went over to Kenneth and kicked him in the shin. She said, 'What the fuck did you bring that here for?'

Kenneth was busy holding his aching shin, so I piped up, 'We figure someone will pay us for it.'

'Yeah, right,' said Teresa. She put her little hands on her hips. 'That thing is disgusting.'

I began to feel embarrassed. 'Oh God,' I thought. 'Just look at me. What a fool.' After all, I was the one holding the bag. I must have looked like some sort of creep.

But Kenneth stuck to his guns. He said, 'Disgusting does not mean undesirable.'

Teresa didn't buy that and she whirled around and stomped back into the house. What a firebrand. See, I knew she was Kenneth's wife, but even so I liked her quite a lot. Thou shalt not covet thy neighbor's wife, right? Well fuck that, I thought, look at Kenneth. He's no Casanova. He collects slugs. Where does he get off marrying a woman like Teresa?

We put the giant slug in one of Kenneth's old fish tanks. Actually, the tank still had fish in it, but Kenneth dumped them out to make room for the slug. He dumped them right on the floor of his garage where they flipped about on the cement.

'I'll show her,' he kept saying. 'I'll make a mint off this slug and then you and me will go off on a trip without her.'

'Yeah, right,' I said. But what I was really thinking was, 'This is my chance.' I know, it was crass of me, but remember, Kenneth had just dumped a bunch of helpless fish onto the ground. Where was the compassion in that?

So, while Kenneth was tending to the slug, I went inside and found Teresa. She was at her loom, weaving. She had an enormous loom in the house. It took up a whole room and there was string and yarn everywhere. She made rugs with it.

I said to Teresa, 'Hey, I've got a surprise for you.'

She said, 'It better not be another fucking mollusk.'

'No,' I said, 'it's a cup, solid silver.'

I held out the cup I had found and Teresa stopped working. She had this way of raising just one eyebrow. It was a very sexy thing to do. She said, 'Are you sure you want to give that to me?'

I wasn't making much money then and she was right, I needed everything I got. So I said, 'Oh, maybe I SHOULD hold onto it,' and she nodded knowingly. What a vixen.

Then Kenneth walked in saying, 'I've got some phone calls to make.'

It turned into night. Outside it grew dark and for hours and hours Kenneth kept at it on the phone.

'Yeah, Leroy,' he would say, 'I've got something very unusual here. I think you're gonna like this . . . Yeah, right . . . We found it this afternoon . . . It's a giant slug . . . over ten pounds, easy . . . What? . . . Oh come on, Leroy . . . Leroy? . . . Fuck.' And then he'd try somewhere else.

Meanwhile, I was doing my best with Teresa.

'That's a nice rug you're making,' I said.

'Thank you,' she said. Her childlike hands scampered up and down the vertical strings. The rug was made of many colors, bright yellows and blazing reds. The truth is it was very ugly. I would have gotten sick having something like that on my floor.

Kenneth: 'Hi, Mr Logan . . . Yes, Bob Willis referred me to you . . . Right, he said your organization might be interested in a scientific find I've come across . . .'

'I'm sorry about the slug,' I said to Teresa.

She said, 'Oh, that's okay. I'm used to Ken's bullshit by now.'

'Bullshit!' I thought to myself, 'she's dissatisfied!'

Kenneth yelled over the phone, 'Oh Jesus! That's awful! You people ought to be gassed!' He slammed down the receiver and came running over to us.

'Those Satanists wanted to burn the slug!' he said. 'They've got some kind of voodoo ritual involving mollusks! Isn't that fucked?' Kenneth looked tired. He'd been pulling his greasy hair this way and that.

'I think you're getting too attached to that thing, honey,' said Teresa.

'Yeah,' I said. 'How much were they going to pay you?'

Kenneth looked shocked. He spun around and stormed off in a huff. 'You Nazis!' he called out. 'Fucking sellouts!'

Teresa turned to me and she said, 'Can you and me go and talk somewhere private?'

I said, 'Sure.' All I could think was, 'Now's my chance, now's my chance.'

There was nowhere to move in that trash-filled house so we ended up in the garage. There was that giant slug, sitting in the fish tank, all lit up and glowing yellow. What a monster! It was too big for the tank. Part of its slimy tail slapped up against the glass.

'I sure hope that thing doesn't escape,' I said.

Teresa looked up at me with solemn eyes and she said, 'I haven't told Kenneth about this yet. I haven't told anybody. I'm with child.'

'Oh, hey,' I said, 'a baby.'

Teresa began to cry and I took her into my arms. I put my hand on her stomach. 'Where's the kid?' I asked her. I couldn't feel it.

'It's not big enough yet,' she said.

'Okay,' I said.

We stood there holding each other in that strange aquarium light. I took my hand off of Terresa's stomach and motioned towards the quivering slug. 'Maybe your baby will come out like that,' I said. I'd intended it as some sort of joke, but Teresa didn't take it like that.

'Oh God,' she said.

I moved a little closer and under my foot I felt the body of one of those dead fishes go 'squish.' It wasn't very romantic, but I leaned down and kissed her all the same.

Teresa didn't push me away, but she didn't seem very turned on either. Her lips were cold, as a matter of fact. So I stopped kissing her. I hugged her tight and pulled her little body close to mine. I whispered in her ear, 'I can take you away from all this, Teresa. I can take care of you.'

Of course, I couldn't. I had always looked up to Kenneth. I don't know why I decided at that moment that I was a better man for Teresa. But it didn't matter. Kenneth walked into the garage as we were hugging like that and he stood there shocked. He looked first at Teresa, and then at me, and then at Teresa again.

Then he looked at the slug. 'Dammit,' he said.

He went over to the garage door and heaved it open. The night air rushed in. Kenneth walked back to the tank and reached his hands inside. With a loud grunt he hoisted the beast up and over his head. He stood there holding it high, like a first-place trophy, or a prize fish, and he looked down upon Teresa and me.

'I'll be damned,' he said, 'if I'm gonna let this slug come between us.'

Kenneth dashed out the garage door, slug in hands, and heaved it with all his strength into the night. It landed with a dull thud out on the lawn.

'I don't care how much they were going to pay me,' he said, almost tearful.

Of course, I let go of Teresa at that point and she rushed over to Kenneth and wrapped her arms around him. Kenneth wiped his hands on his pants, to get rid of the slime, and then he hugged her too. I stood there feeling like a true heel at this point, but I had to admit that things looked better this way.

The slug made its escape that night, leaving a thick trail of ooze which disappeared into the woods. Perhaps it found some other abandoned glove compartment to call home. I found out later that some collector had offered Kenneth five hundred dollars for that slug, so it wasn't an empty gesture, tossing the animal away like that. I was sad at first to hear about that money lost. I thought Kenneth was a fool. But then I thought, who are we to decide the fate of the earth's creatures? It was the Mollusks, after all, who first inhabited this earth. They roamed the land for millions and millions of years before any of us were even born.

The Republic of Marfa

SEAN WILSEY

Isolation

In the middle of what's known as Far West Texas, there is Marfa: a hardscrabble ranching community in the upper Chihuahuan desert, 60 miles north of the Mexican border, that inhabits some of the most beautiful and intransigent countryside imaginable: inexhaustible sky over a high desert formed in the Permian period and left more or less alone since. It's situated in one of the least populated sections of the contiguous United States, known locally as *el despoblado* ('the uninhabited place'), a twelve-hour car-and-plane trip from the east coast, and seven from the west. It is nowhere near any interstates, major cities, or significant non-military airfields; it hosts an active population of dangerous animals and insects (a gas station clerk died of a spider bite the summer I first visited); and its 2,424 inhabitants represent the densest concentration of people in a county that covers over 6,000 square miles – an area larger than the states of Connecticut and Rhode Island combined. The isolation is such that if you laid out the islands of the Hawaiian archipelago, and the deep ocean channels that separate them, on the road between Marfa and the East Texas of strip shopping and George Bush Jr., you'd still have 100 miles of blank highway stretching away in front of you.

I've been in regular contact with the place since the summer of 1996 – when my girlfriend, Daphne, was a reporter for the local weekly, the *Big Bend Sentinel* – visiting as often as possible, and witnessing some of the often volatile ways the town's 2,424 people come together; having coalesced, through strange endeavor and coincidence, into a sort of city-state of cattlemen, artists, writers, fugitives, smugglers, free-thinkers, environmentalists, soldiers and secessionists – making Marfa home to what must be the most uncompromised contemporary art museum in the world; and, nineteen months ago, when a local teenager tending goats on a bluff above the nearby Rio Grande was shot by a Marine patrol, the site of the first civilian killing by American military personnel since Kent State.

Marfa is the name of the family servant in *The Brothers Karamazov*, the book a railway overseer's wife was reading when an unnamed water stop became a town in 1881. This frontierswoman was reading the book a year after its initial publication in Russian, the same year Billy the Kid was shot dead in nearby New Mexico, and during the extended period of border uneasiness that followed the Mexican–American war. But such circumstances are typically Marfan. The town attracts the bizarre: some of the first documentation of the area comes from Indian and pioneer accounts, in the 1800s, of flashing, mobile, seemingly animate luminescences on the horizon – the Marfa Mystery Lights, unexplained optical phenomena that are still observed from a pull-off on the outskirts of town, where a crowd seems to appear every night to socialize. And until the mid-70s the lights were the main attraction. Then the minimalist artist Donald Judd moved to Marfa, exiling himself from what he termed the 'glib and harsh' New York art scene, in order to live in a sort of high-plains laboratory devoted to building, sculpture, furniture design, museology, conservation, and a dash of ranching, until his death in 1994.

Last April the Chinati Foundation, a contemporary art museum Judd founded in the late 70s, and named after a nearby mountain range, invited architects and artists to come to Marfa and discuss the future of collaboration between the two disciplines. Billed as a symposium, it was more like a conflagration. Among the participants were Frank Gehry, whose Guggenheim Museum had recently opened in Bilbao, Spain (architect Philip Johnson has since declared it 'the greatest building of our time'); the Swiss architects Jacques Herzog and Pierre de Meuron, engaged in a massive and controversial expansion of the Tate Gallery in London; the light and space artist Robert Irwin, who had just taken an unexpected creative detour and designed the garden for the Getty Center in Los Angeles; Roni Horn, a wily New York conceptualist who sculpts with words (she's plastic-cast adjectives that describe both emotions and weather and embedded them in the structure of a German meteorological bureau); and the pop artist (and deadpan comedian) Claes Oldenburg. This group spent two days in *el despoblado* showing slides and talking about their work, while two art historians – James Ackerman from Harvard, a hoary emeritus type, and Michael Benedikt from the University of Texas, a searing and somewhat humorless postmodernist – weighed in in a critical capacity, paid homage to Donald Judd, and attempted to shut everyone up. Daphne (her last name is Beal) had assignments to write about it for a couple of architecture magazines, and I went along. They were expecting 600 people, and I was curious to observe what a 25 percent increase in Marfa's population might produce –

the equivalent of 2 million ranchers suddenly arriving for a weekend in Manhattan.

Marfa sits in what seems like ground zero of an ancient impact site – a wide plain with mountain ranges surrounding it at an equidistant remove of about 30 miles. To the west lie the Sierra Vieja, to the north the Davis. The Glass, Del Norte, and Santiago (as well as an extinct volcano) are to the east, the Chinati to the south. These mountains run down to the high desert of cacti and yellow grassland around Marfa, framing an oceanic West Texas sky, with virtually nothing in the way of buildings or tall trees to interrupt it. The result is a big basin full of light and dry heat, where every object takes on a peculiar definition; shapes clarified and detailed, shadows standing out in perfect relief.

The town itself is a rectangle 16 blocks high by 20 wide, with Mexican and Anglo cemeteries (separated by a fence) on the west end, a golf course (highest elevation in Texas) on the east, and satellite neighborhoods protruding to the south and northeast like radar arrays. It contains unexpected delfs and shadows, grand old homes behind tree-shaded lawns, century-old structures whose adobe disintegrates at any elemental provocation, and disused industrial buildings with aluminum siding that ticks in the heat. It operates in a state of oblivion to all the high-concept art that is made and displayed there. The two restaurants, Mike's and Carmen's, are full of ranchers, workmen and border patrol. The two bars do decent business – there's no open-container law in Texas, and both have takeout windows. The streets are wide and for the most part empty.

In order to get to Marfa you fly into either El Paso or Midland/Odessa. Of course, there's almost never a direct flight, so after landing in Dallas or Houston you get on a small twin-prop plane. When Daphne flew down to work at the *Sentinel* the editors met her in Midland. After shaking hands she ran into the bathroom and vomited. When I went down to visit I couldn't wait till landing and had to throw up on the plane.

Unforced Excommunication, Forced Communication

Donald Judd, a cantankerous Scotsblood Midwesterner with a fondness for kilts, had all the fame, respect and financial recompense a visual artist could hope for when he relegated his five-story cast-iron residence in SoHo to the status of a pied-à-terre and abandoned New York for Marfa in 1976.

This was a man with a hankering for space – not to say empire. A book devoted exclusively to Judd's many homes and buildings, *Donald Judd Spaces*, runs to more than 100 pages and contains 15 different beds (less than half the total). Judd held that a bed should always be convenient to a place people might even passingly abide. When he arrived in Marfa he set up residence in two World War I aircraft hangars and proceeded to buy the bank, a 300-acre former cavalry base (now the Chinati Foundation), three ranches (with a total acreage of 38,000), a mohair warehouse, the Safeway, the Marfa Hotel, a handful of light-manufacturing and commercial buildings, six homes from around the turn of the century, and the Marfa hot springs. By the early 90s he was planning on bottling Marfa water (which is said to contain traces of natural lithium), shipping it to New York, and selling it at Dean and Deluca.

Judd's philosophy was both ascetic and profligate – a paradoxical combination of simplicity and mass consumption. He bought everything he could lay his hands on with money from art he'd made with his own two hands. He had an almost feudal arrangement with Marfa, employing a workforce that for a time outnumbered the municipal payroll (and over which I've always unfairly – I have no evidence of such a thing – imagined him exercising some kind of droit du seigneur, what with all those beds). Because of the controlled surroundings he created by purchasing whole buildings and stretches of land, his art in Marfa ingeniously extends its own boundaries to include entire rooms, structures and vistas.

The Brothers Karamazov is a novel about a murder and a family's convoluted relations, played out in a small town. The transposition from the novel's unnamed Russian village to present-day Marfa is an easy one to make. The way the brothers talk to each other – in grandiloquent outbursts of 'excitement' or grave silences full of 'strain' – reminds me of how Marfans communicate. Much of the town's emotion, as expressed in the *Sentinel*'s letters column, is reminiscent of that in the book. One man, writing about Marfa's segregated Anglo/Mexican cemetery, declared it 'a slap in the face to humanity.' A woman, dissecting an exploitative nuclear waste agreement Texas signed with some eastern states, concluded, 'We could have made this same compact with a dog.'

Marfa's mood is Dostoyevsky's. The book and the town contain the same sort of devote, and the same sort of outrage.

In Marfa, the people are restrained, disinclined to conversation, courteous, fractious, and, when they wish to be, extremely generous. There is also a good deal of public eccentricity. A woman roams the streets, roads, and surrounding desert with all her possessions tied to the back of a pack animal. Sometimes she's way out on the blacktop between Marfa and the mountains. Other times she's ambling through town, taking a short cut across the concrete apron of the Texaco station. She sleeps out in the open, wherever she happens to be when the sun sets, and bears more than a passing resemblance to another character from *The Brothers Karamazov*, Stinking Lisaveta, who wandered Dostoyevsky's small-town back alleys, sleeping 'on the ground and in the mud.' Marfans call her the 'Burro Lady.' And she's one of many descriptions and details in the novel that apply almost word-for-word to Marfa. (Although, according to legend, the Burro Lady, unlike Stinking Lisaveta, does have a companion of sorts. A rogue steer drifts through the countryside – the symbol of an unpunished frontier crime. It's supposed to be immortal, and, as a sort of harbinger, it only shows itself to cursed souls: a brand covering its entire flank, from shoulder to rump, reads 'MURDER.')

The town is also a place where mundane interactions unexpectedly take turns for the surreal. Daphne and I once got our car fixed by a gas station attendant who, when I told him I smelled something weird when the car got hot, simply said, 'Let's take a look at that sum-bitchie,' popped the hood, rooted around for awhile, ripped something that looked like a dead snake out of the engine with a flourish (it turned out to be the a/c belt), threw it over his shoulder, and chuckled, 'Re-paired.' In a travelogue by Scottish novelist Duncan McLean, something distinctly Marfan happens when the author checks out of the El Paisano, the only hotel in town:

I stubbed my toe against some clunky bit of litter lying on the sidewalk. It went skittering away in front of me and stopped a metre ahead, long glinting barrel pointing straight at me: A GUN. Next thing I knew I was back at the Paisano's desk, banging on the bell and babbling away to the clerk . . . 'It's out there, a pistol, come on, come on' . . .

The clerk ducked through a hatch in the counter and walked out of the lobby . . .

'There,' I said. 'See it?' . . .

He held up a hand for me to stay, took a step forward, and peeped over my shoulder-bag.

'Ha!' He exhaled.

'What is it?'

He leaned over, snatched up the pistol, and turned back towards me.

'You call this a gun?' he said, and laughed.

'Eh . . . yeah.'

He flicked some kind of catch, then pushed the revolving magazine out sideways.

'This ain't no real gun,' he said.

'What then? An imitation?'

He tilted up the pistol so a shower of little silver bullets fell out and onto his palm.

'This here's a lady's gun,' he said . . . 'Couldn't kill shit.'

When Daphne first arrived, and was living at Chinati, a cowboy gave her a lift into town in his truck. He was a craggy guy in his late 50s who broke horses and raised livestock. When the conversation turned to why he'd settled in Marfa 20 years before, he said it was because the town had a 'genius loci.' It was an expression neither of us had ever heard before, and when we looked it up we found it strangely faithful to the peculiarity that animates the town. In Latin, it means 'genius of the place.' 'Genius,' (says the *OED*) when applied to a locale, indicates 'a presiding deity or spirit.'

It's true – something about the landscape, the strange goings-on, the balance between population and depopulation, lends credence to the belief that Marfa didn't just happen this way – that some unseen force presides.

Renegade Tendencies

The *Big Bend Sentinel* arrives in New York a couple weeks after it's printed in Pecos (100 miles to the north, the nearest town with a printer). The core of its news is crime and the border, with a lot of art, armed forces (jet training for the German and US air forces occurs in county airspace), sports, agriculture, and animal husbandry thrown in. The *Sentinel* covers all of these subjects with curiosity and seriousness, and after a few years of reading it, I'm starting to think it's possible to learn more about the state of the world from a carefully reported small paper than from any other source.

Here are some of the stranger, more significant recent stories:

In 1996, people with multiple-chemical sensitivity, a disease whose sufferers take ill when exposed to synthetic materials, began living in the hills near Marfa and building an all-natural commune – until the members of a yearly Bible retreat (one of the oldest of its kind) arrived upwind and began their annual spraying of Malathion, a DDT-style pesticide that caused the Chemical Sensitives to become violently ill, and engage with the religious group in a small war of ideology and incommunication. Compassion for the sick was ultimately rejected, because it was inconvenient to pray with the mosquitoes.

On a spring night in 1997 a band of Marines on a drug interdiction sortie (part of what locals call the 'militarization' of the US–Mexico border) spent 20 minutes tracking Esequiel Hernandez Jr., a young goatherd who carried a vintage World War I rifle to keep coyotes away from his flock. For some reason Hernandez raised the rifle, in what evidence shows to have been the opposite direction from the Marines, one of whom then shot him 'in self-defense.' The boy bled to death for 20 minutes before the soldiers summoned help. When a deputy sheriff arrived the Marines said that Hernandez hurt himself 'falling into a well.' Unfortunately, soldiers have been a constant presence in the county since the Reagan administration circumvented a law prohibiting military involvement in domestic law-enforcement, and this event, though it enraged the populace, has had little long-term impact on the situation. Last fall the defense department, which still denies any wrong-doing, paid the Hernandez family more than $1 million and washed its hands.

Over the last four years the Texas Low-Level Radioactive Waste Disposal Authority has attempted to push through legislation for a nuclear dump less than 200 miles west of Marfa, on a site that, aside from being both a geological fault line and a watershed for the Rio Grande, is inhabited by an impoverished, not particularly educated populace, key members of which proved amenable to various forms of bribery. The dump looked like a neatly done deal, until an unlikely group of zealous activists (one of them Gary Oliver, the *Sentinel*'s excellent – and legally blind – cartoonist) galvanized the entire six-county area of Far West Texas, as well as a large delegation from the Mexican government, and the measure was defeated. It seemed like a miracle.

A few months ago a local man survived a gas explosion which blew off his roof and knocked down the walls of his house – a story I followed from mystery occurrence, to medical emergency, to amazing recovery, to possible criminal prosecution (he was trying to gas himself, which made the property damage negligent), and, lately, into the real-estate column.

About every other week there's a 400-pound bale of marijuana found on the roadside, an ad taken out by the county informing someone they are 'Hereby Commanded' to appear in court, or a violent fugitive on the lam. (Fugitives are another Dostoyevskian touch. In *The Brothers Karamazov*, there is 'a horrible convict who had just escaped from the provincial prison, and was secretly living in our town.') The bank in Van Horn, about 100 miles to the west, went through a period in 1996 when it was robbed every few weeks. Former Marfa sheriff Rick Thompson is serving a life sentence for smuggling more than a ton of cocaine out of Mexico – he's referred to as 'the cocaine sheriff.' The Unabomber, whose brother owns property in the area, carried on a lengthy and passionate correspondence with a Mexican campesino just over the border.

The *Sentinel* also contains an outspoken, thoughtful, varied, occasionally bombastic opinion section, with letters from the likes of 'Crazy Bear,' George 'Pepper' Brown (who for some reason is the honorary mayor of Wellfleet, Mass., though he lives near Marfa, and his letters to Robert Halpern, the *Sentinel*'s editor, all begin 'Roberto, amigo'), and many members of the large Mexican-American community – names like Lujan and Cabezuela are characteristic – published side by side with a sort of rustic philosophical-observation-cum-chitchat column called 'Wool Gathering,' by Mary Katherine Metcalfe Earney. 'Wool Gathering' is filed from the retirement home, and can take some strange turns. One meandering edition about a pleasant visit to Delaware and Philadelphia, seeing lapsed Marfans, ended like this, 'On the return to Dallas and in between planes, I was stabbed in the hand by an angry woman . . .'

On the back page there's a section for classified ads and public notices. There's a column for mobile homes, a column for garage sales, a column of miscellany ('about 20 goats, all sizes'), and a half-page of real estate. Daphne and I often check to see what houses are going for (usually around $60,000 for a few acres and a couple bedrooms). We imagine moving down to Marfa, becoming some sort of ranch hands, reporting for the *Sentinel* or the daily paper in San Angelo, a town of 100,000 about 200 miles to the northeast, which used to pick up her stories, and living in the 'Judd way,' which we've convinced ourselves involves a pure ascetic harmony with the surroundings.

In fact, Donald Judd, for all his land-grabbing, became something of a holy man. His masterpiece in Marfa is an installation of 100 milled-aluminum boxes – each of the exact same volume (about that of a restaurant stove), but with wildly different interiors, full of sloping metal planes and odd angles. The boxes fill two former artillery sheds that he opened up to the Texas plains with huge windows along their sides, and capped with Quonset roofs. During the day the sheds fill with sun and the boxes warp and change and reflect the landscape. At night they turn liquid in the moonlight. In the distance, between the sheds and the far-off silhouette of the Chinati

Mountains, Judd placed 15 rectangular boxes, each about 10 feet tall, which further link the site to the landscape. This was the artist's favorite (Karamazovian) story about the piece: After a tour, a Jesuit priest turned to him and said, 'You and I are in the same business.'

And Chinati, just outside town, also seems pulled from *The Brothers Karamazov*, resembling the 'neighboring monastery' that 'crowds of pilgrims . . . from thousands of miles, come flocking to see' with Judd – or the spirit of Judd – the presiding elder, called Zosima in the book, responsible for the 'great glory' that has come to the place.

By the time he died, Judd had changed from a sculptor into an almost monastic figure. He was living in deep seclusion, on the remotest of his ranches in the high desert, without electricity, close to the border, surrounded by books on art, philosophy, history and local ecology. 'My first and largest interest is in my relation to the natural world,' he wrote during this period. 'All of it, all the way out. This interest includes my existence . . . the existence of everything and the space and time that is created by the existing things.'

Desert Picnics

Approaching Marfa the temperamentality in the local land-scape quickly becomes apparent. There's an old cowboy poem about a 'place where mountains float in the air,' which may be a reference to the mirages that the dry Marfan climate is known to produce. A local man recalls seeing 'the entire [nearby] town of Valentine appearing in the morning sky.' Another claims to have seen 'the apparition of a Mexican village in the still-light sky just after sunset.' It rarely rains, but when it does the sky is transformed, going from its usual big serene blue to the purple-black of a deep bruise – and letting loose so much precipitation that water suddenly runs in rivers through the streets. You can see it all coming a hundred miles off, like a train down a straight line of track. At night there's a great heaping feast of stars, and meteor showers – 'like confetti' is how Daphne puts it – are a regular event.

Sometimes the sun is so bright that you can't see. I first noticed this while driving back from Balmorhea, a town with a vast spring-fed swimming pool (and ranch-hand brothels) over the mountains about 50 miles north of Marfa. It's typical in Far West Texas to drive 100 miles just to have something to do, the way the rest of the country goes to the movies, and in Balmorhea Daphne and I'd run into some other people from Marfa and spent the day talking in the shade. Coming back, Daphne drove and I stared out the window. As we started coming out of the flatland, up through the Davis Mountains, where the two-lane road twists through a canyon and the desert terrain gives way a bit, I noticed a tree, a salt cedar or something – the first green I'd seen since leaving the pool – standing out with a sort of fluorescent brightness against the canyon's brown rock and scrub. When I pulled off my sunglasses the color disappeared. With a naked eye the tree looked pale, burned and exhausted – almost translucent. The sunlight was so strong that it was shining right through it. But when I put the sunglasses back on the light receded and the tree reappeared – standing out like it was on fire.

Besides the sparse trees, which are more common in town, the terrain supports myriad cacti: yucca and cholla in abundance, but also the odd horse crippler (a nasty, horizontally inclined weed that looks like an unsprung bear trap); nopolito, a cactus with flat pads that are de-spined and sold in fruit bins outside the gas stations; ocotillo, a subaquatic-looking plant with wavy tentacles and sharp thorns that suggests an octopus crossed with a blowfish; and lots of juniper and mesquite. The cholla, or prickly pear, is a thicker, less primordial variant on the ocotillo, with leaves like a pineapple's, and the yucca is a bush with aloe-like spines, each about 2 feet long. When yucca bloom, a 7-foot rod shoots out of the center and bursts into a brilliant yellow flower that stands out brightly, like a flare in the landscape, sunglasses or no.

There are four roads out of Marfa. One leads to Valentine, a comatose place with a post office that receives bags of mail in early February from all over the country, to be reposted before the 14th. A second leads to Shafter, a ghost town waiting for either the governor's order to abolish it or the price of silver to hit $6 an ounce (it's now at $5.30), so as to make it worthwhile for an interested mining concern to tap a vein that was abandoned during World War II. The third road leads to the area's only theater, in Alpine, and the campus of Sul Ross State University, which offers degrees in Range Animal Science, and is the birthplace of intercollegiate rodeo. The last leads to Fort Davis, a boutique town with an observatory dedicated to the spectroscopic analysis of light.

Technically, there's a fifth road, through Pinto Canyon, which leads out of Marfa to the southwest, in the direction of Judd's main ranch, and winds up on the border in a town called Ruidosa (though 'town' is an exaggeration, as there isn't a single amenity in Ruidosa, besides the road; it's more like an encampment). Leaving Marfa down Pinto Canyon, you see a sign that reads, 'Pavement ends 32 miles.' My one experience driving the length of this road was unnerving in the extreme. About an hour out, halfway between Marfa and the Rio Grande, having seen no other cars, we decided to stop where the road crossed a dry creek-bed. This was long after the pavement had ended. The scenery looked a lot like the ocean floor. The temperature was in the 90s. We'd packed a picnic of avocado sandwiches, Lone Star beer, and some local cheese called *osadero*; we spied some tired-looking bushes – the only non-cactus shade in sight – and figured to have lunch under them. After shutting the car off we trudged about 400 feet down the dry creek-bed (I was thinking flash-flood, which is something the area's known for). Away from the road – which was only a spit through the wilderness at this point – we set down our cooler and got out our food. We started to eat without saying much of anything – the silence was so immense it suppressed any conversational impulse.

The picnic was scuttled 15 minutes later when we heard the sound of someone trying to hotwire our car. The starter whined, but the engine wouldn't catch. We looked at each other for an instant, and then jumped up and started tearing back up the creek-bed, more afraid of being stuck out there than of whatever we might find. I got there first, in a gasping, adrenaline-choked rush, and found the car sitting where we'd left it, and with no one in sight. Daphne ran back, packed up our stuff, and we got the hell out of there fast. Whoever was out in that desert on foot, crossing into the US, had to want a car with Texas plates – bad. All we could think was that they gave up trying when they heard us crashing down the creek, thinking to avoid a confrontation: even if the motor caught, the car was headed towards Mexico, and with the road disintegrating into sharp rubble and cacti a foot to either side, there was no obvious way to turn it around.

For the symposium, we came in from the south, via Shafter, and after checking into the Thunderbird Motel, we dragged some chairs outside and watched the motor court fill up with rental cars. Since the Thunderbird's amenities include a plentiful ice machine, we filled a cooler we'd brought and sat out on a concrete walk beneath an overhang for half an hour. Then we went to check out the town. Rob Weiner, Judd's old assistant, who used to spend his every waking hour with Judd and has stayed on in Marfa, stopped his car to say hello. He knew Daphne well when she lived there, and we became friends after I first visited. His causticity and sense of amusement about most things Marfan is combined with a huge knowledge and passion for the place, and if Marfa turns into an art community, he'll have a lot to do with it. He told us that we might be able to stay in a Foundation building later that weekend.

At an ad hoc Chinati Foundation store, which was selling books on all the lecturers in the symposium as well as on the work of artists Judd admired and permanently installed in Marfa (Claes Oldenburg, Dan Flavin, Carl Andre, Richard Long, Ilya Kabakov, and John Chamberlain), we fell into conversation with our first non-Marfan, a half-American-Indian reporter from the *Houston Press* named Shaila. She had driven from Houston and was camping out in the Marfa trailer park.

'Gehry is God,' she told us.

Not in Marfa, I thought. God's Judd.

After that we went by the paper to see Robert Halpern and his wife Rosario, who were busy with an issue but invited us to dinner with the newspaper staff, their kids, and Rusty Taylor, the former chief of police, all of whom had recently been involved in a characteristically unusual chapter in Marfa history.

In July 1996, a photograph in the *Sentinel* showed a tall, lean, rangy-looking man with a circle of white hair wearing a T-shirt that said 'Ask Me about The Republic of Texas.' This was Richard McLaren, described by his neighbors as 'capable of tremendous violence;' a man who, arguing a legal technicality in an 1845 annexation document, considered himself chief ambassador, consul general, and sovereign of the independent nation of Texas. McLaren had become a bullying presence in the hills north of Marfa, given to threats and harassment, filing false liens against property, passing bogus scrip, and accumulating weapons. That day he and his followers were having a picnic in celebration of 'captive nations week,' a propaganda occasion established under Eisenhower in the late 50s to foster dissent under communist dictatorships. In the background could be seen two police cruisers: Rusty Taylor, a couple dozen Texas rangers and other lawmen were keeping an eye on the situation.

Less than a year later, in the spring of 1997, three ROT conscripts, dressed in camouflage and carrying assault weapons, stalked through the mountains from McLaren's trailer home to the house of his nearest neighbors, Joe Rowe – former president of the local neighborhood association – and his wife Margaret Ann. When they arrived in the yard they opened fire on the house, sending shrapnel into Mr Rowe's shoulder, then burst through the door and struck him with a rifle butt, breaking his arm. With the Rowes subdued, the intruders made some long-distance calls, took all the food they could carry (leaving $40 as compensation) and brought their hostages back to McLaren's trailer, from which the group issued a communique describing the action as reprisal for the arrest earlier that morning of another Republic of Texas member, Robert Scheidt, on charges of carrying illegal weapons. McLaren declared war on the United States, and named the Rowes as his first prisoners. Showing considerable restraint, police in Marfa agreed to release Scheidt in exchange for the Rowes, and a trade was made that left the group isolated in their trailer, several miles up a dirt road, surrounded by SWAT teams and Texas rangers.

McLaren had prepared for such an occasion by digging a series of bunkers and stockpiling more than 60 pipe bombs, a dozen or so gasoline cans, 10 long rifles, several pistols, and 500 to 700 rounds of ammunition. He swore to fight to the end, and issued a grandiloquent statement evoking the diary of William B. Travis, commander at the Alamo in 1836: 'Everyone has chosen to stay and hold the sovereign soil of the Republic and its foreign missions. I pray reinforcements arrive before they overrun the embassy.' He would wage an Alamo-style fight to the death. He would kill as many officers as possible. As police reinforcements continued to arrive, McLaren got on the shortwave radio and broadcast: 'Mayday! Mayday! Mayday! Hostiles are invading the Republic of Texas embassy. We have hostiles in the woods.'

After a few days, though, McLaren began to soften. He conceded that he could surrender if the rules of war were applied and the US agreed to treat him under the rules of the Geneva Convention, allowing an appeal to the United Nations. This eventually led to his signing a 'Texas-wide cease-fire document,' essentially an unconditional surrender, with a proviso that the embassy be respected, which he understood to mean that the Republic flag, a lone yellow star on a blue field, would continue to fly – it was lowered and replaced by the Texas flag, in what a local fireman described as an 'Iwo Jima-style ceremony.' McLaren and four others lay down their weapons (though, arriving in Marfa, one of them shouted, 'I was captured, not surrendered, and I'm ashamed I didn't die'). Two other members went renegade and retreated into the hills with rifles and small arms. They were pursued by hounds, all of which they shot. Helicopters then tracked the pair into more remote terrain, and when they were fired upon, police snipers shot back and killed one man. The other, Richard Keyes III, who had quit a job at a Kansas bathroom-equipment manufacturer just weeks before these events, managed to escape. He basically evanesced. And now, almost 20 months later, he still has not been found. One newspaper called him 'a West Texas version of D.B. Cooper,' a hijacker in the early 70s who parachuted out of a 727 with $200,000 in ransom money and was never heard from again.

But a reporter for *Mother Jones* magazine has heard from Keyes, or a man claiming (quite credibly) to be Keyes. He defended the attack on the Rowes, and noted that after inflicting wounds they'd subsequently called a doctor, who'd refused to help, because 'he was concerned about a house full of armed fruitcakes.' Touching on the fact that the kidnappers had left the Rowes payment for food and phone calls, the man declared, 'They were fully compensated for what happened, except for the fact that they had a rather bad day.' He also said that he was safely outside the United States, which, in McLaren terms, probably means he's still in Texas.

As for McLaren, before the surrender he made sure that his

international ceasefire agreement also included a conjugal visit with a woman he'd 'married' a short time before, in a service binding only under the laws of the Republic of Texas. She was also under arrest for her involvement in the siege, so following arraignment by the Marfa justice of the peace, Cinderella Gonzalez, the two were put in the same cell.

In the lonely days that followed, while awaiting trial, McLaren took to writing florid letters to the *Sentinel*, calling his 'challenge to gain national independence . . . the best-executed legal presentation that has ever been accomplished in the 20th century.' He also described his predicament in Marfa as that of a 'prisoner of war' being held in the 'king's jails.' More than a few locals have expressed disappointment that he was not killed during the siege. Though McLaren is going to be away for a long time, some neighbors fear that Keyes might return and retake the embassy.

As Daphne and I left the *Sentinel* and stepped onto Highland Avenue, the main street in town, we could see the old court-house, with its cupola, coffered ceiling, and yard of sprawling almond trees. It's crowned by a statue of justice, which, legend has it, lost her scales sometime in the 20s, after a hungover cowboy, fresh out of jail and reunited with his six guns, shot them out of her hands, yelling, 'Thar ain't no justice in this goddamn country.'

Conflagrations

The next morning, 600 artists, art historians, architects, critics, journalists, and a few townspeople assembled under the corrugated-tin roof of a former ice plant in a neighborhood

called Salsipuedes ('get out if you can'). The place was so full
that they'd dragged in extra chairs from the local veterans
society with phrases like 'AMVETS Salutes USO Post 65
with Pride' stenciled on their backs. Opening the proceedings,
James Ackerman, the art historian from Harvard, tried to
temper the Judd idolatry by describing the artist as a man
'at war' with architecture, given less to collaboration than to
'fulminations against architecture in our time.'

A big man was seated across the aisle from me. It was
Frank Gehry, looking a lot like somebody's Palm Springs
grandfather. He was wearing old loafers that needed a shine,
a white button-down shirt, gray suit pants and a sport jacket.
When the architect Jacques Herzog – thin, hip, dressed with
a Swiss meticulousness, completely in black, Gehry's aesthetic
opposite – got up to give a detailed lecture, I watched Gehry.
Herzog explained the process of 'tattooing' photographs to
concrete in order to give his buildings variegated surfaces.
He'd been talking for half an hour when an El Paso-bound
train came by and drowned him out for a minute. I glanced
over at Gehry. He seemed aggravated. When Herzog resumed
lecturing and began a long series of slides on the expansion
of the Tate Gallery, Gehry, brow furrowed, started fidgeting
with a pencil. The next time I looked, he was up and gone.
Herzog continued lecturing for a few minutes until the director
of Chinati suddenly cut him off. It seemed like Gehry had
heard enough from his competition and put an end to it.

That afternoon, an ornery vibe intensified, and some Judd-
style 'fulminating' commenced when the artists took the stage.
Robert Irwin, opening his lecture with a sustained tangent
about art history, endeavored to make it clear that he didn't
believe in anything beyond modernism. 'Postmodernism: If

that isn't a red herring I'll kiss your ass,' he hollered. He then proceeded to slam Richard Meier, the principal architect on the Getty Center project, saying, 'I chewed him up and left him for dead . . . Though you'd never define a collaboration in that way.'

It was around this time that I heard a groan. It wasn't Gehry, but Shaila, from the *Houston Press*, who had fainted from the slowly intensifying heat. Daphne had to help her outside. When Shaila filed her piece she would blame the incident on side effects associated with her stay in the Marfa trailer park, and its limited culinary options: 'the smell of my own road fare farts.' But at the time we were happily unaware of her condition.

And during all this commotion Irwin didn't ever slow down. Animated with a sort of giddy, profane enthusiasm, the artist reveled in some of the stranger details of his work. He described his relations with his horticultural consultants on the Getty Center garden as 'spending a lot of time going to nurseries and hugging each other.' As evidence of his attention to minutiae he said that he'd made certain that benches in the garden would 'feel good on your ass.' He then explained that he'd fashioned the stream that runs through the garden with heavy stonework because 'I didn't want it to look like some gay bathroom.' With this a disapproving rumble came over the ice plant. (Later, when questioned about the gay bathroom comment, Irwin was both apologetic and cagey. 'I don't get out much. I'm an artist,' he explained.)

The next speaker, Michael Benedikt, the postmodernist, riveted Irwin through his spectacles and said, 'Modernism is male and macho. And that's the problem with it.'

After castigating Irwin, Benedikt called the work of making

art a 'religious project,' and delivered a lecture that delved into the Old Testament. In Benedikt's mind, the burning bush that Moses encountered in the desert was, like successful art, 'burning with its own authenticity.' Then we were released for dinner at Chinati.

Standing in line for food, a man was saying, 'We need to maximize returns for the whole Marfa concept.' This was Judd's old lawyer, John Jerome. Dinner was brisket and Shiner Bock beer in the Arena, a former army gymnasium that Judd rehabilitated. It's difficult to say what exactly the 'Marfa concept' might be. For Judd it meant control: of his surroundings, of his art, of the company he kept. As the Russian installation artist Ilya Kabakov noted, 'When I first came to Marfa, my biggest impression was the unbelievable combination of estrangement, similar to a holy place, and at the same time of unbelievable attention to the life of the works there. For me it was like some sort of Tibetan monastery; there were no material things at all, none of the hubbub of our everyday lives. It was . . . a world for art.' (Although I don't think that's what Jerome meant.)

But Kabakov's presence in Marfa alters the concept significantly. Kabakov, whose installation is completely different from all the other major pieces in Marfa, was an underground artist in the Soviet Union who began to exhibit in the West only in the late 80s. In the early 90s Judd invited him to come to Marfa and do a piece. Kabakov was 'astounded.' The haunting result is 'School No. 6,' a replica of an entire communist-era Russian grade school – desks, display cases, lesson plans, Cyrillic textbooks, musical instruments – installed in a Chinati barracks, exposed to the elements, and encouraged to decay. 'Of course there was nothing more awful than the Soviet school, with all of its discipline, abomination, and militariz-ation,' he has said of the work. 'But now that that system has collapsed and left behind only ruins, it evokes the same kind of nostalgic feelings as a ruined temple.' It also has its serene, even spiritual overtones. As he describes it: 'The entire space of the school is flooded with sunshine and quiet. Sunny squares lie on the school floor. The blue sky is visible in the empty apertures. From all of this, the neglect reigning all around does not seem so cheerless and depressing.' The installation plays the trick of turning Marfa into Russia. And Kabakov's description of its mood is akin to one in *The Brothers Karamazov* wherein the youngest brother repeatedly recalls his mother's face, but always in 'the slanting rays of the setting sun (these slanting rays he remembered most of all).'

In discussing another one of his installations Kabakov has said that 'everything that we see around us, everything that we discover in our past, or which could possibly comprise the future – all of this is a limitless world of projects.' Though he seems to mean it somewhat ironically, the statement pairs nicely with Judd's writing about his interest in the natural world, 'all of it, all the way out.' A radically different interpret-ation of the same artistic impulse.

So Kabakov is also part of the 'Marfa concept.'

And the concept – no matter which of the seminal events or legends in the town's history one follows – always has to do with light.

Light, in fact, is Marfa's last name. Marfa Ignatievna – meaning 'daughter of Ignatius,' which, according to a diction-ary of names, is derived from the Latin word *ignis*, meaning 'fire.' 'Ignatievna' can be broken down to mean 'daughter of fire.' According to Dostoyevsky, the character is 'not a stupid woman,' and early in *The Brothers Karamazov* she gives rise to 'a strange, unexpected and original occurrence' – the birth of a boy that her superstitious husband fears, calls a 'dragon' – fire-breathing, presumably – and refuses to care for. When the baby dies, Marfa takes it stoically. Aside from not being stupid, she's a stoical lady – two desirable qualities in a frontierswoman. And since the woman who named the town after this character must have been reading the book in the original Russian – the first translation, into German, wasn't until 1884, and the English version didn't appear until 1912 – she could not have been unaware of the name's significance.

After going through the food line, Daphne and I sat down with some of the staff and artists in residence at Chinati, who were talking about how the Lannan Foundation was almost finished renovating two homes it had bought to house writers who receive its literary awards. An English poet would be arriving in a month. (He's there now, putting aside the poetry, evidently, to write a book called *Marfan*.) The other major piece of art news was the receipt of Chinati's first NEA grant, towards the renovation of six old U-shaped army barracks, to house a piece that light artist Dan Flavin planned with Judd and completed designing after Judd's death, when Flavin was on his own deathbed, in 1996. There was also talk about Robert Irwin maybe taking a spare building and making a piece from light-capturing scrim veils.

After dinner the evening migrated to Lucy's Bar, where, as the sun went down in Marfa's austere big-sky setting, the gathering's most imposing participant, Frank Gehry, was given a wide, somewhat awestruck berth. Ray, the owner, even allowed him to stand in an off-limits-to-customers spot beside the bartender (blocking the sink). Eventually he left for the dilapidated old El Paisano Hotel, where he was the most famous guest since James Dean spent a week during the shooting of the film *Giant*. As Lucy's started to break up, people either headed home or out to see the Marfa Lights.

The Marfa Lights, not unlike Frank Gehry, are a fairly aloof phenomenon – mostly appearing at a hard-to-quantify distance from a roadside pull-off, near the site of an old military airfield. To most observers they look like a distant swarm of fireflies, constantly changing direction and flashing on and off in random patterns. But there are wild exceptions to this aloofness. In various accounts the lights are animate and even intelligent. They metastasize, hide behind one another, change color, bounce across the desert 'like basketballs,' line up for aircraft 'like runway lights,' and pursue lone motorists between Marfa and Alpine. (Robert Halpern told me about a guy who was descended upon and pursued by a pair of Marfa lights, blazing incandescently, all the way to the town limits, after which he swore that he would never leave Marfa again, and hasn't.) Though the most reliable place to see them is the viewing site, overlooking a vast swath of desert between Marfa and Alpine – where a weather-beaten historical marker details various explanations ('campfires, phosphorescent minerals, swamp gas, static electricity, St Elmo's fire, and "ghost lights"') – the lights have been known to stray as far away as the Dead Horse Mountains, 60 miles to the east, the hills near Ruidosa, an equal distance to the southwest, and the Davis Mountains, the location of McDonald Observatory, one of the country's most sophisticated stargazing facilities, 30 miles due north. According to Marfan Lee Bennett, author of some of the boosterish material promoting the annual Lights Festival (an excuse for yearly outdoor concerts), even the observatory is mystified by the lights phenomenon: 'One night they trained one of their telescopes on the viewing site until they spied some of the glowing lights. Everyone working that night saw them. They pinpointed the location. The next day, they traveled to that exact spot, certain they would find the source. What did they find? Grass, rocks, dirt. That's it. Nothing else.'

Though this history may be a little loose with the facts, more than a few serious science teams have visited the site over the years, eventually arriving at one or more of the hazy explanations engraved on the historical marker. Folktales stretching back to the 19th century explain them as everything from restless Indian spirits to the campfires of perished settlers. Most often close-up observers compare the lights to combustion. 'It was a ball of fire,' said a motorist of the light that kept pace with her car for 10 miles on the way to Alpine. 'I saw three big balls of fire lined up,' reported a woman of lights she witnessed hovering by the side of the road outside town. A former Alpine resident once stopped at the viewing site on a spring night and saw thirteen lights 'coming through the field like little fireballs . . . and rolling out onto the road.' Hallie Stillwell, an Alpine rancherwoman and justice of the peace, spotted some on her property and saw them 'die down and then come up again, brighter. They looked like flames.' Less credible information comes from a recluse living off in the hills around Shafter, who calls them 'agents of Satan' and claims that 'they walk up the side of the mountain' near his house; and a bit of hearsay in which the lights are supposed to have incinerated a truck belonging to a pair of investigating scientists, rendering the men, in the words of a Sul Ross University English professor, 'idiots from that day on.'

Lee Bennett also contributes this story to the Lights Festival material:

I'm the local historian. So when someone in town dies, the families usually give me pieces of history that may have been collected by that person. Well, a special lady on a ranch west of town had kept a little tiny notebook of writings about the local flora and fauna and the general environment out here. But one entry especially caught my attention. She wrote in her own handwriting about driving down an old canyon road – a good 20 miles from the usual viewing site – many years ago. She was rather new to the area, and when she looked to her right she saw Chinati Mountain. 'Isn't that a pretty big mountain?' she asked. Her friend replied that it was one of the highest around. 'And there's a road coming down it?' she asked, amazed. Her friend looked at her strangely and answered, 'There's no road coming down off Chinati.' 'Then why do I see lights coming quickly down that mountain?' The entry went on to describe several lights that shot down the side of the mountain, directly toward them. They danced in the canyon and moved right up to the hood of the car. In her own words she wrote, 'I felt so special. We were never afraid. In fact, we had sort of a warm feeling.'

There have also been a good many lights posses – debunkers who go out to 'get them' and always return humiliated. In the 70s a corporation that figured the site for a uranium cache funded various futile investigations. In the 80s a science professor from Sul Ross University gathered a large party of students and volunteers to converge on the lights, with walkie-talkies and spotter planes to coordinate their maneuvers. But whenever a group got close the lights would wink out or move rapidly out of range. A geologist from Fort Worth named Pat Keeney visited Marfa on business and became fascinated with the lights. Hoping to find their source, he conducted a series of experiments in order to rule out car headlights and other man-made luminosity, and then managed to triangulate the area of the remaining unexplained lights. He then returned with another geologist, Elwood Wright, and together the two drove out on a small ranch road where they encountered a pair of lights moving nearby. Keeney published this account of what happened next:

They looked like they were moving at about a hundred-fifty to two-hundred miles per hour, but of course I had no way of measuring that. The lights spooked some horses, almost ran into them. Those horses started kicking and running through a cactus patch, trying to get away. The lights came to the edge of this road and stopped. Several times I had seen lights around this old hangar they had on the airbase. Well, one of these lights took off for that hangar, but the other one stayed there by the side of the road. It kept moving around a bush, kind of like it knew we were trying to get near it. It seemed to possess intelligence – it was like that thing was smarter than we were. It was making us feel pretty stupid. It was perfectly round, about the size of a cantaloupe, and it moved through that bush like it was looking for something. When the light stopped moving, it would get dimmer, but as it moved, it got brighter. Finally, it pulled out in the middle of the road about twenty yards from us and just hovered there. I had left the engine running, and Elwood said, 'Put it in gear and floorboard it. We'll run over it.' All of a sudden it got real bright and took off like a rocket.

Marfa mayor Fritz Kahl dismisses most accounts of up-close encounters as 'asinine stories' (though he has a certain deference for Keeney). Many years prior to his mayoralty Kahl was a military flight instructor at Marfa Field, and he took after the lights one night in a World War II fighter trainer. Unable to ever get close, he banished them from his thoughts (like most saner Marfans have). 'The best way to see the lights is with a six-pack of beer and a good-looking woman,' he says today.

Still, the lights are out there, and on most weekends (as on the first night of the symposium) people assemble by the roadside while the sun goes down, and stay on into the evening. Only after midnight does the crowd thin out and return the road to the circumstances under which most reports of close encounters have occurred.

Some say that the place was bewitched . . . during the early days of the settlement; others, that an old Indian chief, the prophet or wizard of his tribe, held his powwows there before the country was discovered . . . Certain it is, the place still continues under the sway of some witching power, that holds a spell over the minds of the good people . . . They are given to all kinds of marvelous beliefs; are subject to trances and visions, and frequently see strange sights, and hear music and voices in the air . . . stars shoot and meteors glare oftener across the valley than in any other part of the country.

This is not a description of Marfa, but in every detail it could be. It is how Washington Irving describes Westchester, New York, the environs where the Headless Horseman prowled. And for the late-night driver traveling between Marfa and Alpine, there is always a certain identification with Ichabod Crane's hoping to make it through Sleepy Hollow, with Paisano

Pass, where the lights tend to disappear, subbing in for the church bridge where the Horseman 'vanished in a flash of fire.'

On the last day of the symposium, the big boys, Gehry and Oldenburg, spoke. And the odd, inflammatory statements continued. 'I'm for an art that doesn't sit on its ass in a museum,' Oldenburg declared. He and his wife and collaborator Coosje van Bruggen took turns at the lectern, one talking while the other hit the button for the slide projector. Van Bruggen described the typical architect's ideas about the position sculpture takes in relation to architecture as 'nothing more than a turd on the sidewalk.' Like Irwin the day before, they seemed all fired up. Among their slides was a proposed sculpture of two giant copper toilet floats to be installed on the Thames, near the location of Jacques Herzog's Tate Gallery (for which they soon expressed unequivocal disdain). By the time Gehry took the stage there was tension in the air.

'Don Judd hated my work,' said Gehry, who seemed to find perverse pleasure in the fact. It may have been the spare setting that provoked him, but he made a point of defending the Guggenheim from the charge of upstaging the art it displays (the antithesis of anything that can be said of the unadorned spaces and clean vistas of Judd's Marfa installations), insisting that 'artists want their work in an important place.' (Again, not exactly the 'Marfa concept.') Gehry then talked about his other recent work, like the seafood restaurant topped with a fish that he'd deliberately turned to face the windows of a neighboring five-star hotel. 'The owner told me he didn't want 'em looking up the asshole of a fish,' Gehry explained. Future projects included the Condé Nast cafeteria in New York (a sketch conveying Gehry's idea of a Condé Nast employee showed a leggy woman in a short skirt and shades, blowing a kiss), and a massive gateway for the city of Modena, Italy. Modena's mayor originally offered a design budget of $1 million for the project, 'but you get a few people back and forth and that won't hardly cover airfare,' said Gehry. 'And I ain't gonna stay in no El Paisano Hotel in Modena.'

At the end of the lectures the participants gathered together around a long Donald Judd table to discuss each other's work and riff on the theme. It didn't take long for the ideological lines to clarify. Irwin fired a final salvo at critics who engage in 'ass-kissing.' Coosje van Bruggen lit into Jacques Herzog for his Tate Gallery expansion, calling the whole thing 'a pity.' Pissed off, Herzog glared out at the audience and said, 'It's not bullshit.' But before he could go on, he was interrupted by the artist Roni Horn, who stole the moment by remarking, 'All this architecture is really about sex.' The audience banged its steel chairs, and a beaming Gehry raised his fists above his head like a prize fighter.

'And on that note,' Horn said, 'I'm going back to New York.' Everyone applauded as Gehry and Irwin strode off stage with her, trailed by Herzog (waving a dismissive hand at van Bruggen). The remaining artists soon followed. 'The panel has defected,' said the moderator. The only ones left on stage were the academics, who were still talking to each other into the microphones.

That afternoon, once everyone had left town, Daphne went running and I went back to Lucy's Bar. I heard a local guy tell the bartender he'd 'never seen so many people in black.' The bartender told him, 'We had the most famous architect in the world in here!' I ordered a Lone Star and heard the bartender tell another customer, 'We thought we'd sell a lot of Mexican beer – but all they wanted was Lone Star.'

Something in Marfa had riled up a lot of architects, artists and academics. Six hundred of us had been treated to tongue-lashings, dressing downs, fully amplified upbraiding, storming, and railing – not what anyone had expected out of a symposium. In this vexed atmosphere rumors were circulating about an old feud between an art photographer and the Judd estate breaking into a full-blown multimillion dollar lawsuit (broken in the *Sentinel* the next week).

On the surface, of course, Marfa had hosted celebrated artists and architects. But the way it struck me was that they had hosted Marfa. Marfa had got into them. And they had behaved . . . accordingly: cantankerously, radically, wonderfully, badly, generously, absurdly; in extremis. Like Marfans.

Some other notable people who've come through Marfa:

> Katherine Anne Porter
> John Waters
> Denis Johnson
> Dennis Quaid
> Martha Stewart
> David Kaczynski
> W.S. Merwin
> Neil Armstrong
> Gwyneth Paltrow
> Holly Brubach
> James Caan
> Selena
> Elvis

I wish I could say that the place nourishes artists. It may. But I think it does something stranger. The relationship seems less friendly – more volatile. (I can imagine it destroying some.) Katherine Anne Porter, who lived there as a girl (Judd's son, Flavin, now lives in her house), loathed it. Elvis played a dance nearby and never came back. A cave in the wilderness near the town of Terlingua was a refuge for David Kaczynski, the Unabomber's brother. And W.S. Merwin, who is fascinated with the lights, would rather no one else know about it.

It seems that the best places for artists are places that are themselves; have a certain innate self-confidence – burn with that authenticity that Benedikt was talking about. And Marfa is what it is. Less Kabakov's 'world for art,' perhaps, than a provocative place for all kinds of impulses: creative, destructive, uncharted – by all means authentic.

And it's got better things to do than become aware of its unselfconsciousness. Within the next year there may be a 100-man crew of silver miners in nearby Shafter, drilling on a 10- to 15-year timetable, and eating at Carmen's next to the likes of Seamus Heaney, A.R. Ammons, or William Trevor – all three men are on the small list of Lannan grantees eligible for Marfa residencies. The Entrada al Pacifico, a trade corridor opened up by NAFTA, is altering the regional economy, with border crossings in the country up 100 percent in the last year. Hydroponic tomatoes are being cultivated in massive greenhouses just outside the city limits, turning Marfa into a desert town that exports water, just as Judd wanted. (It's a bizarre sight: huge glass and steel superstructures, sucking away at the aquifer. Though there's undeniably something Marfan about it.) The border patrol, for better or worse, is bolstering its forces in Marfa. Newcomers have bought back the hot springs, and a handful of other buildings from the Judd estate, restoring the former to public use. An ATM was installed this January (the one Marfa had a few years ago was decommissioned, because it never caught on – but this one may). Things are happening. By no means moribund, Marfa is a viable town on its own terms. As Robert Halpern told me by email the other day, 'Pretty much most of the folks who are moving here as well as us locals are reading from the same sheet of music: A town has to change and grow or it dies. Marfa will survive in spite of us all.'

And, of course, 'mystery lights' is not a bad description of these people who continually pass through Marfa. People like Irwin, Kabakov, Judd, and Peter Reading, the inaugural Lannan grantee, an oft-inebriated everyman's skeptic, with a tab at Lucy's, who likes to kick around Chinati muttering about how much all the damn boxes cost; or, in characteristic Marfan style, provoke his benefactors by bragging of his residency, 'I am required to do nothing. This suits me.' But many others also seem to find their way to Marfa. A few weeks after the symposium, a conjunto accordionist, Santiago Jimenez Jr., who, along with his brother Flaco, is one of the more revered traditionalists on the Tex-Mex scene, paid a visit. He walked around town playing for old folks, the community center, veterans, whoever wanted to listen. Fantastic pictures of him doing sessions with local musicians kept appearing in the paper. I don't know how long he was around, but he seemed to just stay and stay and stay – through about four issues of the *Sentinel*, becoming a part of the town. And then he winked out and was gone.

*

For our last night, Rob Weiner at the Chinati Foundation said we could move out of the Thunderbird Motel and into a Foundation building. Fortunately, part of Donald Judd's philosophy about beds also pertains to having one in most every gallery. We wound up in the John Chamberlain Building, a 30,000-square-foot former mohair warehouse full of sculptures made out of crushed cars. 'You'll find it interesting,' Rob said. At 2 a.m., I awoke with a start. The windows were shaking, the air vibrating, and roars and whistles seemed to be coming straight from the bathroom. It got louder and louder until I was sure something was going to come crashing through the door. 'Get up!' I shouted. 'It's the ghost of Donald Judd!' And the El Paso-bound train shot by.

Fire: The Next Sharp Stick?

JOHN HODGMAN

The offices of Ten Men Who Help Each Other But Are Not Brothers, a firm located Near The River That's Not as Wide as The Really Wide River.

(One Who Helps The Hairy One is seated going over some notes. Enter Maker of Fire.)

ONE: *(standing)* Hey, it's good to see you. Thanks for coming by.

MAKER: Thank you, One Who Helps The Hairy One. I'm sorry I'm late. Somehow I ended up by The Really Wide River.

ONE: Really? When we met by The Sticky Tree, I thought I said Near The River That's Not as Wide as The Really Wide River.

MAKER: That is what you said. I must have gotten turned around at The Sharp Shells.

ONE: Oh, yeah. That happens a lot.

MAKER: I must have just spaced.

ONE: No harm done. Do you want a Stick That Tastes Good to gnaw on?

MAKER: No thanks. I just had one. I'm a bear if I don't have one before Hot Part of The Day.

ONE: *(doesn't understand, a little afraid)* Excuse me?

MAKER: *(laughs)* Sorry. Sorry. I'm not actually a bear. I just mean that I'm like a bear if I don't have a Stick That Tastes Good.

ONE: You pretend to be a bear?

MAKER: No. I feel like a bear feels when he wakes up. You know, grumpy, impatient.

ONE: Do you become a bear when you say it?

MAKER: No. I just say it.

ONE: (*still doesn't understand*) Oh. Okay. I see. Well, in a way, that's exactly why I asked you to come down here. As you know, Ten Men Who Help Each Other But Are Not Brothers is a very old and established firm.

MAKER: I do know.

ONE: I mean, for me, it's a real honor to be associated with The Hairy One and to be his Helper. The Hairy One's a visionary, you know. But he's, how do I say it? He's older than The Old One, and as a result, I think that Ten Men needs to think about its future and think about how it can stay competitive in changing times.

MAKER: Naturally, I agree.

ONE: When we met by The Sticky Tree, I immediately thought, here's a guy who's ahead of the curve. Here's a guy who maybe can help Ten Men make the transition into that Day Which Isn't This Day, But Also Isn't The Day Before or The Day Before.

MAKER: At The Shallow Pond With a Terrible Odor, we call it 'Tomorrow.'

ONE: Really? 'Tomorrow?' Very clever. But the point is, we were talking about fire. And it seemed to me after we spoke that this could be just the thing to carry Ten Men into 'Tomorrow.'

MAKER: Well, there's no question that fire has a lot to offer any firm, Ten Men included, and I'm happy to show you why. But I think you need to think seriously about what your fire needs are. The truth is, this technology is so revolutionary that I think the real question won't be whether fire is right for Ten Men, but whether Ten Men is ready for fire.

ONE: (*nodding seriously*) True. True. Well, what I have planned is pretty informal, just a meeting of the minds, so to speak. I've asked The Hairy One to sit in on this meeting, since he'll have to approve anything that might happen Not Now, But Another Time. You may have to take it a little slow with him – he's a bit of a neanderthal when it comes to this sort of thing, if you know what I mean.

MAKER: HA HA HA HA HA HA!

ONE: HA HA HA HA HA HA!

(*Enter The Hairy One, carrying a sharp stick. One immediately stops laughing and falls to the floor completely prostate, arms and legs spread, face down. Maker smirks and does not move.*)

ONE: (*speaking into the floor*) Oh, hey, Hairy One, how are you? Thanks for coming by.

HAIRY ONE: (*grunts. To Maker*) Where are the Sticks That Taste Good?

MAKER: I think they're over there.

(*Hairy One crosses to side table to get a stick and begins gnawing it.*)

ONE: (*starting to raise himself*) I just gathered them, Hairy One, so they're fresh. (*Pauses. Looks to Maker*) You know me: I'm a bear if I don't have one before The Time You Tell Us When We Can Eat.

HAIRY ONE: (*stick drops from mouth in fear*) BEAR! BEAR! (*Raises sharp stick and crosses to begin hitting One with it.*)

ONE: No! Not bear! Not bear!

MAKER: It's just a saying.

ONE: It's just a saying!

(*Hairy One stops his attack and stares at both of them suspiciously.*)

ONE: (*rising, then sitting down*) I'm not a bear.

MAKER: It's just something that he said.

HAIRY ONE: (*completely disinterested*) Whatever. (*Retrieves stick and sits down at head of table.*)

ONE: Hairy One, Maker of Fire. Maker of Fire, The Hairy One.

MAKER: My pleasure, Hairy One. I've followed your work with Ten Men for a long time. It's a remarkable firm.

HAIRY ONE: So you're the one with the fire?

MAKER: Yes.

HAIRY ONE: Is it here?

MAKER: Well, no.

HAIRY ONE: Where is it?

MAKER: Well, in a sense, Hairy One, fire is everywhere. Rather than being an object, say, like your sharp stick, it's really a process, and so it can't really be said to exist anywhere. In a sense, fire exists in its own imaginary, virtual space, where we can only talk about what is not fire, and what might become fire.

HAIRY ONE: Whoa whoa whoa! English, please!

ONE: I think that what Maker of Fire is trying to say is that – and let me know if I have it right – while I may have one fire, and you may have another fire in another place, and The One Who Helps The Hairy One may be planning to make a fire, the truth is that it's all fire. It's all the same thing. It's all fire.

MAKER: That's true, in a rudimentary sense, but for our purposes, it'll do fine.

ONE: What's great about fire, Hairy One, is that it combines many things in one. Light, heat, pain – all in one. It's all those things. It's multi-thing.

HAIRY ONE: I thought you said it was all the same thing.

ONE: It is!

HAIRY ONE: But now you say it's multi-thing?

(One is confused; looks to Maker of Fire.)

MAKER: It is and it isn't. It depends on how you define thing.

HAIRY ONE: And where does the bear come in?

MAKER: It doesn't.

ONE: That was just something I said.

HAIRY ONE: I get that, Okay? I just wanted to know if a bear was involved in fire or not.

MAKER: It isn't.

HAIRY ONE: Good.

MAKER: See, the thing about fire is that it's totally interactive. Fire isn't a bear, but if you put fire on a bear, then the bear becomes fire. It's completely responsive to your needs at a given time, reacting specifically to your fuel input and usage paradigm . . .

HAIRY ONE: Okay, stop right there. Here's the thing. I've heard a lot about this fire already. Everyone is saying how shiny it is and how flickery it is. But you have to agree that that's very specialized. I know you folks at The Shallow Pond With a Terrible Odor are making a whole big deal about this, but we here by The River That's Not as Wide as The Really Wide River, well, we're simple folk. We want to know: what can it do for us? And the thing is, until people really figure out how fire can be used, I just can't see it becoming a staple of everyday life.

ONE: If I can just jump in here for a moment, Hairy One, think of it like the sharp stick. You know, Many Many Many Nights Ago, everyone was using a blunt stick for clubbing and for poking at things we had no name for. We didn't even call it Blunt Stick back then. We just called it Stick.

MAKER: Exactly.

ONE: And then someone came along and said, hey, let's take this rock and push it on the stick and remove parts of the stick at one end until it's different than it was before. Everyone called this one Crazy One, until Crazy One took The Sharp Stick and put it in The Loud One's eye.

HAIRY ONE: Someone didn't do that. I did.

ONE: That's what I'm saying. Once we had The Sharp Stick, The

Loud One became One Eye, and The Crazy One became The Big Hairy One.

HAIRY ONE: I'm The Big Hairy One.

ONE: That's what I'm saying. You don't want to be The One Who Didn't Like Fire. Fire is The Sharp Stick of . . . of . . . Tomorrow.

HAIRY ONE: What's Tomorrow?

MAKER: Well, that's not entirely a correct analogy, since fire can't really be compared to anything that isn't fire, but . . .

HAIRY ONE: (*to One*) Okay, but I think you're both overlooking an important thing: fire is very very scary. Even when Sharp Stick got big, there were a lot of people still using Blunt Stick because they knew what Blunt Stick could do. People still love their Blunt Sticks, and it is Many Many Days and Nights Later. So I can't see how this fire thing is going to work until people have a reason not to be scared.

MAKER: Well, before we go on, we have to all accept that not everything is going to appeal to Johnny Blunt Stick.

HAIRY ONE: Okay, but let me tell you that it's Johnny Blunt Sticks that made Ten Men one of the top firms by The River That's Not The Really Wide River. Johnny Blunt Sticks like me.

MAKER: Look, I didn't mean to offend anyone. Listen, I have to use the dungheap. Why don't I step out for a moment, and you two can decide how you want this meeting to go. Okay?

HAIRY ONE: No offense, no offense. We'll be here.

(*Maker exits.*)

ONE: I'm sure he didn't mean to suggest that . . .

HAIRY ONE: I don't care about that. I know how they are by The Shallow Pond. You know I've met him before?

ONE: You have?

HAIRY ONE: Sure. Many Many Many Nights Ago on a business trip. I was over by The Shallow Pond, and all The Shallow Ponders were laughing at him. You know what they used to call him? I mean, before all this 'Maker of Fire' bullshit?

ONE: What?

HAIRY ONE: They used to call him The One Who Knocks Two Rocks Together Over Dry, Dead Plants.

ONE: Oh, man, really?

HAIRY ONE: He's a complete lunatic. Not just Not Like Us – not like anybody.

ONE: But what about fire?

HAIRY ONE: Oh, he may have fire, but 'Maker of Fire?' He's an idiot. Where did you meet him?

ONE: Over by The Sticky Tree. He wanted to know if Ten Men would want to give him some food and then he would give us some fire.

HAIRY ONE: He what?!

ONE: He called it 'barter.'

HAIRY ONE: Well, I call it bullshit. He's obviously deranged. I thought he was here to invite us to go to The Shallow Pond and kill everyone and take fire.

ONE: No, he wants to 'trade.'

HAIRY ONE: Now I just feel sorry for him.

(Re-enter Maker of Fire.)

MAKER: Well, have you thought it over?

HAIRY ONE: Maker of Fire, you do us great honor by traveling so far to visit we Two Men of The Ten Men Who Help Each Other But Are Not Brothers. But until I get a sense of how fire could ever be useful, I'm afraid we're just going to have to muddle along without it.

MAKER: I understand. Not all are fire-ready.

HAIRY ONE: And I'm sorry about the Johnny Blunt Stick business. Please, come over here and join hands.

(Maker goes to join hands. The Hairy One stabs him with the stick, and then beats him until he is dead.)

ONE: What are you doing?

HAIRY ONE: There, he's out of his misery, poor fellow. Now go through his skins and his magic bag.

ONE: What? Why?

HAIRY ONE: We're looking for fire, my Helper! We're looking for fire!

ONE: Oh, you truly are The Wise and Big Hairy One!

finis.

The Double Zero

RICK MOODY

My dad was for Midwestern values; he was for families; he was for a firm handshake; he was for a little awkward sweet-talking with the waitress at the HoJo's. Until he grew to the age of thirty-four he worked at one of those farms owned by a big international corporation that's created from family farms gone defunct. Looked like a chessboard, if you saw it from the air. This was near Bidwell, Ohio. Don't know if it was Archer Daniels Midland, Monsanto, some company like that. The particular spread I'm talking about got sold to developers later. Guess it was more lucrative to sell the plot and buy some other place. The housing development that grew up on that land, it was called Golden Meadow Estates even though it didn't have any meadows. That's where we lived after Dad got laid off. He'd been at the bar down by the railroad when the news came through.

So he took the job at Sears, in the power tools dept. About the same time he met my mom. She'd once won a beauty contest, Miss Scandinavian Bidwell. They got married after dating a long while. My mom, probably on account of her beauty crown, was eager for my dad (and me, too, because I showed up pretty soon) to get some of that American fortune all around her. She was hopeful. She was going to get her some. The single-story tract house over in Golden Meadow Estates, well, it was a pretty tight fit, not to mention falling

395

down, and they were stuck next door to a used-car salesman nobody liked. I heard a rumor that this guy Stubb, this neighbor, had dead teenagers in the basement. The Buckeye State had a national lead in serial killers, though, so maybe that wasn't any big surprise. My mother convinced my dad that he had to get into some other line of work, where there was a better possibility of advancing. *Was he going to spend his whole life selling power tools?* Her idea was raising Angora rabbits. He went along with it. They really multiplied, these rabbits, like I bet you've heard. They were my chore, as a matter of fact. You'd get dozens of these cages with rabbits that urinated and shat all over everything if you even whispered at them, and then you had to *spin* their fur, you know, on an *actual loom*. If you wanted to make any kind of money at all. I didn't have to spin anything back then. I was too little. But you get the idea. Turned out my mother didn't have the patience for all that.

Next was yew trees. Some chemical in the yew tree was supposed to be an ingredient in the toxins for fighting cancers. Maybe my mother was thinking about that cluster in town. I mean, just about everybody in Golden Meadow Estates sported a wig, and so it wasn't newsworthy later when they found that the development had been laid out on an old chromium dump. Meantime, we actually had a half acre of yew trees already planted on some land rented from the nylon manufacturer downtown, and there were heavy metals there, too, must have been fatal to the yew trees. The main thing is they made this chemical, the yew chemical, in the laboratory by the end of the year.

Mom made a play for llamas. She went down to the Bidwell public library. To the business section. Read up about llamas.

But what can you do with them anyway? Make a sweater? *Well, that's how we settled on ostriches.* The ostrich is a poetic thing, let me tell you. Its life is full of dramas. The largest of birds on planet earth. The ostrich is almost eight feet tall and weighs three hundred pounds and it has a brain not too much bigger than a pigeon's brain. It has two toes. It can reach speeds of fifty miles an hour, and believe me, I've seen them do it. Like if you were standing at the far end of the ostrich farm we had, the Rancho Double Zero, and you were holding a Cleveland Indians beer cup full of corn, that ostrich would come at you about the speed an eighteen-wheeler comes at you on the interstate. Just like having a pigeon swoop at you, except that this pigeon is the size of a minivan. The incredible stupidity on the ostrich's face is worth commenting on, too, in case you haven't seen one lately. They're mouth-breathers, or anyhow their beaks always hang open a little bit. That pretty much tells you all you need to know. Lights on, property vacant. They reminded me of a retarded kid I knew in grammar school, Zechariah Dunbar. He's dead now. Anyway, the point is that ostriches are always trying to hold down other ostriches, by sitting on them, in order to fuck these other ostriches, without any regard to whether it's a boy or girl animal they're trying to get next to. And speaking of sex and ostriches, I'm almost sure that the men who worked on my father's farm tried to have their way with the Rancho Double Zero product. With a brain so small, it was obvious that the ostrich would never feel loving congress with some heartbroken Midwestern hombre as any kind of bodily insult. Actually, it's amazing that the pea-sized brain in those ostrich skulls could operate the other end of them. Amazing that electrical transmissions could make it that far, what with that huge bulky midsection that was *all red meat*, hundreds of pounds of it, as every brochure will tell you, *but with a start- lingly low fat content*. In fact, *it tastes like chicken*, my grandma said before the choking incident. Okay, it was almost like the ostrich was some kind of bird. But it didn't look like a bird, and when there were three or four hundred of them, running around in a herd at fifty miles an hour, flattening rodents, trying to have sex with each other, three or four hundred of them purchased with a precarious loan from Buckeye Savings and Trust, well, they looked more like conventioneers from some Holiday Inn assembly of extinct species. You expected a mating pair of wooly mammoths or a bunch of saber-toothed tigers to show up any moment.

I'm getting away from the story, though. I really meant to talk about ostrich eggs. After ten years of trying to get the Rancho Double Zero to perform fiscally, my parents had to sell the whole thing and declare bankruptcy. That's the sad truth. And it was no shame. Everybody they knew was bank- rupt. Everybody in Bidwell, practically, had a lien on their bank account. When we were done with the Double Zero, we had nothing left but a bunch of ostrich eggs, the kind that my parents used to sell out in front of the farm, under a canopy, for people who came out driving. There were three signs, a quarter mile apart, *See the Ostriches! Two Miles!* And then another half-mile. *Ostrich eggs*! *Five dollars each!* Then another. *Feed the ostriches*! *If you dare*!

I remember giving the feeding lecture myself to a couple from back East. They were the only people who'd volunteered to feed the ostriches in weeks. I handed them the Cleveland Indians cups. They were dressed up fine. *You can either put some of this corn in your hand and hold it out for the ostriches, but I sure wouldn't do that myself, because I've seen them pick up a little kid and whirl him around like he was a handkerchief and throw him over a fence, bust his neck clean through. Or you can hold out the cup and the ostriches will try to trample each other to death to get right in front of you, and then one of those pinheads will descend with incredible force on you, steal the entire cup away. Or else you can just scatter some corn at the base of the electrified fence there and get the heck out of the way, which is certainly what I'd do if I were you.* Who would go from Bidwell to anywhere, I was asking myself, unless they were trying to avoid a massive interstate manhunt? Probably this couple, right here, laughing at the poor dumb birds, probably they were the kind of people who would sodomize an entire preschool of kids, rob a rich lady on Park Avenue, hide her body, grind up some teenagers, and then disappear to manage their investments.

Anyhow, that ranch came and went and soon we were in a used El Dorado with 120,000 miles on it. I was in the backseat, with five dozen ostrich eggs. Dad was forty-eight, or there-abouts, and he was bald, and he was paunchy, and, because of the failure of all the gold-rush schemes, he was discouraged and mean. If he spoke at all it was just to gripe at politicians. He was an independent, in terms of gripes. Just so you know. Non-partisan. And the only hair left on his ugly head, after all the worrying, was around those two patches just above his ears, just like if he were an ostrich chick himself. Because you know when they came out of the shell, these chicks looked like human fetuses. In fact, I've heard it said that a human being and an ostrich actually share 38 percent of their DNA, which is pretty much when you think about it. So Dad looked like an ostrich. Or maybe he looked like one of those cancer survivors from Golden Meadow Estates who were always saying they felt like a million bucks even though it was obvious that they felt like about a buck fifty. Mom, on the other hand, despite her bad business decisions, only seemed to get prettier and prettier. She still spent a couple of hours each morning making up her face with pencils and brushes in a color called *deadly nightshade*.

In terms of volume, one ostrich egg is the equivalent of two dozen of your regular eggs. It's got two liters of liquefied muck in it. That means, if you're a short-order cook, that one of these ostrich eggs can last you a long time. A whole day, maybe. The ostrich shell is about the size of a regulation football, but it's shaped just like the traditional chicken egg-shell. Which is something I was told to say to tourists, *Note your traditional eggshell styling*. The ostrich egg is so perfect that it looks fake. The ostrich egg looks like it's made out of plastic. In fact, maybe the guys who came up with plastics got the idea from looking at the perfection of the ostrich egg. Myself, I could barely eat one of those ostrich eggs without worrying about seeing a little ostrich fledgling in it, because it looked so much like a human fetus, or what I imagined a human fetus looked like based on some pictures I'd seen in the *Golden Books Encyclopedia*. What if you accidentally ate one of the fledglings! Look out! They made pretty good French toast, though.

Over the years, my dad had assembled an ostrich freak exhibition. There were lots of genetic things that could go wrong with an ostrich flock, like say an ostrich had four legs, or an ostrich had two heads, or the ostrich didn't have any head at all, just a gigantic midsection. Maybe the number of genetic abnormalities in our stock had to do with how close the farm was to a dioxin-exuding paper plant, or maybe it was the chromium or the PCBs, whatever else. It was always something. The important part here is that the abnormalities made Dad sort of happy and enabled him to have a *collection* to take away from the Rancho Double Zero, and what's the harm in that. Not a lot of room for me in the backseat, though, what with the eggs and the freaks.

The restaurant we started wasn't in Bidwell, because we had bad memories of Bidwell, after the foreclosure and all. There wasn't much choice but to move further out where things were cheaper. We landed in Pickleville, where it was real cheap, all right, and where there wasn't anything to do. People used to kill feral cats in Pickleville. There was a bounty on them. Kids learned to obliterate any and all wildlife. Pickleville also had a train station where the out-of-state train stopped once a day. Mom figured what with the train station right nearby there was a good chance that people would want to stop at a family-style restaurant. So it was a diner, Dizzy's, which was the nickname we had given our ostrich chick *with two heads*. The design of our restaurant was like the traditional style of older diners, you know, shaped like a suppository, aluminum and chrome, jukeboxes at every booth. We lived out back. I was lucky. I got to go to a better school district and fraternize with a better class of kids who called me *hayseed* and accused me of intimate relations with brutes.

My parents bought a neon sign, and they made a shelf where Dad put his ostrich experiments, and then they got busy cooking up *open-faced turkey sandwiches* and *breaded fish cutlets* and *turkey hash* and lots of things with *chipped beef* in them. Just about everything in the restaurant had chipped beef in it. Mom decided that the restaurant should stay open nights (she never had to see my dad that way, since he worked a different shift), for the freight trains that emptied out their passengers in Pickleville occasionally. Freight hoboes would come in wearing that hunted expression you get from never having owned a thing and having no fixed address. Sometimes these guys would order an egg over easy, and Dad would attempt to convince them that they should have an ostrich egg. He would haul one of the eggs down, and the hoboes would get a load of the ostrich egg and there would be flourishing of *change money*, and then these hoboes would be gone.

My guess is that Dad had concluded that most Midwestern people were friendly, outgoing folks, and that, in spite of his failure in any enterprise that ever had his name on it, in spite of his galloping melancholy, he should make a real attempt to put on a warm, entertaining manner with the people who came into the diner. It was a *jolly innkeeper* strategy. It was a last-chance thing. He tried smiling at customers, and even at me, and he tried smiling at my mother, and it caught on. I tried smiling at the alley cat who lived in the trailer with us. I even tried smiling at the kids at school who called me *hayseed*. But then an ostrich egg ruined everything.

One rainy night I was up late avoiding homework when I heard a really scary shriek come from the restaurant. An emergency wail that couldn't be mistaken for anything but a real emergency. Made goosebumps break out on me. My dad burst into the trailer, weeping horribly, smashing plates. What I remember best was the fact that my mother, who never touched the old man, caressed the bald part of the top of his head, as if she could smooth out the canals of his worry lines.

It was like this. Joe Kane, a strip-club merchant in Bidwell, was waiting for his own dad, Republican district attorney of

Bidwell, to come through on the train that night. There'd been a big case up at the state capital. The train was late and Joe was loafing in the restaurant, drinking coffees, playing through all the Merle Haggard songs on the jukebox. After a couple of hours of ignoring my dad, Joe felt like he ought to try to say something. He went ahead and blurted out a pleasantry,

– Waiting for the old man. On the train. Train's running late.

Probably, Dad had thought so much about this body that was right there in front of him, this body who happened to be the son of the district attorney, that he started getting really nervous. A white foam began to accumulate at the corners of his mouth. And like in your chess games that kind of pile outward from the opening, maybe Dad was attempting to figure out *every possible future conversation* with Joe Kane, ahead of time, so he would have something witty to say, becoming, in the process, a complete retard.

He said the immortal words, – How-de-do.

– How-de-do? said Joe Kane. Did anyone still say stuff like this? Did kiddy television greetings still exist in the modern world of schoolyard massacres and religious cults? Next thing you know my father'd be saying *poopy diapers, weenie roast, tra la la, making nookie.* Just so he could conduct his business. He'd locate in his playbook the conversational gambit entitled *withering contempt dawns in the face of your auditor,* and, according to this playbook, wasn't anything else for him to do but go on being friendly, and he would.

– Uh, well, have you heard the one about how Christopher Columbus, discoverer of this land of ours, was a cheat? Sure was. Said he could make an egg stand on its end, which obviously you can only do when the calendar's on the equinoxes. And when he couldn't make the egg stand, why he had to crush the end of the egg. Maybe it was a hard-boiled egg, I don't know. Obviously, he can't have been that great a man if he had to crush the end of the egg in order to make it stand. I wonder, you know, whether we ought to be having all these annual celebrations in honor of him, since he was a liar about the egg incident. Probably about other things too. He claimed he hadn't crushed the end of the egg when he had. That's not dealing fair.

To make his point, my father took an ostrich egg from the shelf where a half-dozen were all piled up for use at the diner. The counter was grimy with a shellac of old bacon and corn syrup and butterfat and honey and molasses and salmonella. He set the egg down here.

– Helluva egg, Joe Kane remarked. – What is that, some kind of nuclear egg? You make that in a reactor?

– I know more about eggs than any man living, my father mumbled.

– Don't doubt that for a second, Joe Kane said.

– This egg will bend to my will. It will succumb to my powers of magic.

– If you say so.

My dad attempted to balance the ostrich egg on its end without success. He tried a number of times. Personally, I don't get where people thought up this idea about balancing eggs. You don't see people trying to balance gourds or footballs. But people seem like they have been trying to balance eggs since there were eggs to balance. Maybe it's because we all come from some kind of *ovum*, even if it doesn't look exactly like the kind that my father kept tipping up onto its end in front of Joe Kane, but since we come from some kind of *ovum* and since that is the closest we can get to any kind of real point of origin, maybe we're all kind of dumb on the subject of *ova*, although on the other hand, I guess these *ova* probably had to come from some chicken, and vice versa. Don't get me confused. Joe had to relocate his cup of coffee out of the wobbly trajectory of the shell. A couple of times. My father couldn't get anything going in terms of balancing the ostrich egg and so why did he keep trying?

Next, Dad got down the formaldehyde jars from up on the shelf, and started displaying for Joe Kane some deformed ostriches. In his recitation about the abnormalities he had names for a lot of the birds. He showed Joe the fetus with two heads, Dizzy; *she was the sweetest little chick*, and then showed Joe one with four legs. He showed Joe two or three sets of Siamese twin ostriches, including the set called Jack 'n' Jill. *This pair could run like a bat out of hell.* My dad's voice swelled. He was a proud parent. He gazed deeply into yellowed formaldehyde.

Joe Kane tried to figure an escape. He looked like an ostrich himself, right then, a mouth-breather, a shill waiting for the sideshow, where the real freaks, the circus owners themselves, would go to any lengths, glue a piece of bone on the forehead of a Shetland pony and call it a unicorn, for the thrill of separating crowds from wallets. Wasn't there any other place for Joe to take shelter from the buckets of rain falling from the sky? Must have been a lean-to or something. On the good side of the tracks.

– This bird here has two *male appendages*, and I know a number of fellows would really like it if they had two of those. Imagine all the trouble you could get into with the ladies.

Ever notice how in the Midwest no one ever kisses anyone? That little peck on the cheek people are always giving one another back East? *Nice to see you!* Much less in evidence here in the Midwest. It accounts for the ostrich farmhands and their romantic pursuits, turned down by wives, just looking for some glancing contact somewhere, with a mouth-breather, if necessary. They came home, these working men, to wives reciting lists of incomplete chores, because of which they'd just get right back into their pickups and head for the drive-thru. They'd sing their lamenting songs into drive-thru microphones. My father had seen a man once slap another man good-naturedly on the shoulder after a friendly exchange about a baseball. This was at a fast-food joint. He was sick with envy right then. And that's why, since he'd just shown Joe Kane an ostrich fetus with two penises, he decided *to chuck Joe under the chin*, as a sign of neighborly good wishes. My father came out from around the counter – he was a big man, I think I already said, 250 pounds, and over six feet – and as Joe Kane attempted to get up from his stool, my father *chucked him under the chin*.

– Take a weight off for a second, friend; I'm going to show you how to get an ostrich egg into a Coke bottle. And when the magic's done you can carry this Coke bottle around with you as a souvenir. I'll give it to you as a special gift. Here's how I do it. I heat this egg in regular old vinegar, kind you get anyplace, and that loosens up the surface of the egg, and then I just slip it into this liter bottle of Coke, which I also bought at the mini-mart up the road, and then when it's inside the Coke bottle, it goes back to its normal hardness. When people ask you how you did it, you just don't let on. Okay? It's our secret. Is that a deal?

What could Joe say? Dad already had the vinegar going on one of the burners. When the egg had been heated in this solution, my dad began attempting to cram the thing into the Coke bottle, to disappointing results. Of course, the Coke bottle kept toppling end over end. Falling behind the counter. Dad would have to go pick it up again. Meantime, the train was about to come in. Hours had passed. The train was wailing through the crossing. My father jammed the ostrich egg, which didn't look like it had loosened up at all, against the tiny Coke bottle opening, without success. Maybe if he had a *wide-mouth bottle* instead.

– Last time it worked fine.

– Look, I gotta go. Train's pulling in. My dad's –

– *Sit down on that stool*. Damned if you're going to sit in here for two hours on a bunch of coffees, eighty-five cent cups of coffee, and that's going to be all the business I'm gonna have all week, you *son of a bitch*. I know one place I can get this egg to fit. Goddamn you.

And this is where the ostrich egg broke, of course, like a geyser, like an explosion at the refinery of my old man's self-respect. Its unfertilized gunk, pints of it, splattered all over the place, on the counter, the stools, the toaster, the display case of stale donuts. Then Joe Kane, who was already at the door, having managed to get himself safely out of the way, *laughed bitterly*. My father, his face pendulous with tusks of egg white, reached himself down an additional ostrich egg and attempted to hurl it at Joe Kane. But, come on, that was like trying to be a shot-put champion. He managed to get it about as far as the first booth, where it shattered on the top of a jukebox, obscuring in yolk an entire run of titles by the Judds.

Next thing that happened, of course, was the blood-curdling shriek I already told you about. I'm sorry for it turning up in the story twice, but that's just how it is this time. My father, alone in the restaurant, like the proverbial bear in the trap, screamed his emergency scream, frightened residents of Pickleville for miles around, especially little kids. People who are happy when they're speculating about other people's business, they might want to make a few guesses about that scream, like that my dad was ashamed of himself because the trick with the ostrich egg didn't work, or my dad was experiencing a crisis of remorse because he couldn't ever *catch a break*. And these people would be right up to a point, but they'd be missing a crucial piece of information that I have and which I'm going to pass along. My father screamed, actually, because he was experiencing a shameful gastrointestinal problem. That's right. It's not really, you know, a major part of the story, but there was this certain large food company that was marketing some cheese snacks with a simulated fatty acid in them, and that large company was test marketing the cheese snacks guess where? Buckeye State. Where these companies test marketed lots of products for people they thought were uninformed. These cheese snacks were cheap, all right, a real bargain when compared to leading brands, and they had a cheddar flavor. Only problem was, since your large and small intestines couldn't absorb the fatty acid, it was deposited right out of you, usually in amounts close to two or three tablespoons. Right in your briefs, an oily residue that didn't come out in the wash. Depended on how fond you were of the cheese snacks. If you ate a whole bag, it could be worse. So the truth is, on top of having *egg on his face*, my dad messed his pants. It was a rough day.

You'll be wanting to know how I know all this stuff, all these things, that happened to my father in the restaurant, especially since I wasn't there and since Dad would never talk about any of it. Especially not *anal leakage*. Wouldn't talk about much at all, after that, unless he was complaining about Ohio State during football season. You'll want to know how I know so much about the soul of Ohio, since I was a teenager when all this happened and was supposed to be sullen and hard to reach. Hey, what's left in this breadbasket nation, but the mystery of imagination? My mother lay in bed, hatched a plan, how to get herself out of this place, how to give me a library of books. One night she dreamed of escaping from the Rust Belt, from a sequence of shotgun shacks and railroad apartments. A dream of a boy in the shape of a bird in the shape of a story, a boy who has a boy who has a boy: each generation's dream cheaper than the last, like for example all these dreams now feature Chuck E. *Cheese (A special birthday show performed by Chuck E. Cheese and his musical friends!)* or Cracker Barrel or Wendy's or Arby's or Red Lobster or the Outback Steakhouse or Boston Chicken or Taco Bell or Burger King or TCBY or Pizza Hut or Baskin Robbins or Friendly's or Hard Rock Cafe or KFC or IHOP or Frisch's Big Boy. Take a right down by Sam's Discount Warehouse, Midas Muffler, Target, Barnes and Noble, Home Depot, WalMart, Super KMart, Ninety-Nine Cent Store. My stand's at the end of the line. Eggs in this county they're the biggest darned eggs you ever seen in your whole life.

About the Contributors

'Yet Another Example of the Porousness of Certain Borders (VIII)'
By David Foster Wallace
Issue # 1
Copyright 1998
David Foster Wallace's most recent book is *Oblivion*, a collection of short stories. He lives in California.

'Four Institutional Monologues'
By George Saunders
Issue # 4
Copyright 2000
George Saunders is the author of the story collections *CivilWarLand in Bad Decline* and *Pastoralia*, and a children's story, *The Very Persistent Gappers of Frip*, illustrated by Lane Smith.

'The Observers'
By Paul LaFarge
Issue # 5
Copyright 2000
Paul LaFarge is an amateur meteorologist and historian of aviation, and the author of *The Artist of the Missing*, *Haussman, or the Distinction*, and *The Facts of Winter*.

'Walking on the Rings of Saturn'
By Paul Collins
Issue # 2
Copyright 1999
Paul Collins is the author of *Banvard's Folly: A Brief History of Notable Failures*, *Sixpence House*, and *Not Even Wrong*. He edits the Collins Library series for McSweeney's.

'The Girl with Bangs'
By Zadie Smith
Issue # 6
Copyright 2001
Zadie Smith is the author of *White Teeth* and *The Autograph Man*.

'The Hypnotist's Trailer'
By Ann Cummins
Issue # 5
Copyright 2000
Ann Cummins divides her time between Flagstaff, Arizona University, and Oakland, California. She is the author of the story collection *Red Ant House*.

'Tedford and the Megalodon'
By Jim Shepherd
Issue # 10
Copyright 2002
Jim Shepherd is the author of six novels, including most recently *Project X*, and two collections of short stories, including most recently *Love and Hydrogen*. He teaches at Williams College and in the Warren Wilson MFA Program.

'Three Meditations on Death'
By William T. Vollmann
Issue # 9
Copyright 2002
William T. Vollmann's most recent books include *The Royal Family*, *The Atlas*, and *Argall*, the third in his Seven Dreams series. In 2003, McSweeney's published *Rising Up and Rising Down*, Vollmann's seven-volume treatise on violence. He lives in Sacramento, California.

'Up the Mountain Coming Down Slowly'
By Dave Eggers
Issue # 10
Copyright 2002
Dave Eggers has written two books and several pamphlets.

'The Days Here'
By Kelly Feeney
Issue # 5
Copyright 2000
Kelly Feeney has written performance pieces and art criticism. She works as an interior designer in Connecticut and lives in Colorado.

'Haole Go Home!: Small Gestures from the Hawaiian Secessionist Movement'
By Zev Borow
Issue # 1
Copyright 1998
Zev Borow lives in New York. His work appears regularly in *Spin*, *ESPN Magazine*, and *New York*.

'Solicitation'
By Rebecca Curtis
Issue # 5
Copyright 2000

'Fat Ladies Floated in the Sky Like Balloons'
By Amanda Davis
Issue # 2
Copyright 1999
Amanda Davis grew up in North Carolina, and wrote
Circling the Drain, a collection of stories, and *Wonder When
You'll Miss Me*, a novel.

'In the Kingdom of the Unabomber'
By Gary Greenberg
Issue # 3
Copyright 1999
Gary Greenberg lives and works in Connecticut.

'Mollusks'
By Arthur Bradford
Issue # 1
Copyright 1998
Arthur Bradford is the author of *Dogwalker*, a collection of
stories, and the director of *How's Your News*, a documentary.

'The Republic of Marfa'
By Sean Wilsey
Issue # 2
Copyright 1999
Sean Wilsey is at work on a book about his experiences in
reform schools.

'Fire: The Next Sharp Stick?'
By John Hodgman
Issue # 2
Copyright 1999
John Hodgman is founder and host of the Little Gray Book
Lecture series in Brooklyn. He writes for many magazines.

'The Double Zero'
By Rick Moody
Issue # 4
Coypright 2000
Rick Moody is the author of *Garden State*, *The Ice Storm*, and
Purple America, all novels, and *The Ring of Brightest Angels
around Heaven*, a collection of stories.